LOST
BURBANK

LOST BURBANK

WESLEY H. CLARK &
MICHAEL B. McDANIEL

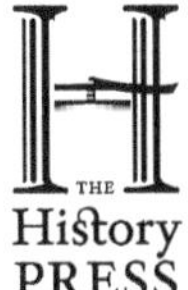

Published by The History Press
Charleston, SC
www.historypress.net

Front cover: The Burbank Building on the corner of San Fernando Road and Olive Avenue, circa 1890. *Burbank Historical Society.*
Back cover, top: Detail of a 1981 "Welcome to Burbank" poster featuring Johnny Carson. *Courtesy of Carson Entertainment Group. Jack Paul Miller, artist.*
Back cover, bottom: Constructing the "Golden Mall" on San Fernando Road, 1967. *City of Burbank.*

First published 2016

ISBN 9781540200778

Library of Congress Control Number: 2016939304

To our parents, who moved us to Burbank;
and to our wives, who put up with our obsessions about the place.

CONTENTS

PREFACE

How, exactly, is Burbank, California, "lost?"

As a global media capital, it is easy to find. In fact, Burbank is, arguably, *the* media capital, as a lot of what gets billed as being from Hollywood is really from Burbank. You encounter it all the time in movies and television, either in front of or behind the camera. (Or, increasingly these days, on the computer or cellphone screen.) In fact, Burbank is rather hard to miss. In 2011, when the city celebrated the 100th anniversary of its incorporation, Mayor Jess Talamantes put a twist on the Las Vegas promotional slogan, "What happens in Vegas, stays in Vegas": "What happens in Burbank is seen globally."

It's important to note that Burbank is very much a part of the vibrant, ever-changing Southern California lifestyle, where fads, interests, hobbies and obsessions come and go with alarming rapidity. Slot-car racetracks give way to drinking-water bars, which give way to Internet cafés, which in turn give way to vape shops.

But that is really not the sort of thing we're talking about in this book. We're primarily concerned with lost lore—the unique experiences and knowledge of everyday Burbankers that make Burbank *Burbank*. For instance, a housewife in wartime Burbank spoke of using some purloined Lockheed blueprints (printed on linen, a scarce material in the early 1940s), which she bleached, as material for a nice, soft pastel blue dress. Another example involved a conversation some years back, when Mike McDaniel casually noted to Wes Clark that an incident had recently occurred near "Turkey

Crossing." Where? Wes had spent fifteen years in Burbank, had attended Burbank schools and had worked there, but he was utterly unfamiliar with the location. And why does it have such a funny name? (As it turned out, Wes walked by the spot every day on his way home from school and later worked there as a Lockheed employee, but he was totally oblivious to the place-name or its funny history.)

All this and more shall be explained in the following pages.

Another question one might reasonably ask is, "Why Burbank?" What is it about a San Fernando Valley community that is special and deserving of a book-length treatment about its lore and history? After all, this is a place that has been (gently) ridiculed in the media for a half century by the likes of the writers of *Rowan and Martin's Laugh-In* and *The Tonight Show Starring Johnny Carson*.

In a word, what makes Burbank special is Burbankers. And we are happy to introduce you to interesting Burbankers and their stories in this book. Some of them you may have heard of, but many you probably haven't. After all, it is our sneaking suspicion that, despite the statue of Dr. David Burbank (dentist and landowner) that presides over a little traffic island at the well-traveled intersection of West Victory and West Burbank Boulevards, many Burbankers suppose that the city was named for Luther Burbank, a prominent botanist. The city fathers didn't help things by naming one of Burbank's junior high schools after the botanist instead of the dentist. Some of these Burbankers fought in wars and paid the ultimate price; they get a chapter of their own. Mike McDaniel has been a tireless chronicler of their identities and service with the city's veterans committee. And there are also Burbank *places*. These are, inevitably, associated with people, but the interesting spots in town get their own chapter.

And, it must be admitted, Burbank is a special place for the authors. On one car ride to a restaurant forty years ago, Wes's parents said something disparaging about Burbank to Wes and Mike, sitting in the rear seat. We boys looked at each other and said, "We like it here. Burbank is cool." Wes's Brooklyn-raised father turned around and said, disbelievingly, "You're just saying that, right? Wouldn't you rather live somewhere else?" "No," we replied. It's hard to believe that teenage males in the 1970s didn't want to live in New York, Los Angeles or somewhere else more hip, but that's how we actually felt.

We liked Burbank then, and we still do. We want to share some of its odd history and lore with you, to discover what's lost and make it known again.

One last note: this is not a history book. It is, rather, a book of some history mixed with lore. If you seek a standard history of Burbank, we recommend *A History of Burbank* (1967), published by the Burbank Unified School District, or the *Burbank Community Book* (1944), by George Lynn Monroe. Those will likely give you what you seek. They can both be found on our Burbankia website at wesclark.com.

Enjoy!

WES CLARK AND MIKE MCDANIEL
Spring 2016

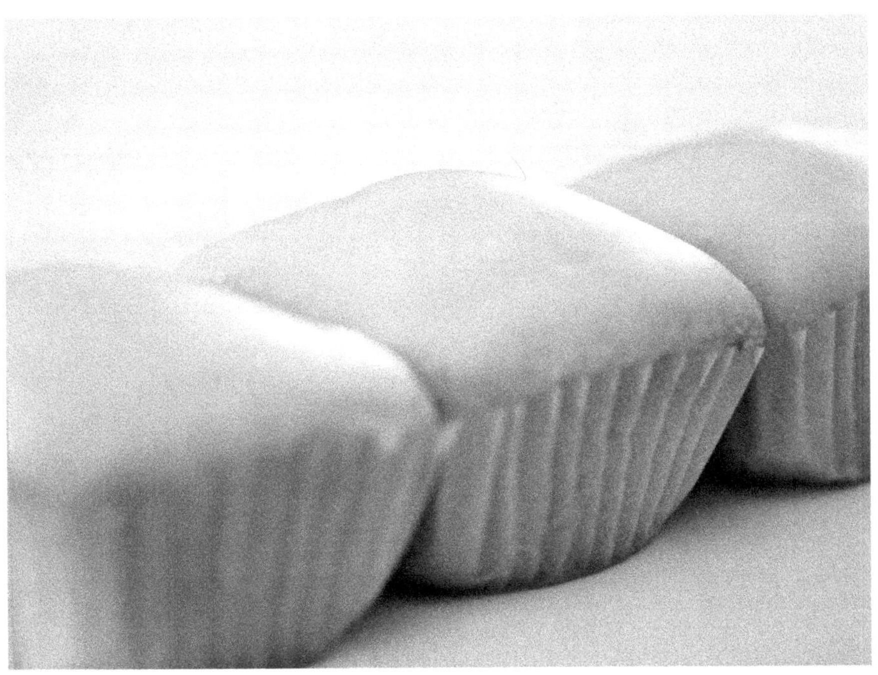

Martino's—and Burbank's—legendary tea cake. *Martino's Bakery.*

ACKNOWLEDGEMENTS

We thank Sue Baldaseroni, Penny Strickland Rivera, Betty Penrod and the other great folks at the Burbank Historical Society, who were kind enough to let us rummage through their files for hours in search of photographs, some of which are published here for the very first time in a book of Burbank history. We also thank Monte Thrasher, who lent many interesting tales to the Burbankia website; the Carson Entertainment Group for permission to reprint a 1981 poster; Greg Aliamo, who supplied his Vietnam photographs; the folks at the various Burbank Facebook groups who have been supportive and who have shared their stories with us; Richard Dixon, a skilled writer who contributed some fine pieces to Burbankia's "Burbankers Remember" article; and Wes Clark's father-in-law, Don Bilyeu (BHS '45), who shared many tales of Burbank in the 1940s as well as his classy P-38 watch. Mickey De Palo of the Burbank Veterans Committee is a constant inspiration, and Doris Vick and Fermer Kellogg shared a lot of great information about "the old days." From the Burbank library system, we thank Louise Paziak and Joan Cappocchi for their support. We think librarians are the unsung heroes of civilization and have spent many an hour enjoying Burbank's fine library system. Jeri Brown, Mindy Ladin and Irene Cabil from the city's records center have also been invaluable. During the writing of this book, Mary Jane Strickland, the Grand Lady of Burbank history and the founder of the Burbank Historical Society, passed away. She is greatly missed. Her dedicated daughter Penny, listed above, survives her and works at the historical society. Thanks also to Megan Laddusaw of The

History Press, who saw a good thing with the Burbankia website and had the vision to turn it into a book.

We are also grateful to George Lynn Monroe for writing *Burbank Community Book* (1944). Seriously, this is a wonderful and lively read; we recommend it to all Burbankers. Readers will observe that we take excerpts from it liberally.

We single out two Burbank High School teachers: Wes would like to thank Roland "Pete" Peterson for his inspirational teaching; it's his fault that Wes lives not in Burbank but in Virginia. (Mr. Peterson's Burbank High School American Civil War class ignited a passionate interest, a move east and a hobby.) Mike would like to thank his printing mentor at BHS, Willard Fredericksen, who printed and gave Mike a copy of the 1967 *A History of Burbank*. "Mister Fred" taught a high school class that led to a vocation for Mike.

Drew McDaniel, Mike's son, was a constant companion in performing veterans' research; fellow 1974 Bulldog Rob Avery looked over the manuscript and made valuable comments; and last but certainly not least, Cari Bilyeu Clark edited this entire work and eradicated her husband's many grammatical errors and sloppy sentence construction.

1
BURBANK'S EARLY DAYS

Remembering the enthusiasm that Pete Peterson, a Burbank High School history teacher, imparted about the American Civil War with slide shows and personal narratives about battlefield visits, Wes Clark headed east after college graduation.

He lives in Virginia, where there are plenty of interesting, historic places to be examined. Mike McDaniel stayed in Burbank. It took years, but Wes finally realized what Mike knew all along: local history is fun, and Burbank has interesting stories of its own—much of it lost to the average resident.

A perceptive quote by historian Will Durant seems to apply:

> *Civilization is a stream with banks. The stream is sometimes filled with blood from people killing, stealing, shouting and doing things historians usually record, while on the banks unnoticed, people build homes, make love, raise children, sing songs and write poetry. The story of civilization is what happened on the banks. Historians are pessimists because they ignore the banks for the river.*

Burbank's First Murder?

From the riverbank of lost history that belongs to Burbank, let's start with prehistory. People have always lived in what is today Burbank (the climate was just as pleasant for them as it is for us). Hundreds of years ago, these inhabitants were Shoshoneans (from *tso* meaning "head" and *so'ni* meaning "curly," describing their headdress). Later, they were renamed Fernandenos, after the mission in San Fernando. While these Native Americans were described as "happy," "carefree" and "gentle" in a 1975 history book, apparently they didn't always get along with others. In 1960, Burbank resident Paul Knapp, a collector of arrowheads and artifacts, described the first arrowhead in his expansive collection. It was discovered in a skull wedged within the roots of a tree stump near what is today North Buena Vista Street. He and his father discovered it when removing the stump; they estimated the death as having occurred hundreds of years before, based on very informal dating. When was Burbank's first murder? Nobody knows, but Knapp's arrowhead provides the first documented evidence of foul play among the earliest Burbankers.[1]

COMPASS TREES

Moving on to what is often called the "Spanish Era" in history books, we note that, sometimes, items of historical interest are often laid out right before our eyes but are still overlooked.

If you drive to the intersection of South Lake Street and West Providencia Avenue, along the concrete-encased banks of the Burbank Western Channel

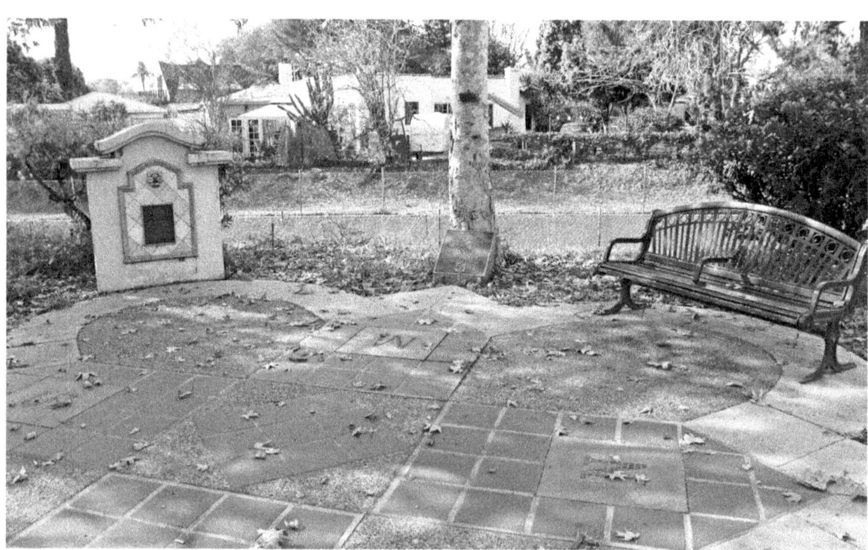

Modern Compass Tree Park. *Wes Clark.*

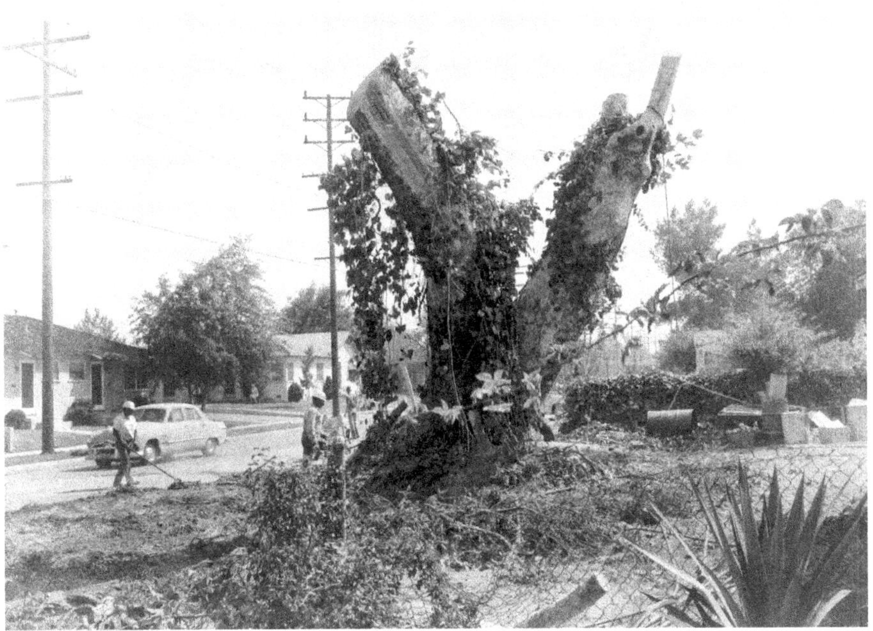

Surviving Compass Tree, 1960. *Collection of Michael B. McDaniel.*

(a 6.3-mile tributary of the Los Angeles River), you will encounter Compass Tree Park, dedicated in 2002. It's small. Don't blink, or you might miss it. It documents where, in 1817, Spanish padres planted sycamore trees as a landmark designating the halfway point between the San Gabriel and San Fernando Missions. There were once four trees here, each corresponding to a compass point. The original trees, sadly, are long gone. Three of them survived until as late as 1944, when they were mentioned in the *Burbank Community Book* of that year. The book states that the fourth was apparently cut down, "sacrificed on the altar of progress before the despoiler apparently knew what he was doing." By 1960, only a stump remained.

DR. DAVID BURBANK

The modern history of Burbank essentially begins with Dr. David Burbank (1821–1895), a dentist and a man whom we will now (humorously) designate as the First True Burbanker. As mentioned in the preface, people commonly

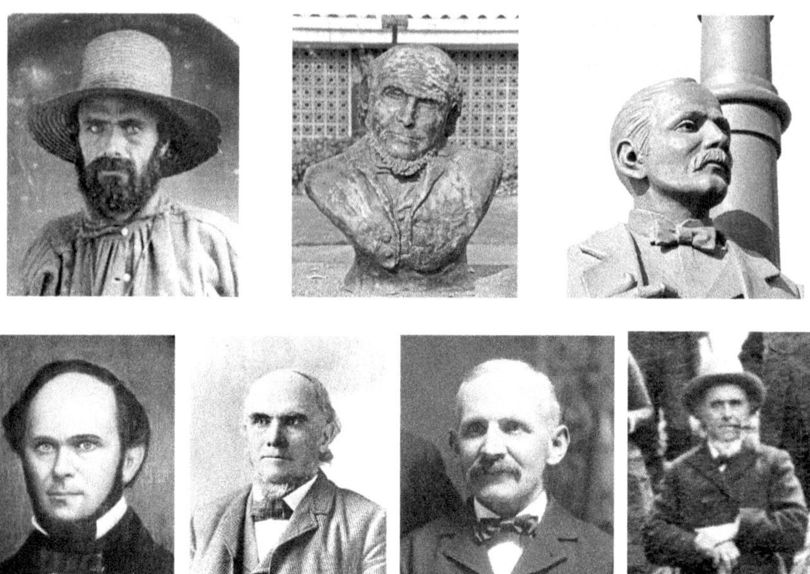

The many faces of Dr. David Burbank. *Burbank Historical Society/Wes Clark.*

suppose that the city of Burbank was named after Luther Burbank, the famous botanist. Actually, it was named after the dentist. (Mike McDaniel recently wrote an impassioned online reply to the History Channel when it aired a piece entitled "Fifty-One Amazing Facts About America" and stated that Burbank is named after Luther Burbank. This from the *History* Channel!) Adding to the confusion is one Amos L. Burbank (1850–1920), a native New Yorker prominent in Southern California real estate. It is not clear if he was related to Dr. David. In his *Los Angeles Times* obituary, Amos was erroneously called the founder of Burbank. Let's clear this up once and for all: it was Dr. David Burbank, not Luther or Amos, who was the founder of Burbank, California.

David Burbank was born in Effingham, New Hampshire, on December 17, 1821; he spent his early childhood in Maine. He became a dentist there, but in 1853 he moved to San Francisco and then, in 1866, to Los Angeles. In each place he was successful, but he decided to also become a landowner. To that end he bought forty-six hundred acres of the Rancho San Rafael from Jonathan Scott (Scott Road in Burbank honors him) and forty-six hundred acres of Rancho La Providencia from David Alexander and Alexander Bell (no streets for them). Burbank combined the two ranchos as one large ranch,

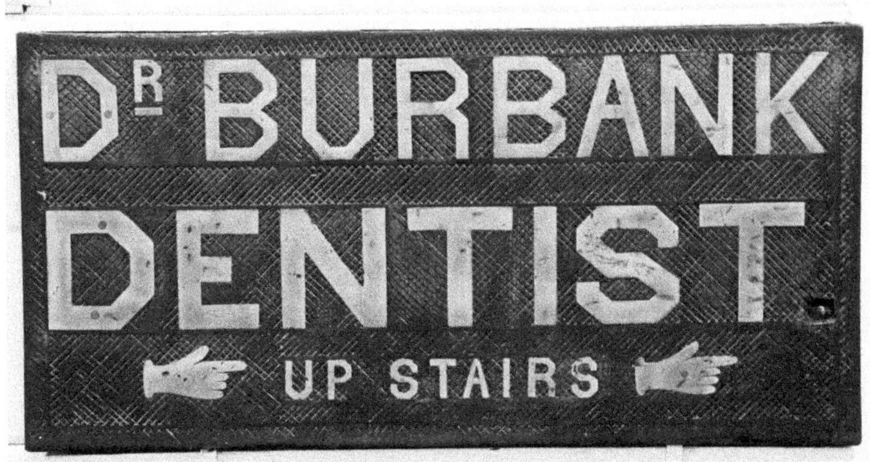

Published here in a book for the first time is the ultimate Burbank artifact: Dr. Burbank's office sign. It is believed to date from his days in San Francisco. *Burbank Historical Society.*

giving himself and his wife, Clara, one of the largest and most successful sheep ranches in Southern California. They also planted wheat.

Their ranch house, near where West Olive Avenue crosses the Los Angeles River[2] at the entrance to Dark Canyon on what was later the Warner Bros. backlot, stood until the 1950s, when it was destroyed in a fire. A fifty-pound metal sign stating "Dr. Burbank, Dentist, Up Stairs"—the very first with the name "Burbank" on it—was affixed thereto, directing toothache sufferers to Dr. Burbank's office. (There is some question as to whether or not Dr. Burbank practiced in Southern California.)

The ranch was so successful that in 1872 Dr. Burbank stopped practicing dentistry and began investing heavily in real estate in Los Angeles. One of his final projects was the Burbank Theatre in downtown Los Angeles, which opened in 1893 and cost $150,000. It soon became the leading theater and opera house in the city. But it wouldn't stay that way forever. By the time *I Was a Communist for the FBI* was released in 1951 (the theater is clearly seen on a street shot), the venue had become a burlesque house. (A postwar marquee advertised "Burbank's Atom Bomb Dancers.") To add to the seediness, Anton LaVey, the founder of the Church of Satan, once played the organ there. After a time as an X-rated movie house, Dr. Burbank's theater was torn down in 1973 or 1974.

Dr. Burbank sold his ranch to the Providencia Land, Water and Development Company for $250,000 in 1886, and he stayed on as a director. (His ranch house, later on the Warner Bros. lot, burned down in a fire in

1957.) Burbank's land was properly surveyed and laid out on paper, and a proper business district, along San Fernando Road,[3] was started. Residential lots surrounded the business district.

David Burbank died in his home on South Main Street in Los Angeles on January 21, 1895, aged seventy-three. After the fashion of the times, his obituary in the *Los Angeles Times* is quite detailed regarding his cause of death:

> *His first illness was neuralgia of the heart, but he recovered from it sufficiently to be about for a few days when he was taken down again, this time with a complication of diseases that ended his life. To his first illness were added others....He died of organic disease of the heart, angina pectoralis and chronic bronchitis and gastritis.*

One other matter about our famous dentist remains: There is a good, circa 1888 photograph of him that has been reprinted widely in books and serves as a reference image. He appears as a bald man of middle age with a sparse beard and no mustache, with deep-set eyes. He is wearing a checkered suit coat. He's not fat, but he's not lean, either. And then there is the twelve-foot-tall statue of Dr. Burbank, commissioned by the city, sculpted by Andrea Favilli and erected on January 13, 2010. Do these two likenesses really depict the same person?

BURBANK BOOSTERISM

The last decades of the nineteenth century were a time of promotion and land sales for the Providencia Land, Water and Development Company. A 1944 history of Burbank describes the unfettered creativity used by Victorian-era admen in promotional literature to induce settlers to move to Burbank, such as this excerpt from an advertising prospectus:

> *Providencia—17,000 acres of the Finest Fruit and Alfalfa Lands in the San Fernando Valley—Only Six Miles from Los Angeles—An Abundance of Water—Three Railroads to Los Angeles—Main Line of Southern Pacific Railroad Passes through These Lands—Burbank—The Sightliest Location in Southern California—Eight Miles to Los Angeles—Twenty-eight Trains to and from Los Angeles Every Twenty-four Hours—$5 for Thirty Round Trip Tickets—Plenty of Pure Mountain Water Now Piped to Each Lot—Lots Have Advanced 400 per cent in Six Months—Sales*

in Burbank in Six Months, $250,000—For Maps, Prices, Terms, Etc., Apply to Providencia Land and Water and Development Co., No. 12 South Spring Street, Los Angeles, California.

In the same prospectus, the descriptions of the health-giving virtues of a home in Burbank were equally fulsome:

Designed for one vast Sanitarium. Conditions favorable to longevity nowhere more numerous. Prolongs the lives of the feeble and enhances the enjoyment of the robust. One must know the name of the month in order to distinguish winter from summer. December as pleasant as May. The invalid is constantly induced to eat, exercise, digest, and recuperate.

Ponce de Leon, eat your heart out.

A KID-AND-DOG STORY

The 1944 *Burbank Community Book* has a charming, but somewhat mind-blowing, story about the community in its sleepy, Pollyannaesque period in the 1880s, 1890s and the turn of the century. It's too good to pass up.

The neighborhood was enjoying a picnic in what apparently was the grove of pepper trees now made up of Vickroy Park. The Morro family was there in full force, consisting of the parents and their brood of children. Early in the afternoon four-year-old Mamie became homesick and started to walk home by herself. Unfortunately she started in the wrong direction. When the rest of the family were ready to leave they were unable to find Mamie. The more they looked, the more the mystery of her whereabouts grew deeper. Darkness came on and searching parties with lanterns and blood-hounds, on foot, on horses and in buggies, scoured the country for miles around. The search was continued all night and most of the next day. In the afternoon of the next day—24 hours after the child's disappearance—she was found in the vicinity of Pacoima, asleep by the side of the road, with her arms around the neck of the likewise sleeping family dog, which instinctively had followed her in her travels in the capacity of protector. The searchers who found the two had quite a hard time to get the child from the dog, so intent it was in its role as sentinel.

Reflect that the straight-line distance from Vickroy Park to Pacoima is about seven and a half miles. How on earth was a four-year-old able to walk that far alone?

Dr. Thompson's Brush with Death

That invaluable resource, the 1944 *Burbank Community Book* by George Lynn Monroe, contains an interesting tale that we cannot ignore. It involves a prominent early Burbanker, Dr. Elmer Thompson, MD, who arrived in town in 1905 and founded the Burbank Hospital (now gone) in 1907. The story is undated, but it perhaps took place between 1910 and 1920.

> *It is quite possible that if Dr. Elmer Thompson, Burbank's first physician and surgeon, had looked up in a tree on a certain occasion he would not be with us today. In the early days before automatic burglar alarms were in fashion, Ralph Church, the town banker, had an arrangement with Dr. Thompson to somewhat take the place of this lack. It was his habit to leave a kerosene lamp in a certain position at the cashier's window in the bank. As the doctor was on the go at all hours of the night as well as the day, he was supposed to note whether the lamp was in its usual position as he passed the building at night. If not, it would be taken for granted that there was something unusual going on. On a certain occasion the lamp showed symptoms of having been moved. Dr. Thompson noticed this and proceeded to investigate. Not finding anything wrong he passed on. It developed the next day that at the time the doctor was investigating, there was a burglar in the bank in the process of blowing open the safe. In a pepper tree near the bank a boy with a gun was keeping watch, as an accomplice of the burglar, to warn him of danger of being apprehended. Later the boy was caught and through him the burglar—an ex-convict. In his testimony in court the boy told about being in the tree at the time Dr. Thompson was looking around the bank. He said he was expecting the doctor to look up in the tree at any moment, and if he had he would certainly have shot him. The door of the vault not being locked the burglar entered but hadn't gotten into the safe before being scared away. He secured about $55 which had been in the vault but not in the safe.*

1911 INCORPORATION

While the official launch of the town was on May 1, 1887, Burbank became an incorporated city on July 13, 1911 (the centennial of this event was duly celebrated on July 13, 2011). This may be considered a milestone for the official start of the modern city.[4] Shortly thereafter, on September 6, 1911, a photograph was taken that shows a bucolic, tree-lined San Fernando Road with American flags and a banner stretched overhead. (The banner reads, "Burbank Boosters, monster free barbeque celebration, everybody welcome, Sat. Sep 23.") The festive occasion was the arrival of the first Pacific Electric Railway car between Burbank and Los Angeles.[5] The *Burbank Community Book* described the occasion:

> *The city was colorfully decorated for the occasion.... The first car that rolled into the Burbank terminal was greeted by a crowd estimated at 1000 people, with the blare of trumpets of a brass band, the ringing of bells, the discharge of firearms and other evidences of joy.*

It must be noted that since then, the discharge of firearms in town has not been a significant part of Burbank festivities but rather a matter for the police to concern itself with.

The members of the chamber of commerce put their heads together and came up with a slogan highlighting Burbank's new arrival as a city to be

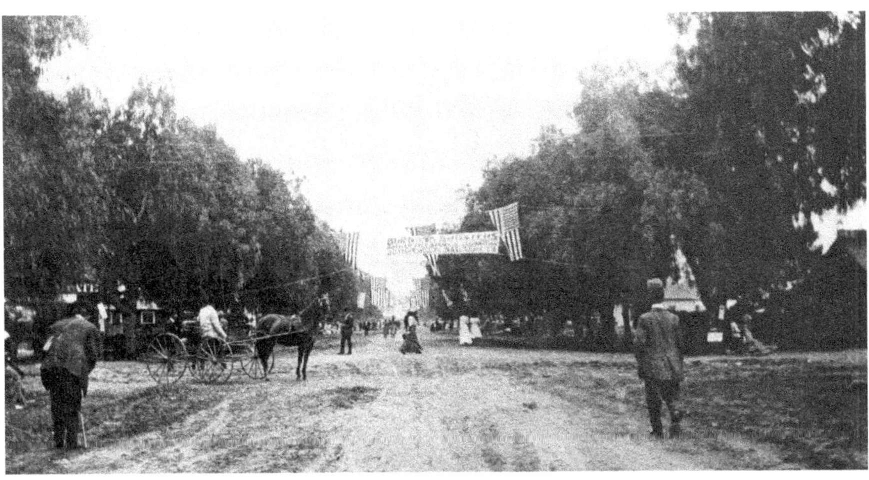

The Pacific Electric Car is coming to town! This view looks up Olive Avenue on September 6, 1911. Bells were rung and firearms were discharged. *Collection of Michael B. McDaniel.*

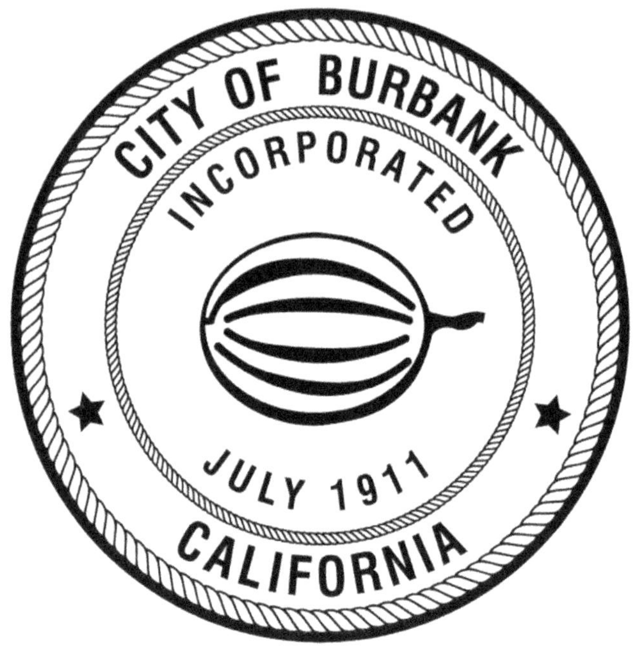

The first city seal, suggestive of a rural economy. That would change. *Collection of Michael B. McDaniel.*

reckoned with: "Burbank: 45 minutes from Broadway." In our era of American highway interconnectedness, it's hard to believe that a simple twelve-mile trolley line from one place to another would seem so significant. But it's important to remember that, in 1911, Burbank was very rural. The city was only slowly making the transition from a farm economy to an industrial economy.

(The authors, growing up in the fast-paced 1960s and 1970s, were amazed to learn that Burbank once had wineries—Brusso, Grangetto, McClure, Randisi, Gai—and that the last major one, the Brusso Winery on Thornton Avenue and Ontario Street, closed as late as 1967. The community that produced the advanced, high-tech Lockheed SR-71 "Blackbird" also made wine at the same time? Wow.)

INDUSTRIAL BURBANK

You can read about the rise of industries in Burbank in many local history books. Among local firms have been the Moreland Motor Truck Company, the Empire China Company, the Jergens Soap Corporation, the Lockheed Aircraft Company, Menasco, Warner Bros., Disney and, more recently, Cartoon Network and Nickelodeon. All brought modern industry to Burbank. But our favorite tale about a local industrial firm is that of Coopers Ltd.

Who were they? You might know the company better by its modern name: Jockey International, Inc. A quaint promotional pamphlet entitled *Burbank—Its Place in the Sun* was produced around 1930. In it, under a section entitled "Textiles," is this:

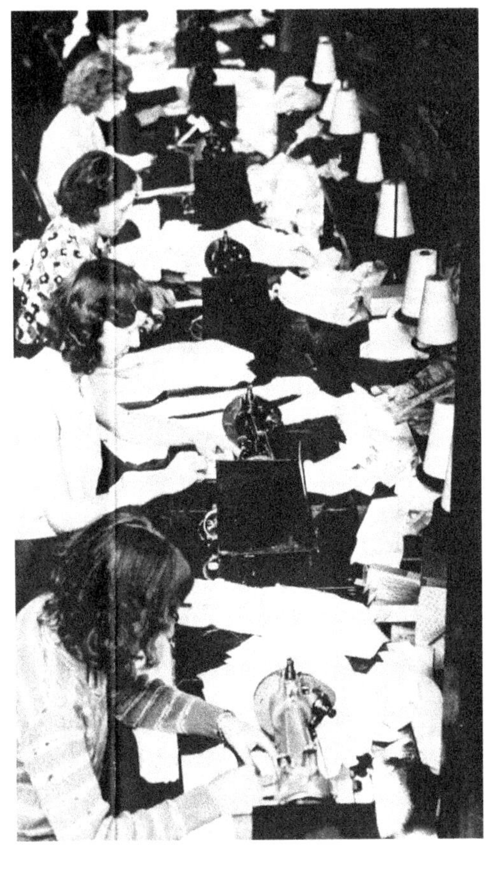

The Coopers cutting table, 1930s. Underwear—lots of it—was made here.
Collection of Michael B. McDaniel.

> *Burbank serves the territory west of Denver from this ultra-modern plant of Coopers Ltd.—for 60 years one of the largest makers of underwear and pajamas with headquarters in Kenosha, Wisconsin and St. Joseph, Michigan. This plant has the world's longest cutting table. In its operations, its labor is largely women. Operators state that the type of help furnished by Burbank is exceptionally efficient.*

So there you go—Burbank: Underwear Giant of the West Coast and site of the World's Largest Cutting Table. Who knew?

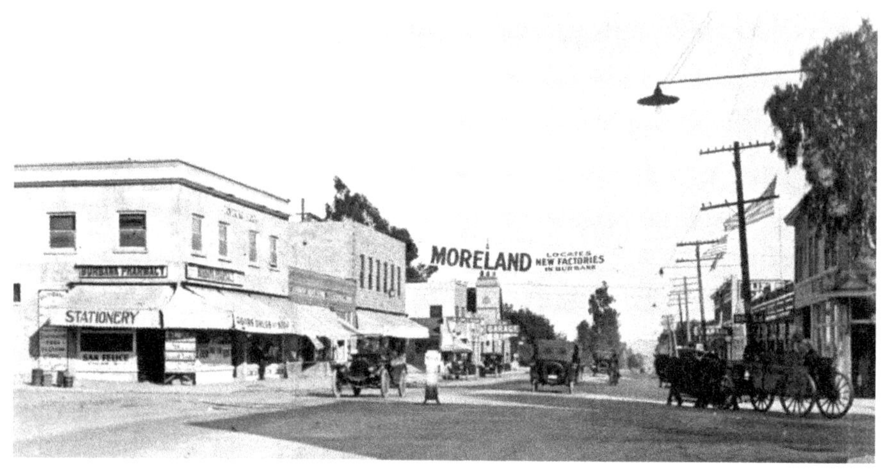

1917: The Moreland Truck Factory is coming to town! *DeLos Wilbur.*

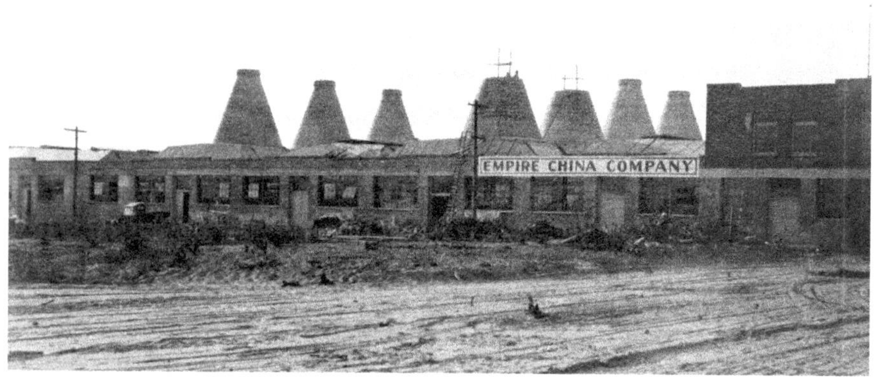

The Empire China Company, before Lockheed bought it, around 1928. *Collection of Michael B. McDaniel.*

Two Burbank Might-Have-Beens

Here's some lost lore, or an urban legend: When Wes Clark's family moved into Burbank in 1965, he recalls hearing stories by his father about how Burbank might have been an even greater community had the foolish city fathers not turned down offers for the city to be the site for Disneyland and/or the University of California at Los Angeles (UCLA). Is there any truth to this?

It is well known that Walt Disney got the inspiration for the world's first modern theme park during visits to amusement parks with his daughters in the 1930s and 1940s. Disenchanted with the usual dirty and badly run amusement parks, he sought to capture some of the charm of places like Tivoli Park, in Denmark. When movie-struck folks and animation buffs wrote letters to Walt Disney about the possibility of visiting the Walt Disney Studios in Burbank, he realized that a working movie studio wouldn't be much of a tourist attraction. So he began to consider that perhaps a park, located near the studios along Riverside Drive, might be a better attraction. Hence was born, according to an internal company memo from 1948, "Mickey Mouse Park." The park concept evolved to include a boat ride and themed areas. But as Disney's thoughts and concepts matured, he realized that the land simply wasn't available in Burbank for the park of his dreams. He hired a consultant, who ran the numbers for predicted crowds, and Disney finally determined that he wanted 160 acres of orange groves and walnut trees in Anaheim instead. This, of course, became Disneyland in 1955. So Mr. Clark was wrong in blaming the Burbank City Council for shortsightedness—it was really a matter of space being obtained quickly and inexpensively. A Burbank location was in the cards only initially.[6]

It's interesting to note that in the 1950s, famed animator Bob Clampett ("Beany and Cecil") had plans to team with a major television station to develop a "Beanyland" in Burbank. The site was envisioned to be near a swimming pool, possibly at Pickwick. It never came to fruition.

As for UCLA in Burbank—once again, the true story is nuanced.

In the early 1920s, developer Ben Marks acquired several hundred acres of Burbank land sloping from the Verdugos and into the foothills and canyons that he christened Benmar Hills. His plan was to make the site into one of the great cultural and educational centers in the country, even to the point of establishing a "University of International Relations," which would be associated with music, art, literature and other high-minded pursuits. The famous Vollmer String Quartette—a much classier outfit than a quartet without the additional letters on the end—performed concerts for free at a temporary auditorium at the site.

It was rumored that the University of Southern California was considering moving from Los Angeles to the Benmar tract in Burbank, but this came to naught. However, when a new, larger site for the University of California at Los Angeles was pursued, Benmar Hills was a natural contender. The list of sites was whittled down to either Burbank's Benmar Hills tract or a Los Angeles location at Westwood, and for a time it appeared that Burbank

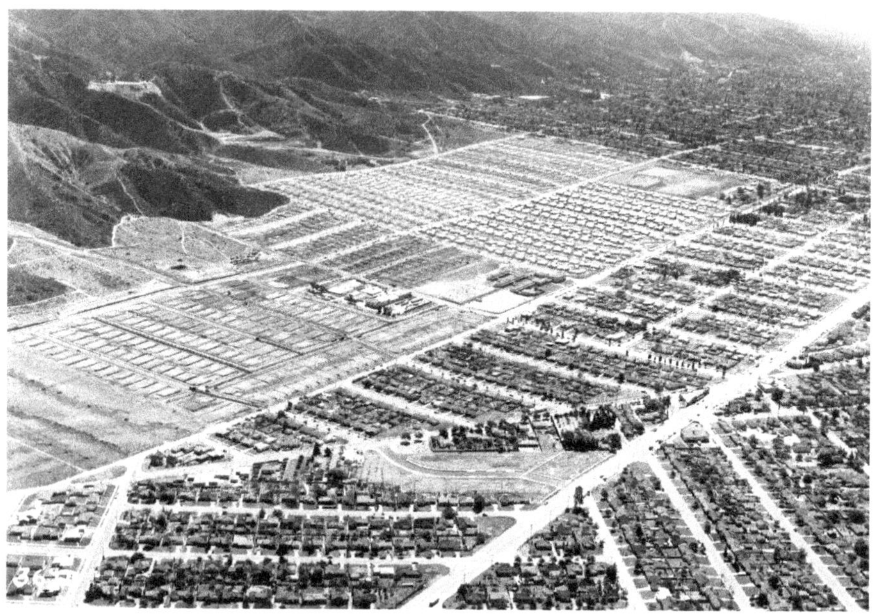

An aerial shot of the Benmar tract on May 4, 1951. The John Muir School site is being graded at upper right. *City of Burbank.*

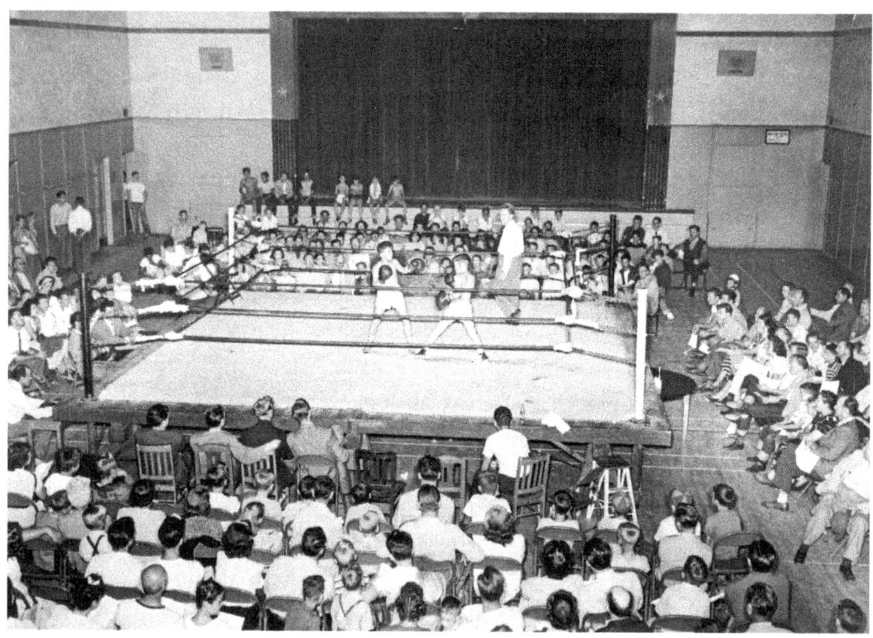

How tough were old-time Burbankers? They enjoyed watching their boys box each other at the Olive Recreational Center, as here in the 1950s. *Collection of Michael B. McDaniel.*

had the edge. However, in the end the university regents decided on the Westwood site by a slim margin, and that became the university's permanent home in 1925. Sorry, Mr. Clark: Short of offering bribery, it is unclear that the Burbank City Council could have done anything more to influence UCLA.

The Great Depression set back the grand educational and cultural plans of Ben Marks, and the development languished. The story has a happy ending, however. Woodbury College—now Woodbury University—happily claims a Burbank campus. Wes Clark's father-in-law is an alumnus.

As for the Vollmer String Quartette, a Google search turns up nothing. *Sic transit gloria mundi.*

With the arrival of World War II—the cataclysmic event that made modern geopolitics, for good or evil, into what they are today—we close our chapter on early Burbank. But first, a digression into the early nineteenth century and a discussion about when Burbank itself was a battleground.

2
WARTIME BURBANK

Nothing defines a place like a war. Who would have heard of Agincourt, Waterloo or Gettysburg had it not been for the mortal combat that took place there? Comedian Paul Rodriguez once opined, "Sometimes I think war is God's way of teaching us geography," and his point is well taken.

While it is true that Burbank's fame did not come about by the bellicose actions of martial men, the face of war has indeed been seen in Burbank.

Sort of.

The Second Battle of Cahuenga

The occasion we're referring to is what some historians call the Battle of Providencia (1845), or Second Battle of Cahuenga.[7] Our guess is that not one Burbanker in a thousand is aware of it. To describe it, we first take a short detour into California history as described by E. Caswell Perry in his book *Burbank: An Illustrated History*:

> *In 1842 an unpopular governor, Manuel Micheltorena, was appointed by Mexico City. Supported by his army of 300 cholos, or convict soldiers, he was bitterly resented by the Californios. In November 1844 an active revolt against him was initiated by both Northern and Southern Californians, themselves rivals but united in their desire to oust Micheltorena. Micheltorena defeated the northern*

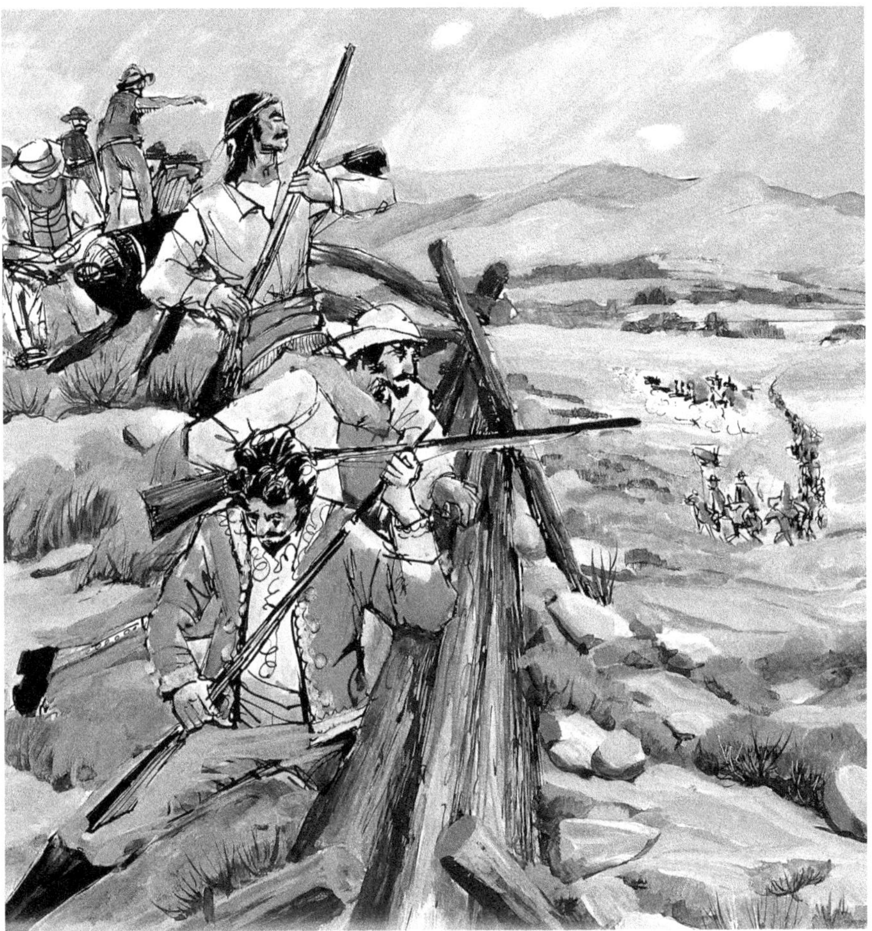

The Battle of Providencia, depicted in the 1976 City of Burbank civic calendar. *City of Burbank.*

> *faction, led by Jose Castro, near San Jose. But coming south to Los Angeles, even after building up his army to about 400, he was met by about the same number of Californios led by Juan Bautista Alvarado. The two small armies met between February 19–20, 1845, in the so-called Battle of Cahuenga.*

One has to be amused by the lineup of combatants: *Cholos* and *Californios*! Perry continues:

> *One side had two small cannon, the other had three, and they limited their combat to a long-range artillery duel. The casualties totaled one horse and*

one mule, and both sides soon ran out of ammunition. The action could only be continued by each side's recovering the cannon balls of the other. Even today, an occasional cannon ball turns up when excavations are made in the battlefield area.

Frank M. Keffer, in his 1934 *History of San Fernando Valley*, gives this dramatic detail:

The display of daring horsemanship and the noise from the cannon and rifle fire must have been very impressive, for on the hillside, women and children with crosses in their hands were weeping and wailing, invoking the saints for the safety of their loved ones who were engaged in the battle. Most of the foreigners in both contingents, who had enlisted merely in the hope of securing grants of lands, early decided to get out of danger and, deserting their commands, fraternized among the spectators on the hillside.

The whole thing sounds like an especially farcical modern battle reenactment; all that was missing were theatrical "deaths." But then, of course, nobody was killed in the Second Battle of Cahuenga.

For reasons that are not tactically apparent, Governor Micheltorena withdrew his forces, signaling the end of the battle. On February 22 he agreed to leave California, taking his army with him. Politically, this meant that Mexico no longer controlled Alta California. Pio Pico was made the governor at Los Angeles.

Why did Micheltorena quit the battle? In 1927, the Burbank Branch of the Security Trust and Savings Bank produced a pamphlet with this bit of information: "The real reason for his surrender was the desertion of a company of Yankees with him to the Yankees headed by (Pico's men) on the other side." Perfidious Yankees!

Where, precisely, in Burbank did this epic conflict occur? Accounts vary somewhat, but author Jackson Myers, in his *Burbank History*, notes that fifteen acres of land along fourteen hundred feet of Riverside Drive between Mariposa and Main Streets was a part of the battlefield site. Other accounts describe the forces being located near the Los Angeles River, not far from where Warner Bros. studios is now located.

A colorful and fanciful illustration of the Second Battle of Cahuenga appeared on the 1976 Burbank City Calendar; we reproduce it in this chapter.

Burbank in World War II

Let's advance the clock nearly one hundred years to the time of an infinitely greater conflict known as the Second World War.

You can't crack open a book of Burbank history without reading how important the presence of the Lockheed Aircraft Company (in all its various names, incarnations and divisions) was to wartime Burbank. Lockheed manufactured Hudson bombers, P-38 Lightnings and other aircraft for the war effort, and this tale is neatly captured in Lockheed's internally produced 1957/1958 corporate historical publication, *Of Men and Stars*.[8] Indeed, there is so much information about Lockheed's stay in Burbank that the authors have to constantly make sure that their Burbankia website doesn't turn into a Lockheedia website.

You might think that everyone—or nearly everyone—in Burbank knows something about the impact of the corporation to the town's history. Yet, the authors are flummoxed to discover that young people often wonder about the Lockheed aircraft outlines used on the tops of the signs designating the Empire Center on West Empire Avenue, which now occupies the space formerly held by Lockheed.[9] Clearly, there is much lore that is well on the way to being lost.

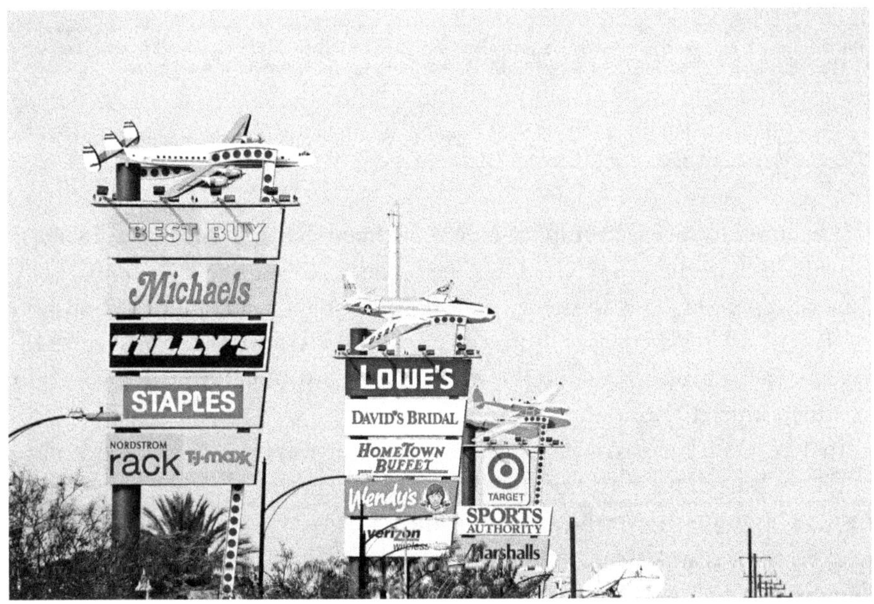

Signs at the Empire Shopping Center. Burgers and doughnuts are now made where, once, Lockheed Constellations and P-38s were built. *Wes Clark.*

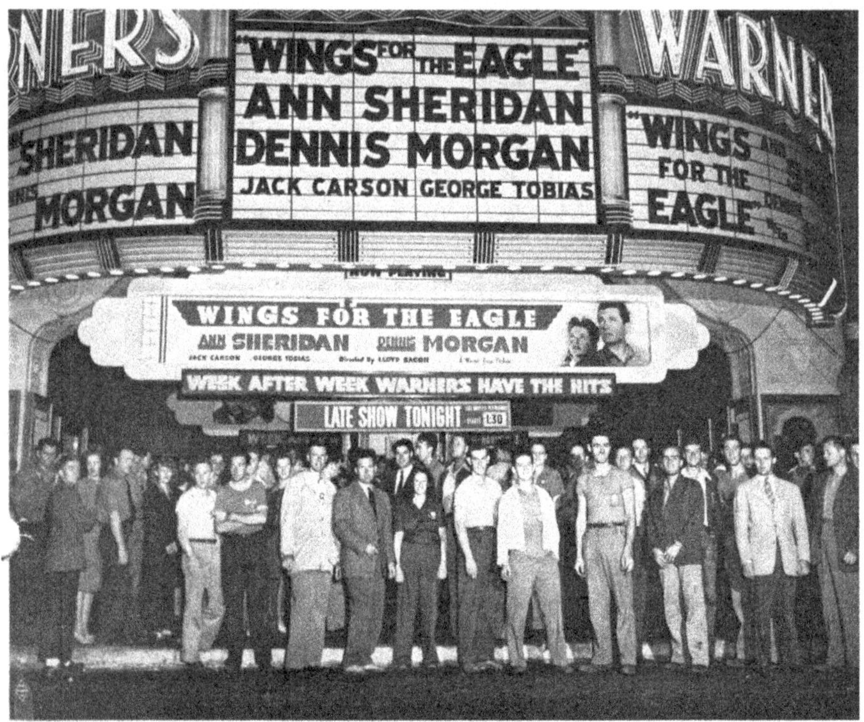

More than 4000 Lockheed and Vega swing shifters turned out at 1:30 a.m. Wednesday for the premiere of "Wings for the Eagle," Warner Bros. picture filmed at Lockheed. Here are a few. A second showing had to be held at 3:28 a.m. to accommodate everyone.

An image from the July 10, 1942 *Lockheed Vega-Star* about the Warner Bros. feature film *Wings for the Eagle*. *Collection of Michael B. McDaniel.*

The most noticeable impact that Lockheed had on Burbank involved crowds and traffic. In 1937 Lockheed had a workforce of about thirty thousand people. This number more than doubled to sixty-three thousand by 1939 and reached an all-time peak of ninety-four thousand in 1943. (Thirty-five thousand of these workers were women—the beloved and greatly admired "Rosie the Riveters.")

In 1942 Warner Bros. produced a dated but rather charming love note to fellow Burbank entity Lockheed Aircraft Company entitled *Wings for the Eagle*. Many scenes were shot within the Lockheed factory, and Lockheed workers served as extras. The authors love the introductory scene, where Dennis Morgan and Don DeFore hop off a freight train halted in Burbank, stroll over to the Lockheed employment office while having an expository chat and quickly get hired. (Yes, it was actually that easy back then. As

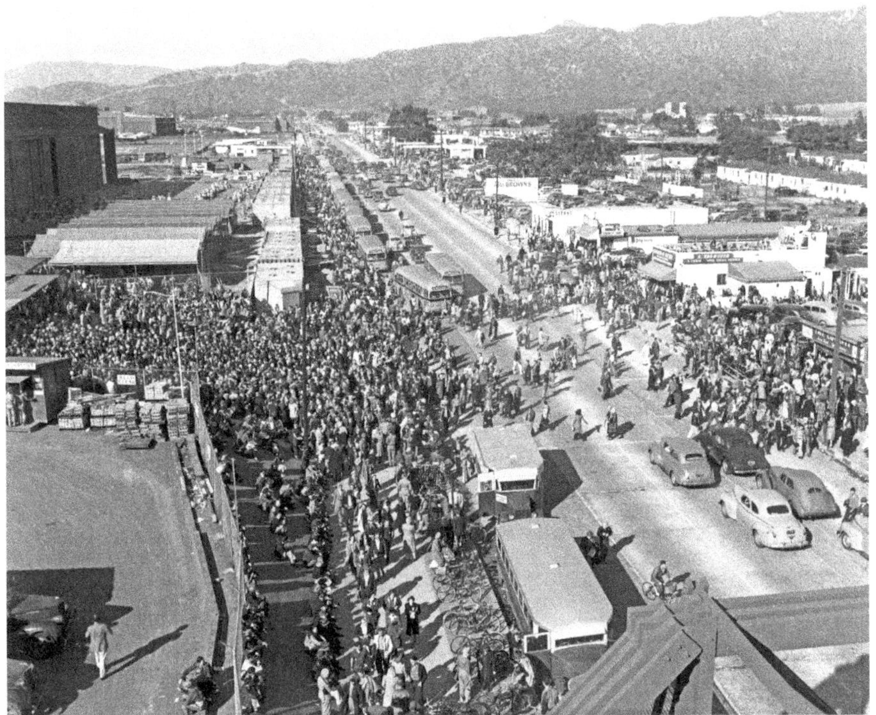

Lockheed shift change at the Hollywood Way gate, February 3, 1943. *Collection of Michael B. McDaniel.*

reported in *Of Men and Stars*, employment interviewers admitted that, in times of manpower shortage, "If the applicants are warm we'll hire them. We've even come close to hiring a few that were cold.") Our heroes blend in with the crowds and seek housing. Drama ensues.

Even in the early 1970s, the authors remember sitting patiently at traffic lights while the Lockheed plants disgorged workers transitioning shifts. For decades, it was a good idea to plan your neighborhood trips around the 3:30 p.m. shift change. These crowds disappeared when Lockheed moved its operations to Georgia and elsewhere in the 1980s.

While it was located there, Lockheed played an indelible part in the culture of Burbank. Wes Clark's father was a Lockheed worker who retired in 1976; his mother ran a café/beer bar just off the corner of Lincoln Street and Empire Avenue that catered to the Lockheed crowd.[10] The Clark home was filled with Lockheed-related items: L-1011 promotional material, models of various aircraft, coffee mugs and various aircraft parts given as souvenirs.

THE P-38 LIGHTNING

Was there ever another wartime aircraft like the Lockheed P-38 Lightning? A brainchild of famed aeronautics engineer Clarence "Kelly" Johnson, it quickly gained recognition for its speed (360 mph), unusually quiet flight (a by-product of its turbo supercharged engines), its murderous firepower (enemy pilots soon learned not to get in front of one), adaptability (it could be used as a fighter, bomber, photo-reconnaissance craft, a glider tow plane or even an ambulance), extended range (due to droppable extra fuel tanks) and reliability (one successfully made it home after a head-on collision with an ME-109—the P-38s were nicknamed "the round trip ticket"). One flier reported to the *Los Angeles Times* that German pilots were terrified of the P-38 and refused to face them head-on. Anything that terrified Nazis had to be a notable product. Indeed, the Germans called the P-38s "the fork-tailed devil." (The Japanese had an equally interesting name: "Two airplanes, one pilot.")

The authors' favorite praise of the P-38 Lightning, however, exists as a poem, written by Technical Sergeant Robert H. Bryson, a radio operator/gunner aboard an unescorted Flying Fortress over North Africa. It was printed in the October 29, 1943 *Lockheed-Vega Star*.

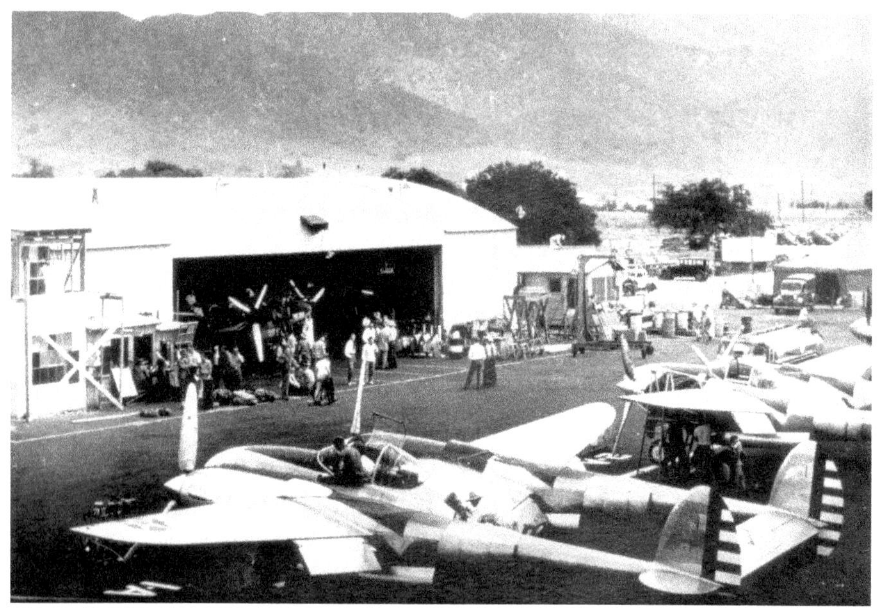

P-38s at final assembly near Buena Vista Street, around 1943. *Collection of Michael B. McDaniel.*

Friday, October 29, 1943 THE LOCKHEED-VEGA STAR Page 3

P-38 Most Dreaded Fighter Says Alex. F. Gribbon

"Many Japanese prisoners say that the P-38 has the reputation among Jap pilots as being the most dreaded American fighter they have to meet. If the Japs can jump first they'll still fight a P-38, but if they can't they usually run for a cloud bank."

This was the word brought back from the Southwest Pacific this week by Alex F. Gribbon, Lockheed Service Division field representative home from more than a year in Australia, New Guinea, New Caledonia and Guadalcanal. Gribbon supervised the reassembly of the first squadron of P-38's to go into action against the Japs during the heavy fighting on Guadalcanal and, later, in New Guinea.

"No Jap plane has much chance against a P-38 if the Lightning pilot keeps his head, sticks to the proper tactics and is not too greatly outnumbered," Gribbon reported. "Most of that criticism of American fighter airplanes in the early days of the war was not justified. The planes, though supplanted now by far better ones of later design and modification, were pretty good—but our tactics were all wrong for meeting a highly maneuverable plane like the Zero. We've changed those tactics long since and our planes are blasting the hell out of the Japs at every meeting.

"I have seen some nose-panel pictures of what happens when a P-38 opens upon a Jap plane. The pictures show the wings of Nip bombers flying off under the impact of steel, and the Zeros just simply explode and there's practically nothing left. Many times our planes have come back with pieces of Zero stuck in the prestone radiators.

Lightning Strikes Terror In Jap

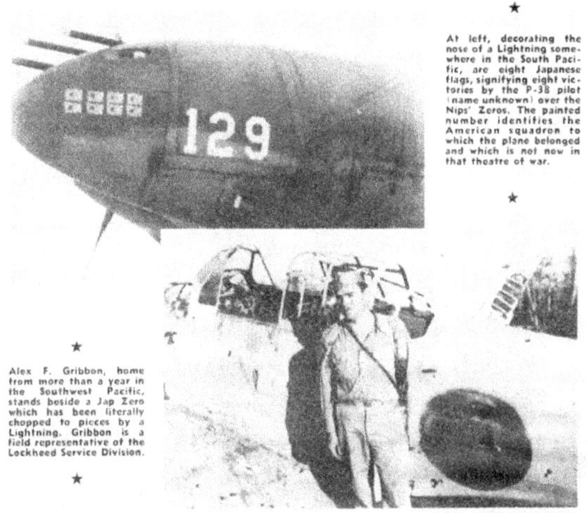

At left, decorating the nose of a Lightning somewhere in the South Pacific, are eight Japanese flags, signifying eight victories by the P-38 pilot (name unknown) over the Nips' Zeros. The painted number identifies the American squadron to which the plane belonged and which is not now in that theatre of war.

Alex F. Gribbon, home from more than a year in the Southwest Pacific, stands beside a Jap Zero which has been literally chopped to pieces by a Lightning. Gribbon is a field representative of the Lockheed Service Division.

ARMY JEEP DRIVERS ADVENTURE ON RADIO

How two U.S. Army jeep drivers accidentally uncover an enemy spy ring in North Africa will be told in dramatic style next Sunday, October 31, on "America—Ceiling Unlimited."

With Joseph Cotten in the starring role, the story-of-the-week is Mindret

LIGHTNINGS TO AID BLITZ ON GERMANY

(Continued from Page 1)

in the Lockheed plants, the dispatch is reprinted here, as follows:

"The big aerial news tonight in London

Above: A page from the October 29, 1943 *Lockheed Vega-Star. Collection of Michael B. McDaniel.*

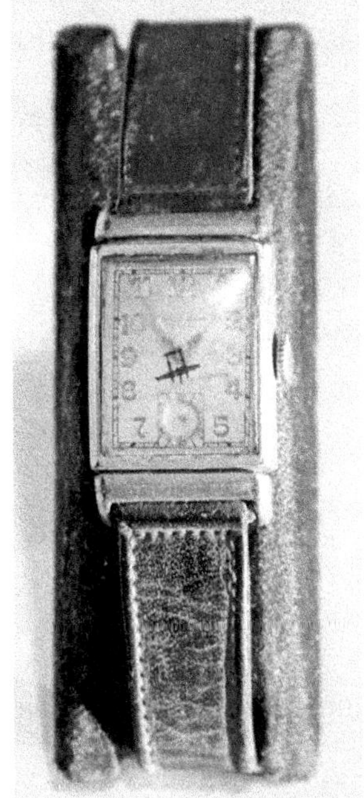

Right: Don Bilyeu's wartime watch, with a P-38 decal on the crystal, from when he worked at the Vega plant. He said that the decals were quite the fashion back then. *Don Bilyeu.*

Lightnings in the Sky

Oh, Hedy Lamarr is a beautiful gal, and Madeleine Carroll[11] *is too!*
But you'll find if you query, a different theory, amongst any bomber crew.
For the loveliest thing of which one could sing (this side of the pearly gates)
Is no blonde or brunette of the Hollywood set—
But an escort of P-38s.
Yes, in days that have passed, when the tables were massed
With glasses of scotch and champagne,
It's quite true that the sight was a thing to delight
Us, intent on feeling no pain.
But no longer the same, nowadays, in this game,
When we head north from Messina Straits,
Take the sparkling wine—every time, just make mine
An escort of P-38s.

Byron, Shelley and Keats ran a dozen dead heats
Describing the view from the hills,
Of the valleys in May when the winds gently sway
An army of bright daffodils.
Take the daffodils, Byron—the wild flowers, Shelley—
Yours is the myrtle, Friend Keats;
Just reserve me those cuties—American Beauties—
An escort of P-38s.

Sure we're braver than hell; on the ground all is swell—
In the air it's a different story:
We sweat out our track through the fighters and flak;
We're willing to split up the glory.
Well, they wouldn't reject us, so heaven protect us
And, until all the shooting abates,
Give us courage to fight 'em and—one other small item—
an escort of P-38s.

As a part of the Burbank centennial celebrations in July 2011, a P-38 flew over city hall; it was great to see this representative of Burbank technological know-how being flown in local skies once again!

LOCKHEED UNDER WRAPS

If the Japanese could bomb Pearl Harbor, it stood to reason that they might also try bombing Los Angeles. Indeed, in February 1942 a Japanese submarine appeared off the coast of Santa Barbara and fired some shells at an oil facility—the first enemy shells to land on the continental United States in World War II. A likely additional target for destruction was the American aircraft industry—by 1941 battles were fought and won in the air (as the Japanese would learn the next year at the Battle of Midway). With this in mind, the Army Corps of Engineers enlisted artists, set dressers and painters from the studios to make Lockheed disappear. The results were impressive. Where before stood a large, modern aircraft factory now stood alfalfa fields, trees and a perfectly rural landscape. Lockheed employees, perhaps the same who got their acting experience as extras in *Wings for the Eagle*, were also required to play along by putting up and taking down laundry on the clotheslines.

The effort to conceal Lockheed from enemy bombers was partially hampered by fellow Californians. As related by the (uncredited) author of a book about the 121st AAA Gun Battalion, *A History of the Desert Wolf: 1940–1945*:

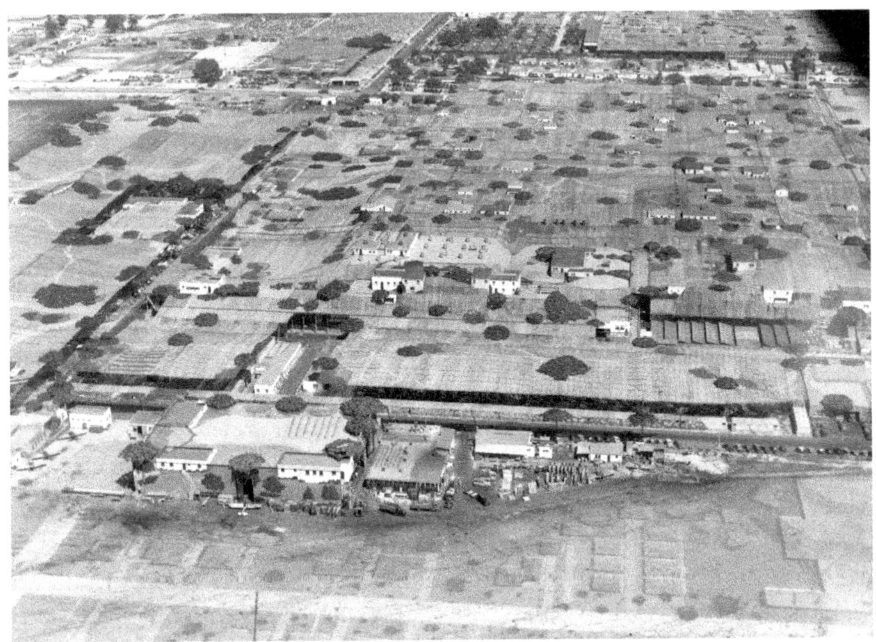

The Lockheed facility is camouflaged to look like a rural area, 1942. *Burbank Historical Society.*

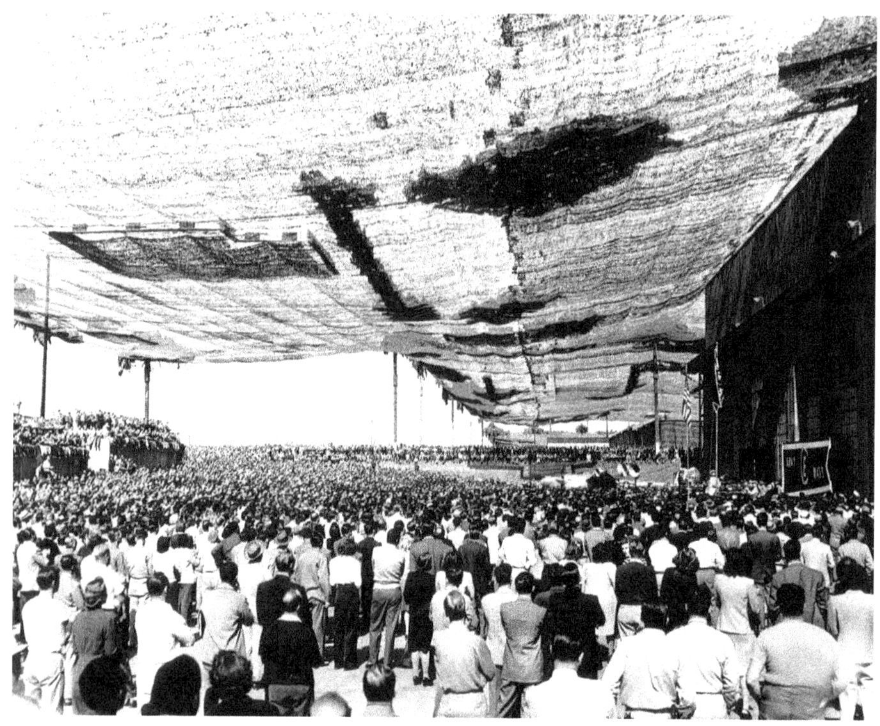

Lockheed employees attend a function under the camouflage netting, 1942. *Burbank Historical Society.*

The FBI and military authorities were checking on Japanese civilians on the coast at that time, and in this work our S2 section played an important part. Remember the time the men discovered the short wave radio set in the Jap[anese] *florist shop in Glendale? And not far away, German espionage agents were found hard at work gathering information on airplane production for transmission to Der Fatherland.*

Recall the morning the Japanese families of the Burbank-Glendale area lined the sidewalk along Magnolia Boulevard and San Fernando Road awaiting government transportation to the Tule Lake Relocation Center and other inland camps established to place all Jap[anese] *under close supervision? I remember seeing an air photograph of the L.A. coastline which showed that the Nip*[ponese] *farmers had plowed their soil and planted their crop in such a manner that from the air distinct arrows would point out to enemy bombers that location of Lockheed, Douglas, North American, and other vital industries of Los Angeles.*

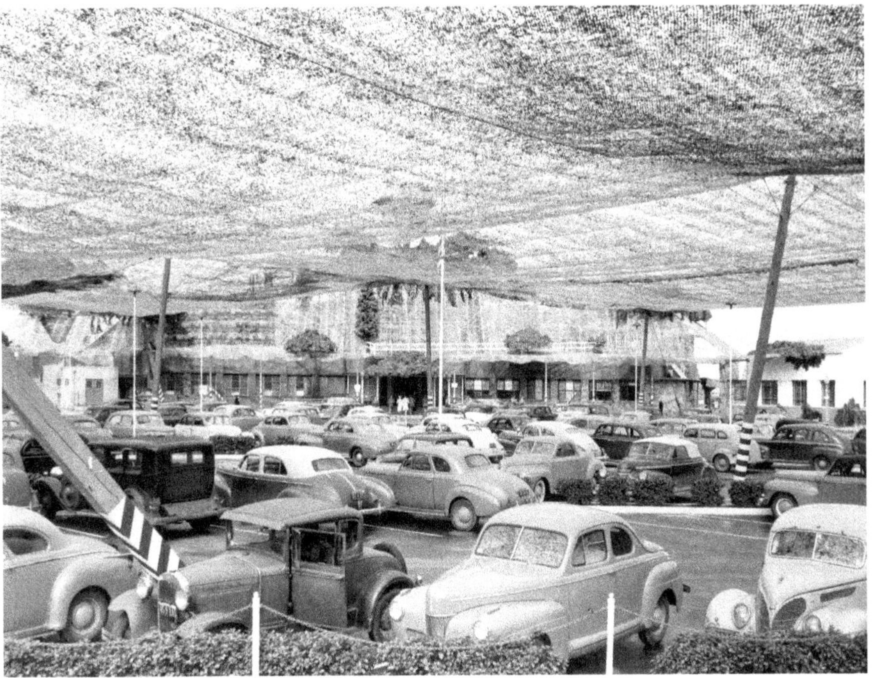

Beware of the chicken feathers! *Burbank Historical Society.*

And, as incredible as it seems, management at Warner Bros.—specifically movie mogul Jack Warner—had the bright idea of painting a sign on the top of his studio: "Lockheed—That a Way." Apparently he feared the Japanese, thinking the Warner studio complex was Lockheed, would bomb there. Needless to say, the sign wasn't up for long. Was Warner Bros. in a 1940s version of what we now call damage control?

The camouflage was occasionally a nuisance, as Wes Clark's father-in-law, Don Bilyeu, describes: "The camouflage over Lockheed was chicken wire suspended from large poles and covered with painted chicken feathers. The main complaint was when it rained, all the cars in the parking lot were covered with wet chicken feathers!"

FORTRESS BURBANK

The possibility of a bombing run over Lockheed was countered with the placement of artillery units within the plant and also in the Verdugo Hills

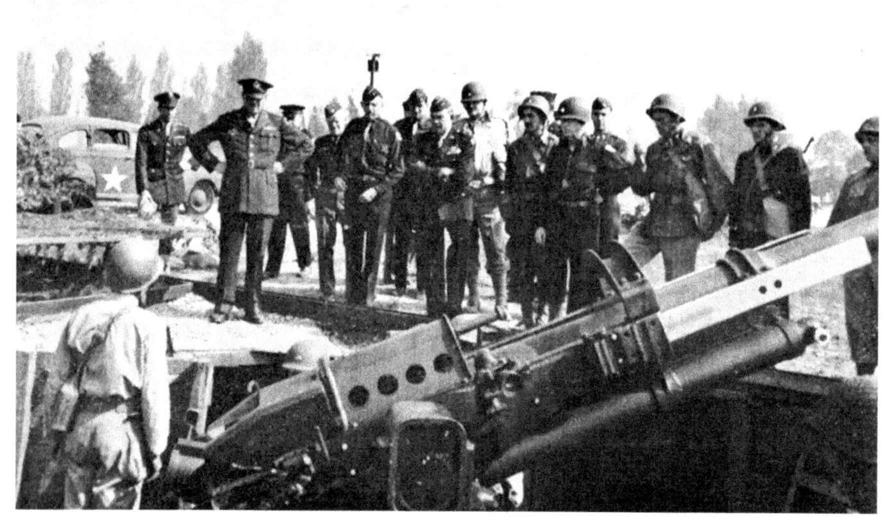

Major General Homer and staff inspect a member of the 121st Anti-Aircraft Artillery battery, stationed in Burbank. *Collection of Michael B. McDaniel.*

bordering Burbank. The unit stationed there was variously called the 421st Rocket FA (Field Artillery) Battalion, the 121st Separate Battalion CA (Coast Artillery) AA (Anti-Aircraft), the 121st AAA (Anti-Aircraft Artillery) Gun Battalion and, finally, the 1st Rocket Battalion. But the men in it called it simply the "Hut-Two-Hut" (121st). A passage from their unit history describes the deployment of various batteries:

> *Few of us who made that trip will forget our "invasion" of the Los Angeles area. Headquarters Battery and Battery A pitched shelter halves behind the hangar at the California National Guard airport in Griffith Park; Battery B, which had in its possession all four of that Battalion's total of four 3-inch AA guns, set up in a position behind the Lockheed Aircraft plant; Battery C moved into the nearby Vega Aircraft area* [also in Burbank]*; and Battery D bivouacked in the Greek Theatre in Griffith Park. It seemed odd to be maneuvering in the very heart of a thriving metropolis.*

Battery A later also found lodging in Burbank of a sort that would probably form the basis for many family tales after the war:

> *Battery A had moved in with Mickey Mouse, Donald Duck, and Snow White and the Seven Dwarfs in an empty studio building generously made*

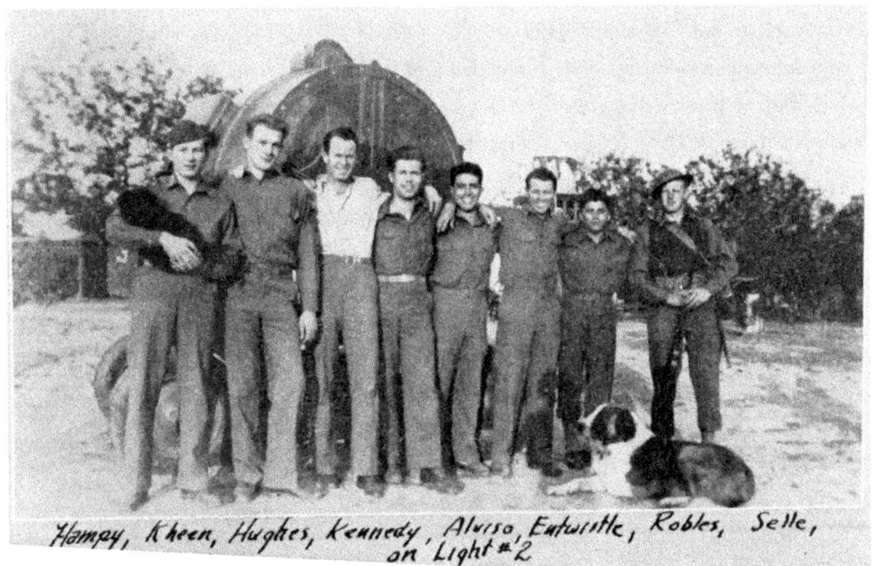

You can't hit what you can't see: Hut-Two-Hut members with a searchlight. *Collection of Michael B. McDaniel.*

> *available by Mr. Walt Disney, and Captain Duncan had contributed his powerful lights to the already large number established in the area. During that period of the war, the lights were taken to the positions in the late afternoon, manned all night, and returned to the well-camouflaged bivouac area in Griffith Park the following morning. Remember the beautiful girls at Disney's; the weekly shows and the cartoon previews in the Disney theater; late breakfast in the studio commissary?*

Interestingly, one of the Hut-Two-Hut's anti-aircraft batteries was posted at the intersection of Burbank Boulevard and Victory Boulevard, at the site Burbankers have always called the Five Points. Today, a McDonald's stands at the battery location.

After the war, the boys of the Hut-Two-Hut spoke well of the patriotism of the average Burbanker:

> *None of us will forget the generosity and "all out for defense" attitude of the citizens of Burbank and Glendale in those early stages of the war. They invited us into their homes for dinners and parties, although alert restrictions prevented our accepting all of the invitations; they brought home-cooked food to us in isolated positions; they knitted woolen sweaters*

and sox [sic] *to supplement our GI clothing during the winter months; before our positions were completed and we had no facilities for bathing and washing, they opened their homes to us and allowed us to use their showers and other conveniences; they made it almost impossible for a soldier to pay for his own drinks in a bar. When she found that we could not leave our positions for entertainment, Eleanor Frank of the Burbank Theatre Guild arranged short comedy skits for her troupe and toured our individual positions, often having her audience suddenly leave in the middle of the performance in a mad dash back to the guns as the alert siren sounded.*

Dick Lane, RKO motion picture star[12] *and his friend, Mr. Langdon, brought radio, stage, and screen stars into our areas for Sunday afternoon performances. When Neal Parker, president of the Burbank Junior Chamber of Commerce, discovered that our guns and lights were manned throughout the night, he sold his organization on the idea of sponsoring a truck carrying trays of doughnuts and gallons of hot coffee to visit the men who were on the watch for enemy aircraft. We of the midnight cavalry, especially, soon began to look forward to the nightly arrival of the doughnut*

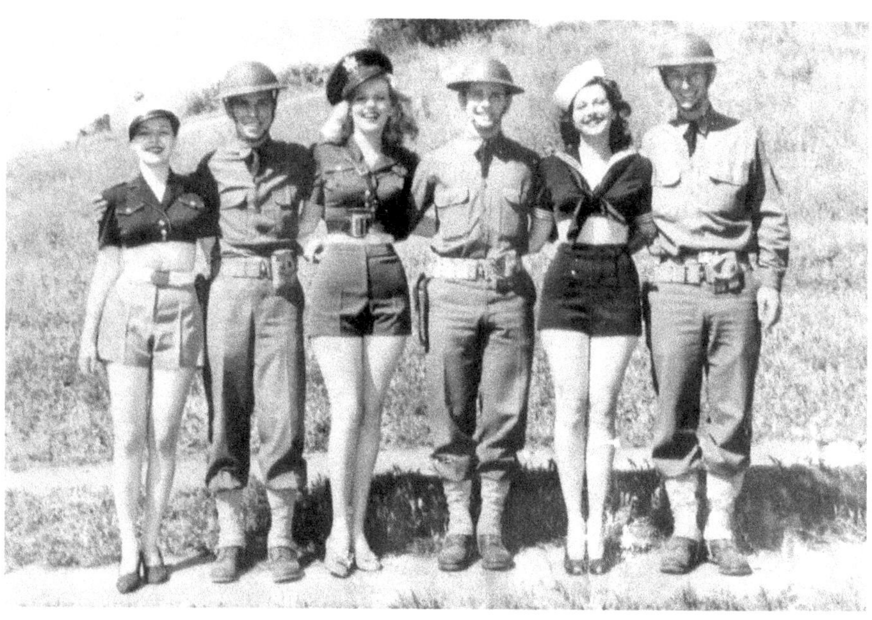

Starlets Donna Reed (USMC), Marilyn Maxwell (Army) and Julie Bishop (Navy) gather with members of the 635th Tank Destroyer Battalion: Ernie Rousellot (left), Earl Francis (center) and Harold Senne (right) were stationed in Burbank in the summer of 1942. *Ernie Rousselot.*

> *truck. Often there would be pretty girls—sometimes movie starlets—to serve us. Churches and other civic and social organizations did their best to make life a little more pleasant for us.*

In addition to the Hut-Two-Hut, the 635th Tank Destroyer Battalion also took up temporary lodging in Burbank. Its men were treated to the same visits and photo ops from the local starlets. Justin Rousselot sent the authors a photo of one such visit involving Donna Reed (in a fetching abbreviated version of a Marine Corps uniform) and his grandfather Ernie. Clomping around the Verdugo Hills on hot days for Uncle Sam clearly wasn't all drudgery.

Mystery Formation

Burbanker Lou Schirm describes what he calls the "First Real Blackout in Burbank" in the pages of the *Burbank Senior Bulldogs News* (December 2006):

> *On January 25, 1942, I was returning a date to her home on the flat part of Burbank, south of Lockheed. While sitting in the car at 12:30 a.m. we heard the air raid warning sirens, which meant off with all lights and shortly after my date's father walked out of the house with his white helmet on to be sure all lights were off. I asked, "What's up?" He said, "Have a look." I looked up to see the sky full of searchlights, searching for something heard by one of the twelve listening ears, each with a searchlight attached. Soon one found its target and all the search-lights focused on nine small dots of white seeming to be flying in formation towards Lockheed. Soon AA artillery was firing 3 inch shells toward the formation. I personally saw several explode within the formation. Yet the only things that came down were pieces of shrapnel of the 1,400 projectiles that exploded in this defense. The pieces scattered all over Hollywood. The formation broke up over Griffith Park and returned again. That's twice the formation came over Burbank. And to this day, nothing has ever been acknowledged as to what was up there and not hit.*

BALLOON BOMBS

Wes Clark's father-in-law, Don Bilyeu, has this entertaining tale about Burbank during World War II:

> *There was much concern about air raids on Lockheed and other defense industry sites in the greater Los Angeles area. On one occasion it was announced in school that balloons carrying bombs were unleashed; these were designed to float over California and detonate, causing, if nothing else, fear. It was emphasized that this caution was to be spread by word of mouth and we students were to tell our parents, friends and relatives. That night in the newspapers were big headlines expounding the danger of "Balloon Bombs."*

THE "BATTLE OF BURBANK"

The media love a good catchphrase—it sells papers. And when, on an unusually warm day on Friday, October 5, 1945, a bloody riot broke out between set decorators represented by the Conference of Studio Unions (CSU) and Warner Bros. security augmented by the Burbank, Glendale and Los Angeles police, the newspapermen dubbed it "Black Friday," "Bloody Friday" or the "Battle of Burbank." Involving some one thousand

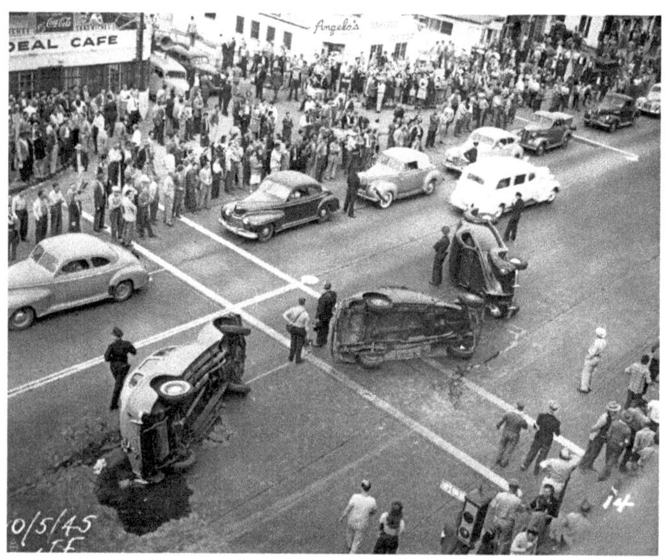

A civil disturbance outside the Warner Bros. Studios at the Battle of Burbank, October 5, 1945. *Burbank Historical Society.*

participants wielding hammers, chains and pipes on the union side and tear gas, high-pressure hoses and nightsticks on the police side, about forty injuries were reported and cars were overturned on Olive Avenue.

A TASTE OF BURBANK

Before closing our narrative about Burbank during World War II, it's probably worthwhile to note that the Burbank city prosecutor, in August 1945, led a drive to initiate legal action against horsemeat sellers in local cafés. (This was an attempt by café owners to overcome meat-rationing shortages.)

BURBANK DURING THE VIETNAM ERA

It's March 1968. Antiwar protests are held with alarming regularity in major cities across the United States, and rifts are opening in society across economic, ethnic and generational lines. But what's happening in Burbank? It's Marine Corps Day! Far from ostracizing these brave men, the city fathers organized a celebration at the recently completed Golden Mall. Disney Studios arranged for Goofy and Pluto to attend, pretty local girls served as tour guides (the Marines

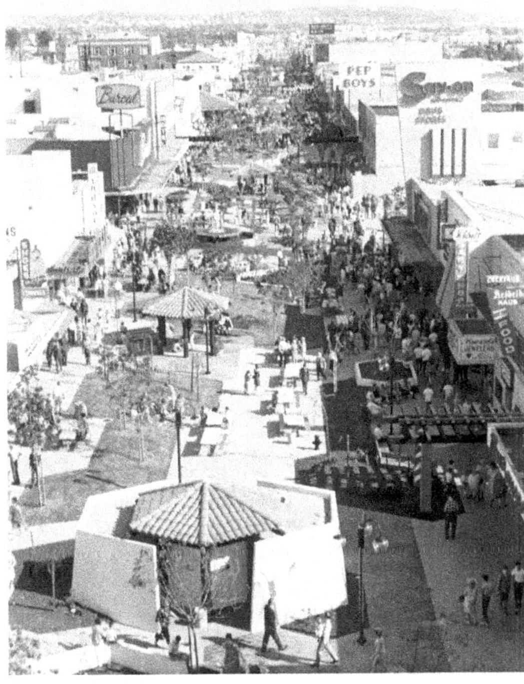

Burbank's Golden Mall is filled with people attending Marine Corps Day on March 23, 1968. *Burbank Historical Society.*

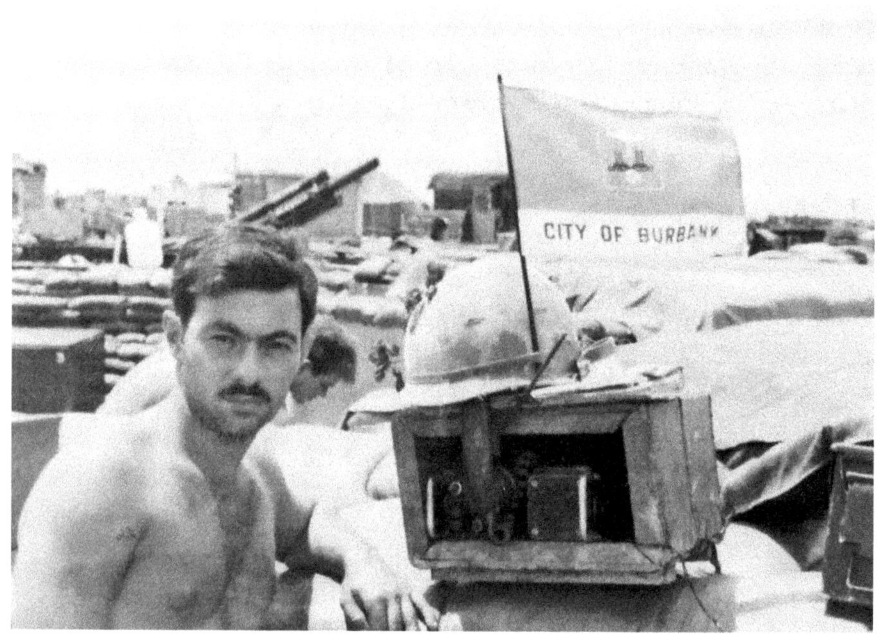

Soldier Greg Aliamo displays pride in his hometown while stationed north of Saigon and below the Cambodian border in Vietnam, 1969. *Greg Alaimo.*

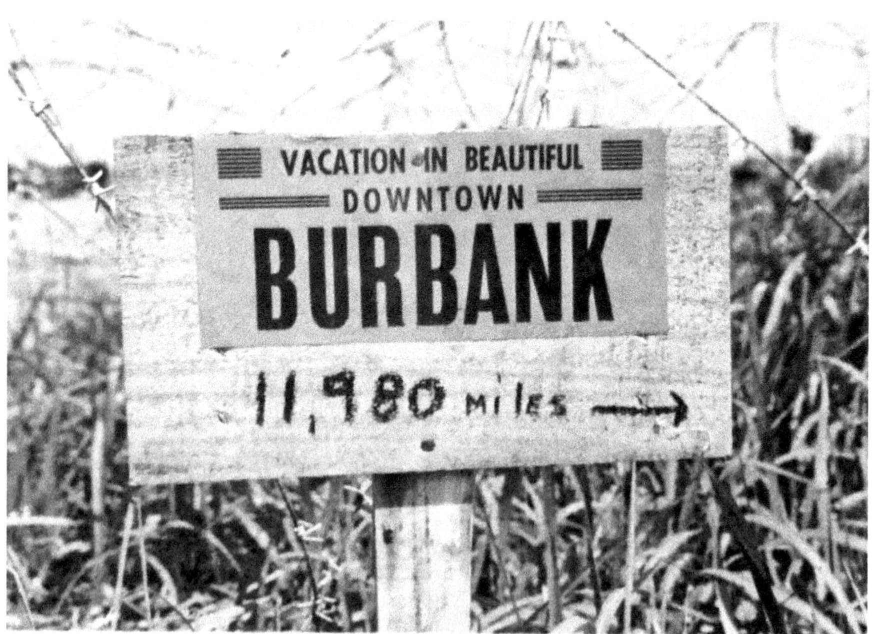

So far away.... *Greg Aliamo.*

must have appreciated that) and Bob Hope greeted the visiting warriors. What a gala affair!

The year before, Burbank High School graduates who were serving in Vietnam benefited from "Operation Cookie Lift," wherein various Burbank service organizations baked and packed cookies for shipment to Vietnam and other overseas destinations. (Burbank's Gold Star Mothers—women who had lost a son in war—contributed to postage and wrapping costs.) The cookie tins had a novel, Burbank-style, approach: they were film cans donated by various local studios.

THE CURRENT WARTIME ERA

As of this writing (March 2016), the United States is at war, with troops posted overseas in Afghanistan and Iraq, among other far-flung places. Battle fatalities, while not at the peak they were in earlier years of the Global War Against Terror, still occur. As always, Burbank has been notable in being an American city that supports the troops, with an active veterans committee.

The Burbank Veterans Committee is a group of citizens who, with the city's Parks and Recreation Department, maintain the veterans' memorials and organize events on Memorial Day and Veterans Day each year. Highlights include patriotic music, speakers,[13] aircraft flyovers and the Memorial Day Ceremony of the Rose. In this, committee members read the names of those from Burbank who have lost their lives in the defense of freedom. While the names are read, members of a local Scout troop place a rose on the monument where the person's name is inscribed. The ceremony takes place at the McCambridge Park War Memorial and is attended by over five hundred people from the community each year.

The Burbank Veterans Committee started a program in the late 1990s called "Hands Across the Battlefield," sort of a modern-day Operation Cookie Lift. Burbank citizens donate items to the veterans committee, which stores them to ship to troops whose addresses have been given to the committee. Once a year a local real estate company opens its parking lot for a November box-packing party, for shipment in time for the packages to arrive by Christmas to soldiers stationed across the globe. Burbankers are treated to a free barbecue with live music while they pack boxes. Thousands of packages have been sent since the inception of the program.

Why all this effort? It's an attempt to remember the sacrifices of citizens, to ensure that their memory is *not* one of the things lost in Burbank.

The authors provide "The Ultimate Sacrifice: Burbank's Warriors," chapter 10, based on the work of the veterans committee and the research of Mike McDaniel.

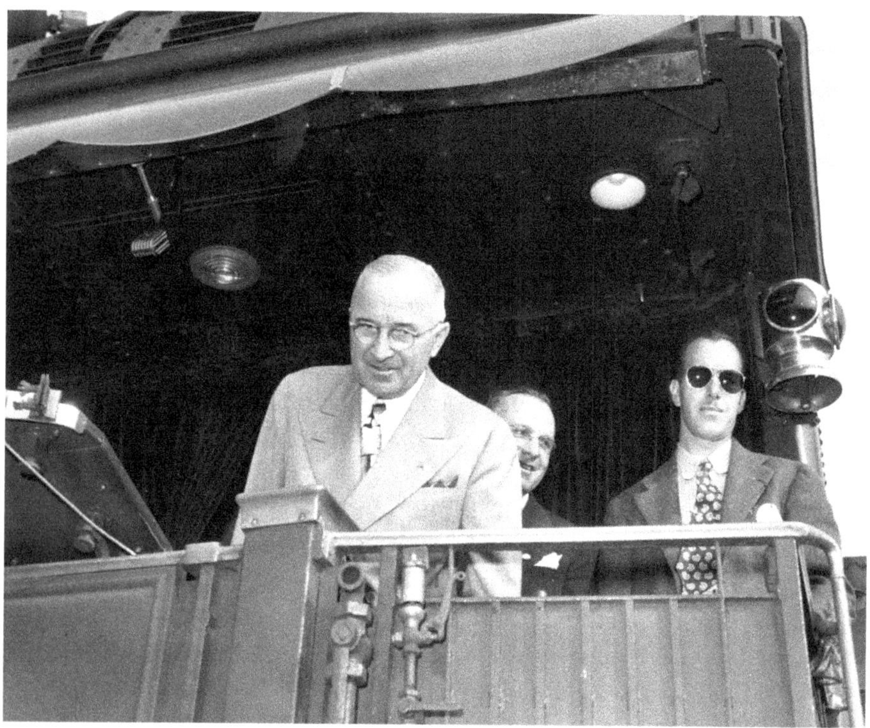

Harry S Truman on a whistle stop tour, back when U.S. presidents actually spoke from trains. This is presumably at the Burbank Depot, in the late 1940s or early 1950s. Is that a Secret Service agent with the shades? *Burbank Historical Society.*

3

THE MEDIA CAPITAL OF THE WORLD

Burbank is sometimes called the "Media Capital of the World," and this is no idle claim. It is, in fact, one of the major American cities in the worldwide entertainment industry. Burbank hosts many media and entertainment companies, and the Walt Disney Studios, Warner Bros. Entertainment, Nickelodeon, DC Comics and the Cartoon Network are all headquartered in town. Many smaller film production labs, audio studios and technical firms also call Burbank home.

First National Pictures

The *Burbank Community Book* of 1944 records the day Burbank was about to become a media capital:

> *One day, according to Howard Martin, who with his parents, Mr. and Mrs. S.A. Martin, owned and occupied the old David Burbank homestead near where Olive Avenue crosses the Los Angeles River and enters Dark Canyon, they saw a wagon unloading a load of lumber on the property of August Handorf, their adjoining neighbor. This was the first inkling the Martins had that they were to have a moving picture studio in the neighborhood. It was likewise the first inkling that the citizens of Burbank had that their city was to be the new home of the First National Studios.*

With the exception of *A Quiet Day in Burbank*, a lost eleven-plus-minute short shown in an unlocated Rose Theater,[14] Burbank's entry into the world of motion pictures by a major studio began on paper in 1924, when the Associated First National Pictures Company expanded from only distributing films to producing them. In 1924 the company changed its corporate name to First National Pictures, Inc., and in 1926 it built a sixty-two-acre studio lot in Burbank on the Handorf property alongside Olive Avenue, where alfalfa and onion fields thrived. Most of the soundstages are still there.

The only First National film you are likely to recognize by name is an important one. Indeed, it is one of the greatest films of the silent era: Charlie Chaplin's *The Kid*, produced in 1921. You might be forgiven for assuming that because it was a First National film and because First National was located in Burbank this important movie was filmed there. It wasn't—it was filmed in Los Angeles and Pasadena, California.

After purchase by Warner Bros. in 1928, *The Dawn Patrol* (1930) and *Little Caesar* (1931) were First National's most famous films. *Little Caesar* was filmed in Burbank.

Warner Bros.

Warner Bros. Studios has been an undeniable presence in town since it merged with First National. Who hasn't driven down Olive Avenue to Barham Boulevard, heading to Hollywood, and seen those enormous promotional signs hanging on the sides of the soundstage buildings?[15]

Angels with Dirty Faces, a Warner Bros. gangster/social issues film from 1938, opens with a splendid sequence showing a New York City street. A man's newspaper is opened, and in large font, we can see that Harding has been nominated—it's mid-June 1920. The camera moves along as we see, incredibly, laundry flapping in the breeze from nearly every open tenement window; fruit trucks move slowly up and down a crowded street. The camera moves down, and a street sign becomes visible: it's Dock Street. Fittingly, a

Opposite, bottom: The Dead End Kids, called in this photograph the Plagues of Burbank, stride with mischief in mind on the Warner lot while filming *Angels with Dirty Faces* in 1938. *Left to right:* Leo Gorcey, Bernard Punsley, Billy Halop, Bobby Jordan, Huntz Hall and Gabriel Dell. *Collection of Michael B. McDaniel.*

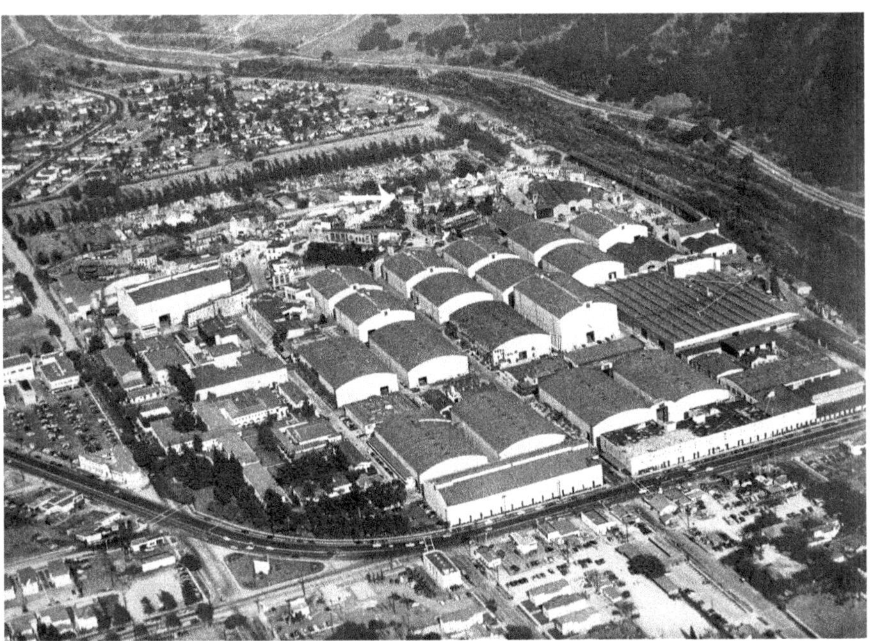

The back lot of Warner Bros. in the late 1930s. The arrow shows the location of Dr. David Burbank's ranch house. *Burbank Historical Society.*

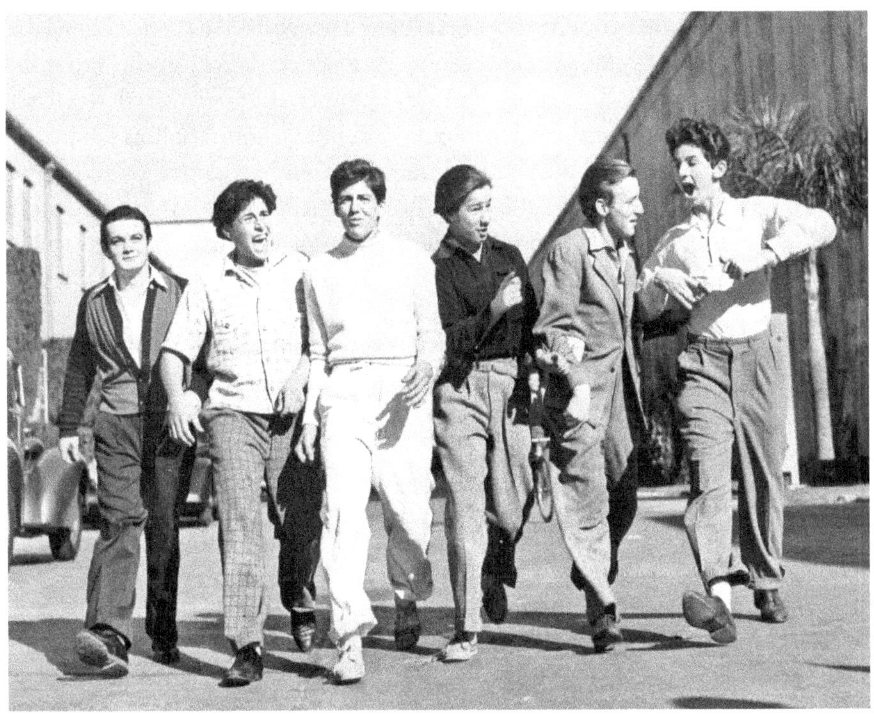

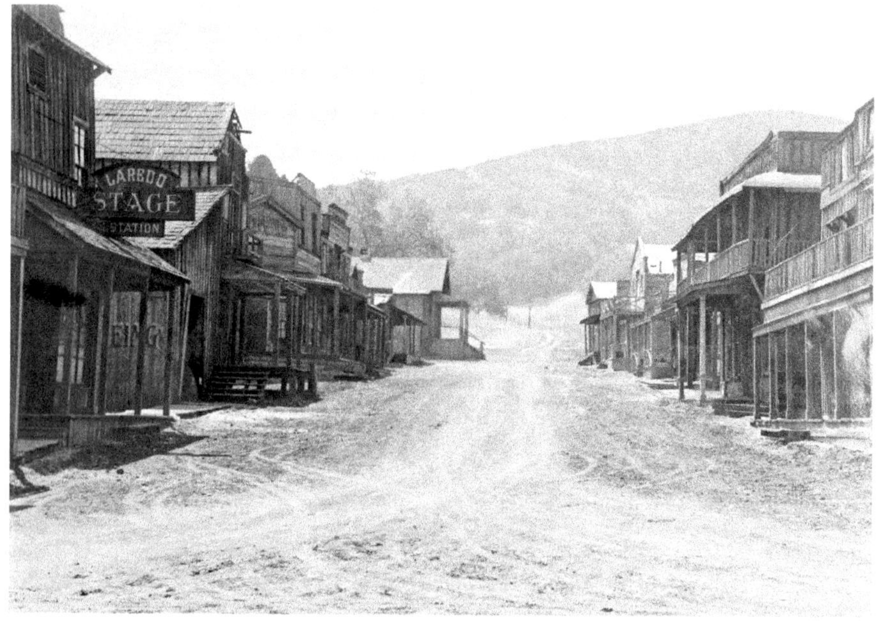

The western set on the Warner Bros. back lot in the 1920s. Three miles behind them thar hills is Hollywood! *Burbank Historical Society.*

barroom piano is heard playing something that sounds like "The Sidewalks of New York." An organ grinder is shown; two girls dance on the sidewalk to the music he makes. The camera moves up onto a fire escape balcony, and two boys are shown: one is clearly intended to be the young James Cagney.[16] The dialogue begins. It's all vivid, visually rich and evocative of old New York. But it's not New York City at all. The set dressers and production people have fooled you. It's the Warner's back lot in Burbank, California! What you've just seen represents the artistic height of the old studio system, when infinite care was taken with the smallest details.

Everyone loves *Casablanca* (1942), the quintessential Bogie flick. That famous farewell scene on the airport tarmac is iconic. But that was no airport, and that was no tarmac. That was a Warner's soundstage. In Burbank. And if you ever watched a Warner's production that included jungle scenes, you probably saw the area that Burbanker Richard Dixon, a valued contributor to the authors' Burbankia website, describes in his delightful memories of Warner Bros. in the 1940s:

> *We often talked of how, one day, we would plan a secret mission into that unknown jungle where so many of the old "B" jungle movies and Saturday*

afternoon serials were filmed, "Warner's Jungle." Although Warner's was not as famous for serials as the smaller studios like Monogram, they did produce their share of really bad black and white jungle movies. There were always a lot of natives in these awful films and you would notice right off that they were all white guys with burnt cork smeared on their bodies. Even we kids saw through this.

Studios in those days had no tours at all. These were mysterious places where movie magic was made and they did not really want anyone to know how it was all done. An operation such as sneaking into Warner's was nothing to be taken lightly. We had heard rumors about kids who had been caught inside the fence and they were not funny stories…at all.

Planning for "Operation Warner's Jungle Adventure" took place in our fort…the plan was complex and detailed and we drew diagrams of how we would carry it out, although by the time we decided to execute it we had lost all of these "Eyes Only" documents. And so, at the appointed time, which, I believe was a Saturday morning, Darrell Woodhouse and I, along with Burton Pines and some other foolish neighborhood kid calmly strode down Olive Avenue to where it intersected with Verdugo Road and, after checking both directions, smoothly and stealthily slipped under the security chain link fence surrounding the back lot. Crouching down, we ran a few yards and disappeared into the steaming hell of the jungle.

When our eyes became accustomed to the darkness we saw huge tropical trees of every kind (not real, of course) and vines that you could actually swing on as well as a clear stream winding through the area. Large elephant ear plants and other tropical vegetation loomed up in front of us. Unfortunately we did not have one of those machete knives they use in the movies so we had to duck under enormous plants as we went. We followed the stream which led us to a clearing at the edge of the jungle and, to our surprise, found ourselves staring at a full size submarine! Forgetting that we were trespassing and in mortal danger we began playing submarine games as if we were in a movie. We must have made quite a racket because suddenly we heard bursts of machine gun fire. We all froze, realizing someone was shooting at us so we dove for cover back into the dense jungle and raced along tracing our path to our entry point, which was about fifty yards from the submarine set. We slipped under the fence and raced across Olive Avenue, all the while still hearing the guns firing at us.

I'm not sure where the others went but I ran into Sanford's market which was right across Olive Avenue from the back lot jungle. I ran through the store and must have knocked down several elderly shoppers, although I don't clearly remember. I hid in the men's restroom at the back of the store for what seemed like several hours. Finally, I slipped out the back service door and walked up the alley which ran parallel to Olive Avenue. This took me up to Catalina Street within three houses of my home. I sat on the edge of our fish pond and relished in the thrill of what we had just done...and we had come out with our minds and bodies intact. Mission accomplished!

Mr. Woodhouse got quite a chuckle out of our story, and when we told him about the machine gun fire he laughed even more, which confused us. He then told us that the guards who patrolled the fences of the back lot had recordings of gun fire to scare off intruders and had been "shooting" just to scare us. We, of course, knew what we had experienced and did not for one minute believe him. From that day forward we felt sort of like veterans who had lived through some very dangerous battle.

HONORARY BURBANKER: TRIGGER

Richard Dixon describes how rural the Burbank outskirts near Dark Canyon looked in the late 1940s:

My father had taken a job as manager of part of this movie ranch which was just across the L.A. River from Warner Brothers Studio. We lived up at the foot of Mt. Lee, just over the crest from the Hollywood sign. We were on the east side of the mountain facing the San Fernando Valley....The area covered a thousand acres of mountain oaks and sycamores with standing sets here and there. Dry stream beds ran down deep gullies and there were mountain lions living in the caves up on the bare face of Mt. Cahuenga to the west. Although Hollywood was only a twenty minute drive from our home, coyotes howled outside our house in the night. It was a child's living fantasy.

Dixon goes on to describe the Hudkins Brothers Ranch, located near here. The ranch was composed of stables that housed movie horses—some of the most famous in history, including Roy Rogers's Trigger and the Lone Ranger's Silver. In fact, Rogers purchased Trigger from the Hudkins Stables on September 18, 1943, for the sum of $2,500.

While it's true that, technically, the Hudkins Ranch was located just over the Los Angeles River past the city boundary into Hollywood, the authors give Trigger honorary Burbanker status. (We're sure Trigger roamed over the river for a drink or two; he was quite intelligent and intrepid.)

COLUMBIA RANCH

The Ranch started in 1934 as a forty-acre lot purchased by Harry Cohn, who, at the time, was head of Columbia Pictures Corporation. It's located on North Hollywood Way and is presently owned by Warner Bros. It is now called the Warner Ranch.

As was the case with various Warner Bros. films, you've seen Burbank before in Columbia productions but just didn't realize that it was Burbank. *Father Knows Best*, *The Donna Reed Show*, *Dennis the Menace*, *Hazel*, *Bewitched*, *Gidget*, *I Dream of Jeannie*, *The Monkees*, *The Flying Nun*, *Here Come the Brides*, *The Partridge Family*...all were filmed on the Columbia Ranch lot in Burbank. Movies filmed there include *Lost Horizon* (1933),[17] *High Noon* (1952), *Mr. Deeds Goes to Town* (1936), *You Were Never Lovelier* (1942), *The Wild One* (1953) and *Autumn Leaves* (1956).

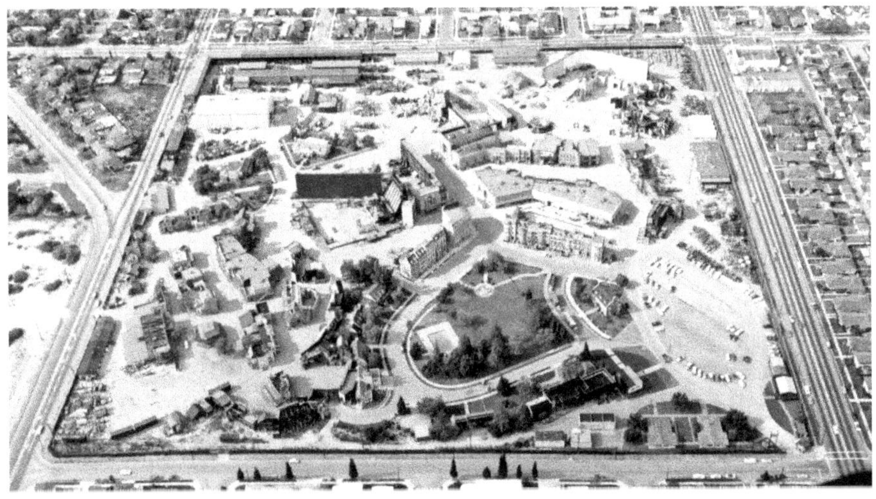

Columbia Ranch in the 1950s. The street at bottom is West Oak Street; the major street at right is Hollywood Way. Verdugo Boulevard is at top. Shangri-La from *Lost Horizon* (1937) once stood at the upper right-hand corner. *Collection of Michael B. McDaniel.*

Part of this historic site is, indeed, lost. By 1970 portions of the lot were in disrepair, and a fire destroyed about a quarter of the ranch. In 1974 eight acres of the original forty were sold off to developers, and in that same year another fire destroyed the entire New York City set. About a third of the ranch was gone—never to be rebuilt.

COLUMBIA FILM TRICKERY

It's always fun to spot Burbank locations in television and in movies. On April 17, 1946, Columbia Studios took film footage in and around Burbank, Glendale and downtown Los Angeles to be used in its Rita Hayworth film *Down to Earth*, which was released in 1947. The story is about a Greek muse coming down to Earth to involve herself in a Broadway production.[18] Rear-screen projection shots were made by Columbia cameramen mounting cameras on railroad trains making their way at night alongside San Fernando Road through Burbank; at one point, some hoboes lounging by the tracks are seen. The finished product is interesting if you know what to look for. In the film, Hayworth steps out onto a train platform for a chat, and the old Burbank train depot on North Front Street can be seen passing by—no less than three times in a few minutes of dialogue. Was this a sneaky visual joke by the Columbia Studios film editor? (The footage may be viewed in the "Videos" section of the Burbankia website.)

The Columbia television division produced a series that ran from 1973 to 1978 called *Police Story*. In one memorable episode,[19] a squad car is shown barreling down Olive Avenue after a fleeing criminal. At one point the squad car is atop the Olive Avenue Bridge. It suddenly appears heading down the Magnolia Boulevard Bridge. Quite a feat, in that the squad car must have traveled sideways two entire city blocks! Also, it impossibly passes the Burbank Ford dealership three times in quick succession.

WALT DISNEY STUDIOS

Snow White (1939) was the first feature-length animated film, and it was a major financial success for the Walt Disney Studios. Using the profits from this film, Walt Disney moved from his Hyperion Street, Los Angeles address

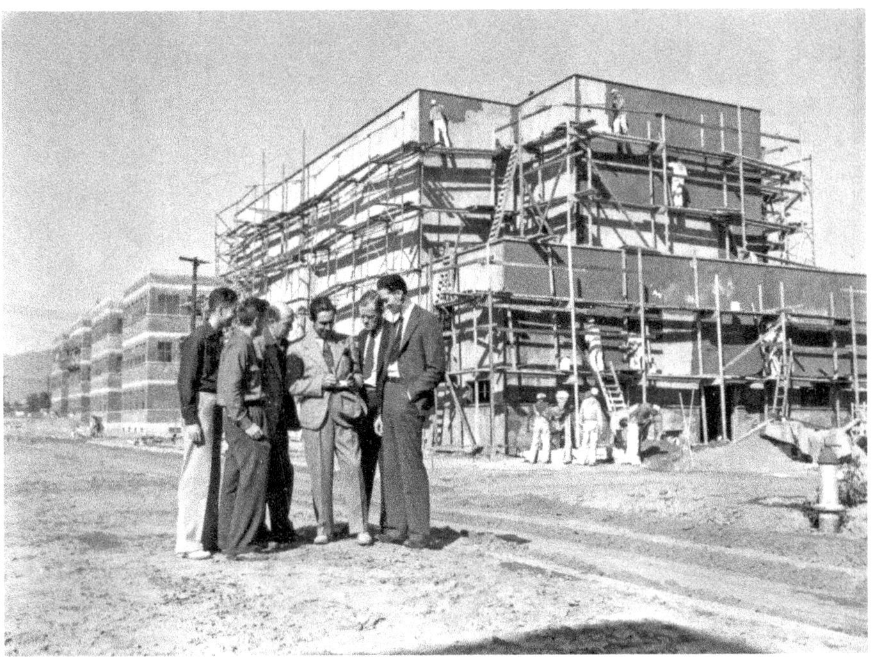

Walt Disney *(center)* visits the construction site of his new studio in Burbank, 1939. *Burbank Historical Society.*

to a fifty-one-acre Burbank location on Buena Vista Avenue in 1939. The company is headquartered there to this day.

The studio has always played a part in the Burbank community, and Disney artists have lent their talents to various city functions and institutions. In fact, during the 2011 centennial celebrations at city hall, Mickey and Minnie Mouse served as Disney representatives.

We return to Richard Dixon's childhood memories, this time of the Disney lot in the 1940s, for some wonderful lore:

> *Sometimes, in the summer, when we weren't cooling off at Pickwick Swim Park we would cross Olive Avenue and walk over to the back of the Walt Disney Studios lot, which was only five blocks away, and swim in the amazingly crystal clear pond which was created from the water runoff from Disney's cooling system. In those days air conditioning was not yet available. Disney had installed water sprinklers on top of all the offices and sound stages, which cooled them. This water runoff was then piped out the back of the studio and into a large pit which formed a perfect swimming pond of crystal clear water at the edge of the L.A. River, which had only dirt banks back then.*

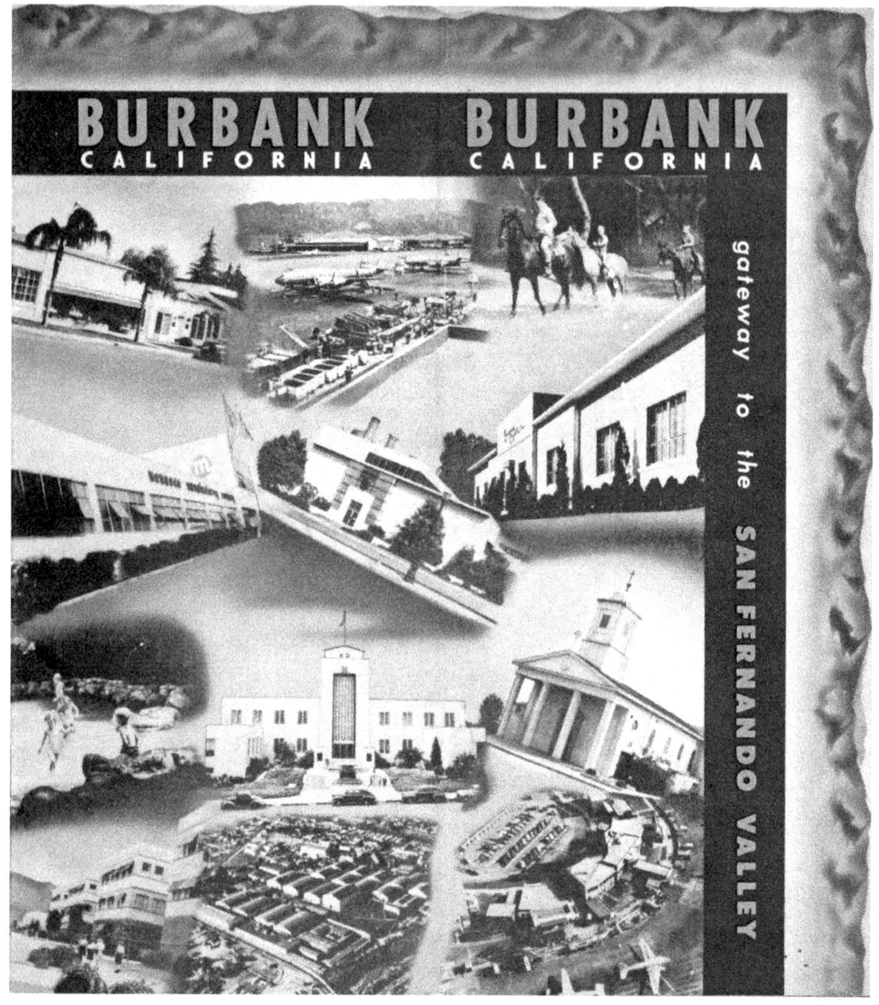

Burbank booklet given to new employees by Walt Disney Studios in 1947. *Collection of Michael B. McDaniel.*

> *Next to the pond was a huge burn pile where the studio burned all the thrown away film clippings, sketches and cells from the animation department. I have always wished I had collected these drawings that were lying all over the place, as they would be worth a fortune now.*

When the Disney Company looked for talent, it looked locally. Kathryn Beaumont, the ten-year-old model for *Alice in Wonderland* (1951), was later a Burbank High School student (class of 1955).

As a matter of interest, Walt Disney died on December 15, 1966, in the St. Joseph's Hospital in Burbank. When he died, his Burbank office was sealed, but you can see it preserved at Disneyland, down to the paperwork left on his desk.

COLOR CITY

The first purpose-built color television studio in the United States was erected by RCA, the parent company of the National Broadcasting Corporation (NBC), in March 1955 on West Alameda Avenue. It was nicknamed "NBC Color City" and occupied forty-nine acres of land (thirty of it purchased from Jack Warner).

Burbanker Jimmy Koren has a funny story about this facility:

> *My first pair of cowboy boots is buried under the NBC building! I was ten years old when they were building that place, and we were playing shoeless in the piles of sand. Lo and behold along comes a tractor to start pushing the sand around....Goodbye boots! Imagine getting home and 'splaining to Mom why you're barefooted.*

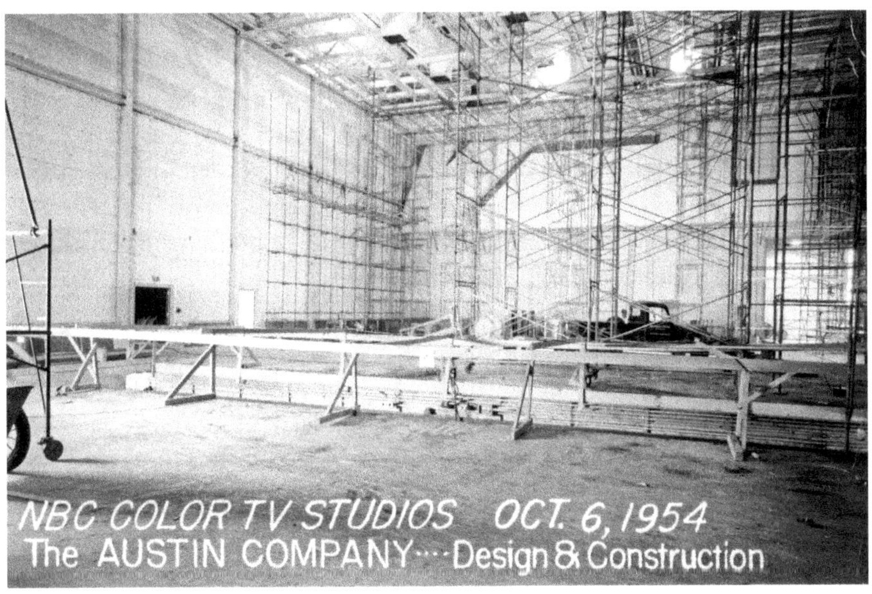

A progress postcard showing the construction of the NBC Studios on West Alameda Avenue, 1954. One gets a good idea of the interior volume of a television sound stage from this image. *Collection of Michael B. McDaniel.*

ROWAN AND MARTIN'S LAUGH-IN

The entire run of the show was filmed at the NBC Studios, and as noted in just about any work about Burbank, the phrase "beautiful downtown Burbank" was first coined on the show by Gary Owens, who served as the announcer. It was a funny moment when, at the ceremony for the 100th anniversary of the city's incorporation, held in front of city hall, Owens once again cupped hand over ear in his characteristic fashion and uttered the famous catchphrase, to wild cheers.

The show almost always opened with some reference to Burbank, including the following examples: "From the lovely Coconut Room high atop the Unemployment Building in beautiful downtown Burbank, it's *Rowan and Martin's Laugh-In*!"; "From the recovery room of the beautiful Uptown Hospital here in beautiful downtown Burbank, it's *Rowan and Martin's Laugh-In*!"; "Coming to you from the beautiful downtown Burbank Bird Sanctuary and Rifle Range, it's *Rowan and Martin's Laugh-In*!"; "From the steam room of the beautiful downtown Burbank Post Office and Maternity Ward, it's *Rowan and Martin's Laugh-In*!"; and "From the beautiful downtown Burbank Municipal Court House and Topless Bowling Alley, it's *Rowan and Martin's Laugh-In*!" There were many more.

A *Los Angeles Times* article from May 16, 1968, notes that the Burbank City Council, knowing a good publicity angle when it saw one, voted unanimously to invite Dan Rowan and Dick Martin to ride on the city's Tournament of Roses float that year. "Beautiful downtown Burbank" soon caught on and put Burbank on the map with television viewers all across the country. It wasn't long before postcards began to be printed with the phrase, allowing visitors to document to folks back home whether or not they had found the place beautiful. The city also became the butt of jokes on *Rowan and Martin's Laugh-In*; one memorable spot featured Eve Arden commemorating Burbank's many famous and historic vacant lots.[20]

The joke, of course, is that beauty is in the eye of the beholder. While there are many who insist that Burbank is indeed beautiful, others, like Frank Zappa, have claimed that the San Fernando Valley is the ugliest and most charmless place in the country.[21] Whether that is the case, you, Gentle Reader, may decide.

It is worth noting that the phrase "beautiful downtown Burbank" was, for a time, a registered trademark owned by the Burbank Chamber of Commerce. The trademark is now dead—additional comedic fodder for those who wax cynical about Burbank.

The Tonight Show Starring Johnny Carson

From 1972 to 1992, announcer Ed McMahon began each broadcast of *The Tonight Show Starring Johnny Carson* with a bald-faced lie that caused Burbankers' jaws to clench: "From Hollywood." No, no, no…it was broadcast from the NBC Studios in Burbank. The show moved there from New York City on May 1, 1972.

In 1979 Dan Remy, a city councilman, claimed, "Burbank is the current Hollywood. Hollywood is simply a name." As true as that may have been, it didn't stop Carson from constantly ribbing Burbank in monologues: "Burbank leads the nation in the number of squirrel suicides." "Burbank was founded by Dr. David Burbank, a dentist—apparently he thought it was a great place to have a toothache." "Burbank has an official flag—a deceased crow." "Burbank has a nightclub for senior citizens: the Slipped Disco—if you put your drink down somebody will put his teeth into it." "You can kill a weekend in Burbank by taking the Forest Lawn Tour."[22] "On New Year's Eve in Burbank everyone gathers around and watches the mayor drop a Ring Ding from the roof of a 7-Eleven." "Burbank's favorite Italian restaurant is Vinnie Abruzzi's Little Touch of Newark—a table with a view is near the ladies room with the door opened." And there were many others.

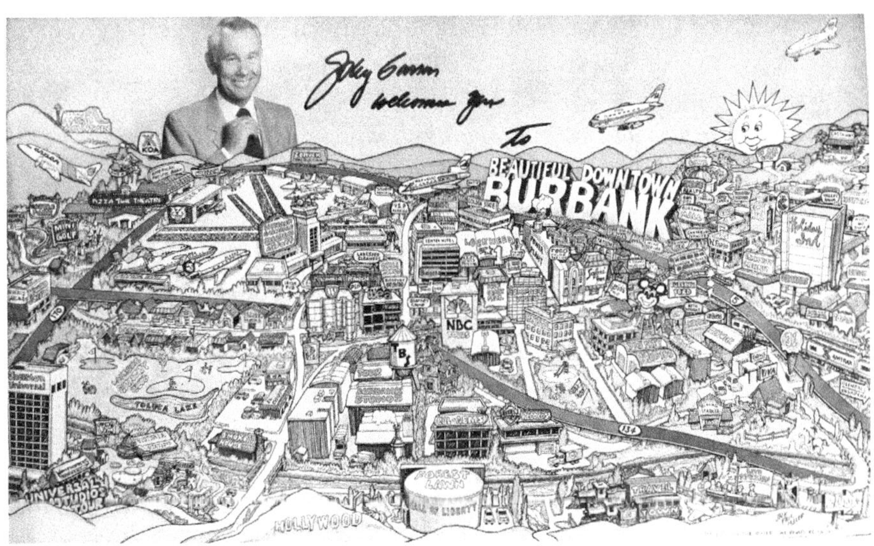

Johnny Carson looms over Burbank in this whimsical 1981 poster welcoming visitors. *Courtesy of Carson Entertainment Group. Jack Paul Miller, artist.*

Burbank, unfazed, made Johnny Carson an official Burbank Ambassador (with all the rights and privileges thereunto pertaining), and in 1981, there appeared a "Beautiful Downtown Burbank" poster featuring Carson looming over the Verdugo Hills. In 1992 Burbank renamed Buena Vista Park, across the street from the NBC Studios, as Johnny Carson Park.

The Burbank Studios

What's "lost" about this site? It's no longer owned by NBC. Universal Studios merged with NBC in 2003 to form the current NBCUniversal. This being the case, Universal moved its television operations to a newer and larger studio a few miles away (the *Tonight Show* moved back to New York City), and by 2008, NBC had sold the facility. It is now known, generically, as the Burbank Studios. Currently, only the daytime soap opera *Days of Our Lives* is produced there—a far cry from its busy earlier history.

The Patsy Awards

You've heard of the Oscar, Emmy and Tony Awards. Have you ever heard of the Patsy Award? The award's Wikipedia page states:

> *The Patsy Award was originated by the Hollywood office of the American Humane Association in 1939. They decided to honor animal performers after a horse was killed in an on-set accident during the filming of the Tyrone Power film* Jesse James. *The letters are an acronym, and stand for Picture Animal Top Star of the Year.*
>
> *The very first recipient of a Patsy was Francis the Talking Mule in 1951. The award now covers both film and television and is separated into four categories: canine, equine, wild and special. The special category encompasses everything from goats to cats to pigs—Arnold Ziffel of TV's* Green Acres *was a two-time winner. Arnold's trainer, Frank Inn, was the proud owner of over 40 Patsy awards, thanks to his work with Orangey, the cat from* Rhubarb *(1951) and* Breakfast at Tiffany's *(1961); Higgins, the dog (who played the lead in the* Benji *movies and "Dog" on* Petticoat Junction*); Cleo the Basset Hound; and Lassie, to name a few.*

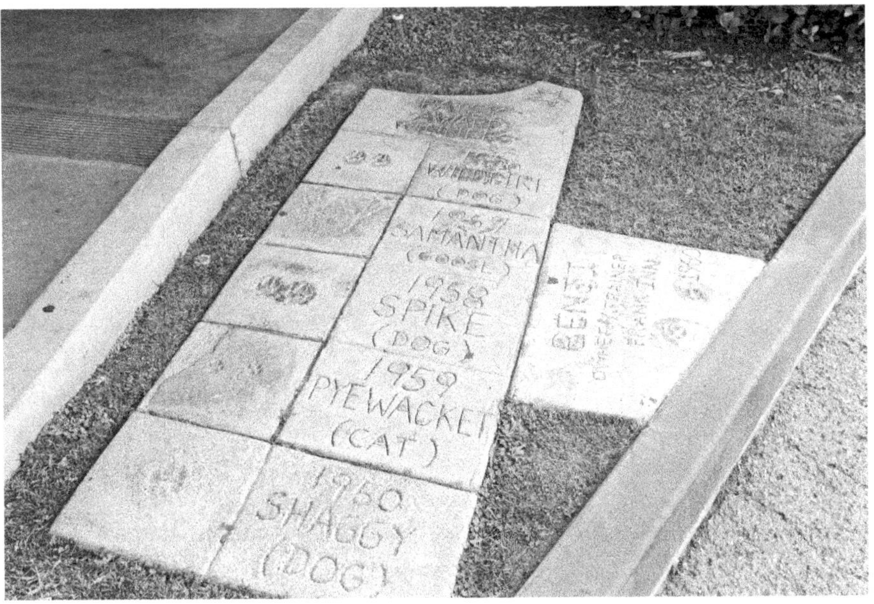

Some of the various Patsy Award winners' paw prints enshrined at the Burbank Animal Shelter. *Wes Clark.*

> *Bob Barker served as host for the Patsy Awards but eventually resigned in protest of the cruel methods some trainers use when training animals for films. The awards ended in 1986 due to lack of funding.*

The movie award recipients from 1951 to 1960 have their names and paw prints in the courtyard of the Burbank Animal Shelter at 1150 North Victory Place. The shelter used to be located under the Burbank Boulevard overpass at the Five Points; when the shelter was moved, so were the paw prints.

BORING PORN, UNEXPECTED PORN...AND TOILET PAPER

Given all the film industry labs in town and the fact that the San Fernando Valley of California is the pornography capital of the United States,[23] it stands to reason that Burbank probably has some entertaining porn industry stories. And so it does. There is a bizarre July 10, 1977 *Los Angeles Times* article about the owners of the Allied Color Laboratories in Burbank playing tricks on one another. One such trick involved toilet paper—six hundred

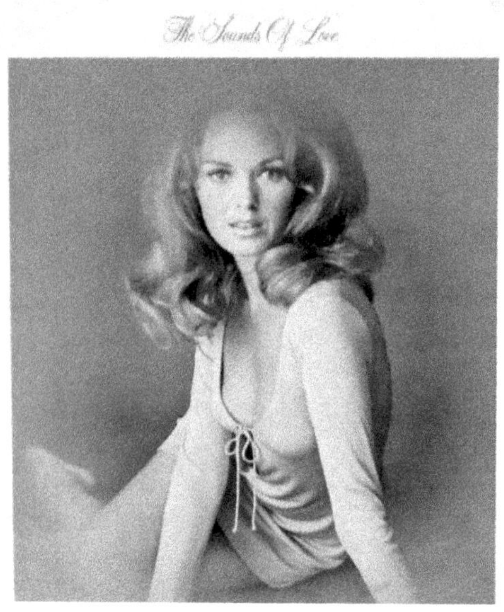

The 101 Strings: *The Sounds of Love.* Not a Grammy winner. *Wes Clark Collection.*

rolls of it—wound around a home on Elmwood Avenue, entirely obscuring it from view. What caused this outsized retaliation was the filling of one of the tricksters' 1977 Porsche with pornographic films (such films being a product of the Allied Color Labs) and an exterior plastered with "the lewdest, most horrible photographs we could find." The neighbors had mixed reactions. One, a resident since 1940, called it "the greatest thing to ever happen" (it topped Lockheed in World War II?). Another called in the Burbank fire and police departments as well as the city zoning folks. Burbank officials demanded that the toilet paper be entirely removed by nightfall. The victim was recorded as stating, "I'll get my revenge. We have to do something to break the monotony of this work." So there you have it: processing pornography is *boring*. Who knew?

Admittedly, the next Burbank porn tale is pretty lightweight and involves the otherwise staid 101 Strings, a musical ensemble famed for recording vinyl albums of the "easy listening" genre with such titles as *The Emotion of 101 Strings at Gypsy Campfires*, *101 Strings Play the Sugar & Spice of Rudolph Friml*, *101 Strings Plays Hit Songs for Girls* and *Million Seller Hits of 1966*. These budget discs usually went for $1.99 each and could be found in grocery store record bins all across America. While the recordings were produced in Germany (the 101 String Orchestra was, in fact, the Orchester des Nordwestdeutschen Rundfunks Hamburg), the vinyl was pressed in Burbank by A/S Records (Alshire Records). Enthusiastic buyers of these albums skewed toward the sixty-five-and-over demographic. It was especially odd, then, when the group released its most infamous record: *101 Strings: The Sounds of Love*. Meaning, literally, the sounds of love as gasped and moaned by one Bebe Bardon, female vocalist. The authors tried listening to *The Sounds of Love* one night.

It's pretty horrible. Cascading strings mixed with porn vocals just doesn't make for a meaningful musical experience. (Hear for yourself. Some of these cuts are on YouTube.) Sometimes, "lost" is not a bad thing.

Finally, there was the time in October 1994 when surprised Burbank Water and Power employees arrived at work to find that the area was the site of the filming of a pornographic movie. The police department clerk, when approving a request for what she thought was an ordinary film, granted the permit. (Burbank grants filming permits for 175 to 200 productions each year.) Among the memorable quotes from interested parties are the following: "That's not the type of image we want for the city." (Ron Stassi, general manager of the Public Services Department.) "We never, ever, ever, ever, ever—and I will say that double emphatically—shoot [X-rated movies] without having permission, without being up front about it." (Nick Pinkowski, porn movie producer.) "I guess they got to film it somewhere, but it's different than if you spend $20 on a nudie bar and are pretty well liquored up and don't care what's going to happen. It's different than coming stone sober to work. It shouldn't occur in the workplace." (Surprised BWP employee.)

FALCON THEATRE

Most Burbankers are aware that the Falcon Theatre, located on 4252 West Riverside Drive, was founded and owned by famous producer Garry Marshall. Befitting a man who may be regarded as an elder statesman of

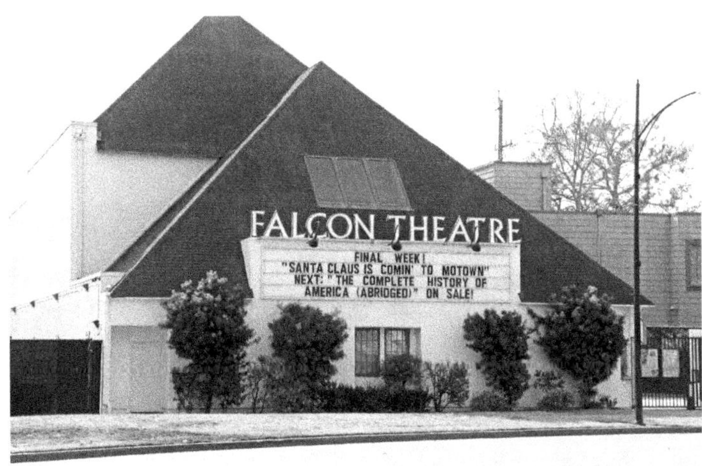

Garry Marshall's Falcon Theatre on 4252 West Riverside Drive. *Wes Clark.*

entertainment, it's a venue that specializes in new work by emerging artists. But why is it called the Falcon Theatre?

As a teen, Marshall was familiar with the gang scene in the Bronx, where he grew up. (In fact, the character of Arthur "The Fonz" Fonzarelli on *Happy Days* was based on an especially charismatic youth he knew named Pete Wagner.) It's simple: The Falcons was the name of Marshall's gang; it was a 1950s Bronx street gang that morphed into a sports club when the boys grew tired of getting beaten up.

FAMOUS BURBANKERS IN THE ENTERTAINMENT INDUSTRY

Wikipedia and notes kept by the Burbank Historical Society give a list of notable Burbankers from all career fields. The ones you might know from the entertainment industry are noted here, in no special order:

> *Debbie Reynolds, Jane Russell, Ann Sheridan, Roy Rogers, Johnny Grant, Peggy Ryan, George Putnam, Glenn Strange, Frankie Laine, Angie Dickinson, Vic Tayback, Don Grady (Agradi), Gary Grimes, Dan Haggerty, Jennifer Love Hewitt, Rene Russo, Angela Cartwright, Anson Williams, Sterling Beaumon, Juice Newton, Eddie Rabbitt, Kim Fields,*

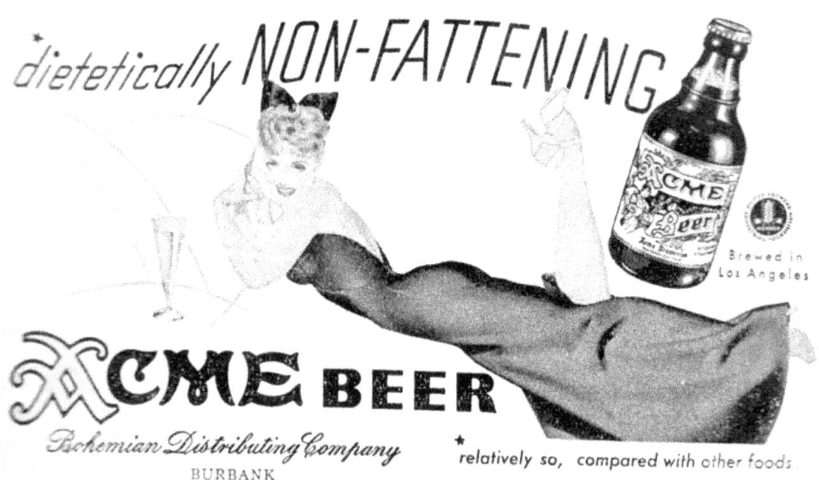

Only in Burbank could beer be (relatively) nonfattening. *Collection of Michael B. McDaniel.*

> *Tyler Blackburn, Kelly Blatz, Tim Burton, Debbe Dunning, Masiela Lusha, Mark Harmon, Ron Howard, Clint Howard, Kristy McNichol, Erin Moran, Elijah Wood, Mitch Vogel, Blake Lively, Chris Marquette, Cady McClain, Hayley McFarland, Eve Plumb, Jason Ritter, John Ritter, Wil Wheaton, and Anton Yelchin.*

There are undoubtedly others, but we shall rely on the constantly updated Internet for those.

4

NOTABLE BURBANK PLACES

Burbank is a jurisdiction of 17.379 square miles. Founded in 1887, it is now 129 years old. That being the case, there are indeed a number of interesting Burbank places. But, often with cities Burbank's size, you have to do some digging to discover where the interest lies. Some of these places are indeed lost, some of them are still with us and one of them has been moved to Buena Park, California.

Jeffries Barn

James J. Jeffries was considered one of the great heavyweight boxers of his era. He owned Burbank property on the corner of West Victory Boulevard and North Buena Vista Street. On that property stood the Jeffries Barn, where Thursday night boxing matches were held from 1931 until Jeffries's death in 1953. It is interesting to note that John Garfield's big boxing scene in the Dead End Kids film *They Made Me a Criminal* (1939) was filmed in the Jeffries Barn. After Jeffries's death the barn was dismantled and moved to the Knott's Berry Farm amusement park in Orange County, where it still stands as the Wilderness Dance Hall. A Ralph's grocery store parking lot occupies the barn's original location. The land for the Jeffries home, across North Buena Vista Street, was one of Burbank's many vacant lots until 1976, when the Landmark Center shopping plaza was built on the site.

Jeffries gradually sold parts of his ranch, until only his home and barn were left when he died on March 3, 1953. The barn was moved to make room for a labor union building that was near the site. The home deteriorated after Jeffries died and was torn down.

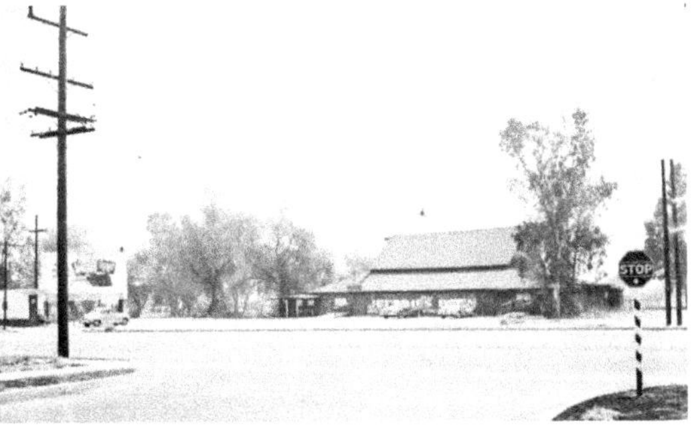

The Jeffries Barn on the corner of Buena Vista Street and Victory Boulevard, 1940s. The site of many a fine bout. *Collection of Michael B. McDaniel.*

BURBANK BUILDING

Without a doubt the most striking edifice of Burbank's earliest days is the Burbank Building on the corner of San Fernando Road and Olive Avenue, with its distinctive circular turret that resembles a medieval Russian helmet.

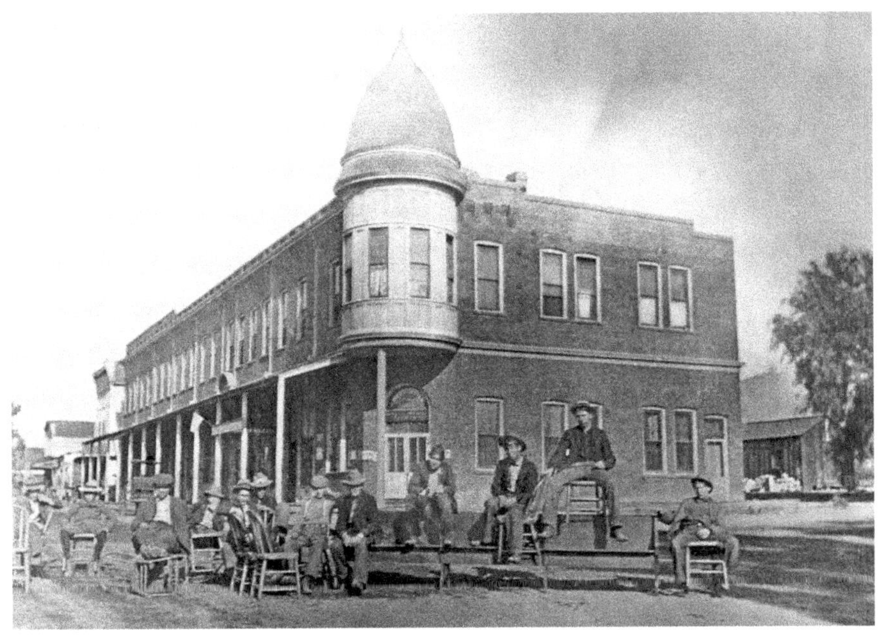

The Burbank Building, 1890s. Why are there raffish young men on church pews blocking San Fernando Road? We don't know. *Burbank Historical Society.*

Built prior to 1888, it still stands—minus the odd roof feature, which was deemed structurally unsafe and removed after an earthquake. The building was originally planned as a bank, but the Burbank Post Office was, for a time, located on the ground level. The city fathers met upstairs to conduct business, and a wooden sidewalk ran in front. A 1967 Burbank history by the Burbank Unified School District gives this charming note: "When the boardwalk was torn up in 1911, the children skipped school at the ten o'clock recess to go down to look for money which they had heard was under the sidewalk. They had to stay after school to make up the time."

THE DIP AT THE FIVE POINTS

If you want to start a long conversational thread in any Burbank-related Facebook group, just introduce the subject of one of Burbank's most fondly remembered greasy-spoon diners, The Dip. It stood as a landmark at a well-known intersection in town, where North and West Victory Boulevards,

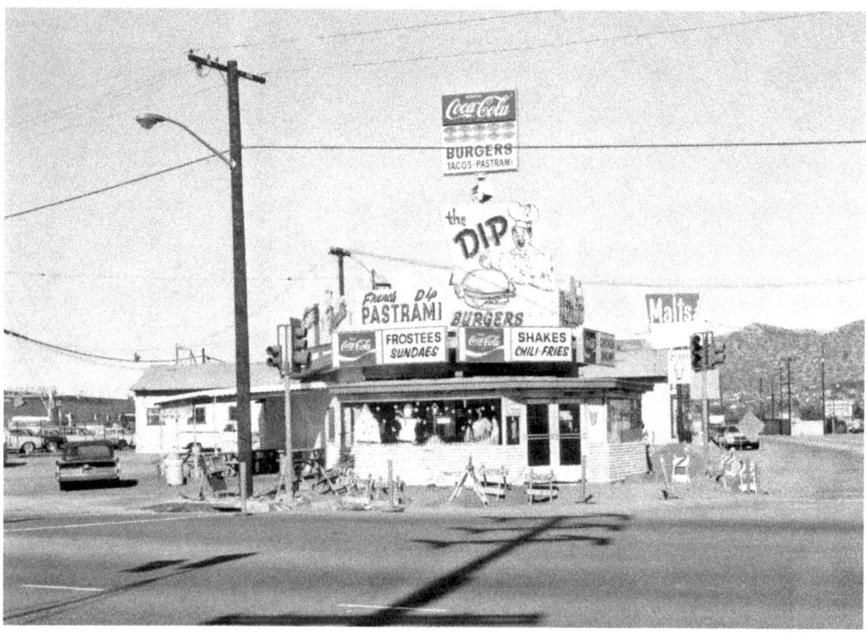

The famous Dip at Burbank's Five Points (where North Victory Place, North and West Victory Boulevard and West Burbank Boulevard all met before the realignment), December 13, 1972. *Collection of Michael B. McDaniel.*

North Victory Place and West Burbank Boulevard met at the southwest end of the Burbank Boulevard Bridge—the "Five Points." The electric sign was memorable: it featured a leering neon cook with lightbulb eyes gesturing grandly at a giant hamburger. But the dish that defined the place was the dipped pastrami sandwiches. In the early 1970s, when Wes Clark patronized The Dip daily on the way home from school, the business was run by the brother-and-sister team of Paul Rosen and Gail Ptack. Gail, the wife of a Burbank policeman, enchanted customers with the graceful way she moved from station to station behind the counter. She was, after all, a trained ballet dancer. Sadly, Paul and Gail died some years ago. Burbanker Nickolas Carreon remembers: "At five points—the most dangerous intersection on the planet—there was a hand-made sign in the median in the middle of two-way traffic on Victory Boulevard that read: 'Left Turn OK For The Dip.' I don't suppose we'll ever know how many people lost life and limb crossing oncoming traffic from multiple directions in an attempt to get a pastrami sandwich." As Gail's husband was a cop, the sign must have been okay. Right?

THE OWL AND THE TURKEYS: TURKEY CROSSING

Turkey Crossing is the traditional name for the bleak industrial spot where San Fernando Road intersects the railroad tracks in Burbank, but there are very few Burbankers who know why it was called this; it is truly lost history.[24] A *Los Angeles Times* story from December 20, 1899, tells the tale: On December 18, a thirty-eight-year-old rancher named Daniel Curtis was making the fifty-five-mile trip to Los Angeles with a wagon full of live Christmas turkeys, hoping to sell them in order to make his own family's Christmas bright. Curtis made it all the way to Burbank and was crossing the tracks when the Owl—the name given to the Southern Pacific passenger train traveling from San Francisco to Los Angeles—hit his wagon amidships, demolishing it. Most of the turkeys were killed (some escaped), as were the two horses, and Curtis himself was seriously injured. The engineer of the Owl, seeing the damage that the train had wrought, reversed the train, picked up the stricken rancher and brought him to Los Angeles for medical attention. His right thigh was broken in two places, and two of his ribs were fractured.

Curtis mended and returned home. In a February 16, 1925 follow-up article in the *Times*, he recounted his accident and the reason for the now

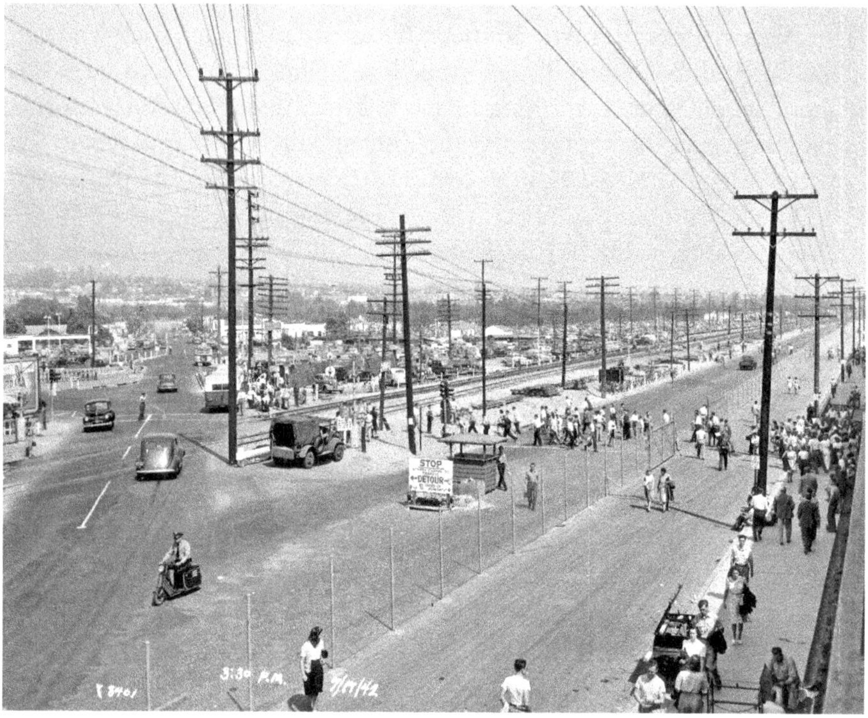

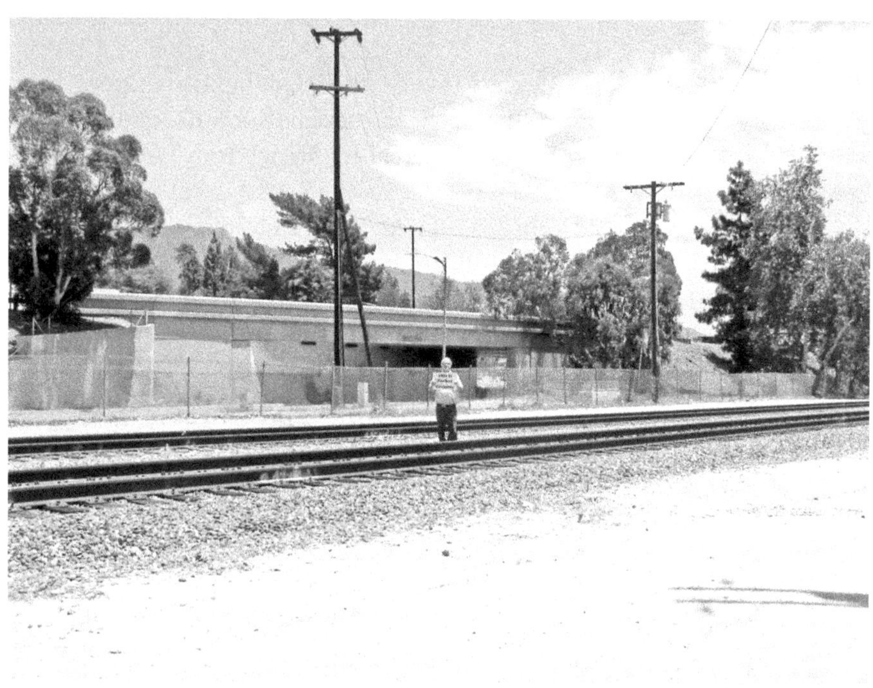

common name for the site. Did he not see or hear the train coming? No. Trees and bushes growing near the track hid the train from view, and the wind was from the wrong direction to hear the locomotive. His brush with death was indeed close: Curtis recounted that the springed seat of his wagon flipped him twenty feet into the air, where he came down near the tracks between the tender of the engine and the first coach. Fortunately he had the presence of mind to see the steps of the coaches whizzing by over his head and did not attempt to stand until the Owl had passed.

As is often the case with accidents, legal action followed. Curtis sued the Southern Pacific Railroad for damages and even retained a former U.S. senator as his attorney. The suit took years to resolve and only resulted in nominal damages being recovered. But it's a great story!

The Turkey Crossing location was the site of another accident, this time in December 1920. In a December 31, 1920 *Los Angeles Times* article partially entitled "Keeper of Booze Warehouse Injured," the story is told of John Tressider, the keeper of a general bonded *warehouse* (a euphemism for the Prohibition-era liquor cabinet in Los Angeles). Failing to see the sneaky and elusive Owl, his car was struck at the intersection, coincidentally on Tressider's eighteenth wedding anniversary. The auto was demolished, and Tressider and his two passengers were seriously injured. The authors could not find a follow-up article to discover if all three passengers survived their injuries, but the article concluded with a statement that Tressider's set of keys to the government liquor warehouse—the only ones—were returned when the revenue collector dispatched a deputy to pick them up at the hospital. They took no chances with something that important falling into the wrong hands, and there would be no riotous parties in Burbank that night.

Perhaps not surprisingly, a March 9, 1924 *Los Angeles Times* article describes the "Turkey Neck Curve" as "obnoxious" and in need of straightening. (The pictorial name suggests that the original meaning of

Opposite, top: Turkey Crossing appears in this photograph from July 17, 1942. It's at left, where the cars cross the railroad tracks. Note the interesting sign: "Street closed to traffic by order of the U.S. Army!" *Burbank Historical Society*.

Opposite, bottom: Mike McDaniel shows conclusively where Turkey Crossing is located. (His sign says, "This is Turkey Crossing.") This area, currently undergoing great change as a result of freeway improvements, will be harder to place in the future. *Erin McDaniel*.

the name as a place where turkeys were once hit was becoming lost.) The straightening never happened.

Fast-forward to 2014, when, as a result of traffic-improvement work by Caltrans, the historic Turkey Crossing site is apparently scheduled to be graded out of existence. As of this writing (spring of 2016), the site is a mess, and traffic around the construction is miserable.

The way you find the historic site is to line up a position on the tracks so that you can see down San Fernando Road. In other words, continue the line of the road to where it intersects the tracks—that's the 1899 Rancher Curtis Turkey Crossing site. But this is dangerous, and we don't recommend it!

HOTSIE ALLEY

This is a site on West Jeffries Avenue between North Pepper Street and North Hollywood Way, fondly remembered by Wes Clark as he walked home from Luther Burbank Junior High School as a thirteen-year-old in 1969. One of Burbank's countless alleys, suspicious-looking teens used to congregate there after school. If stared at, the girls radiating defiance with blue eyeliner, too

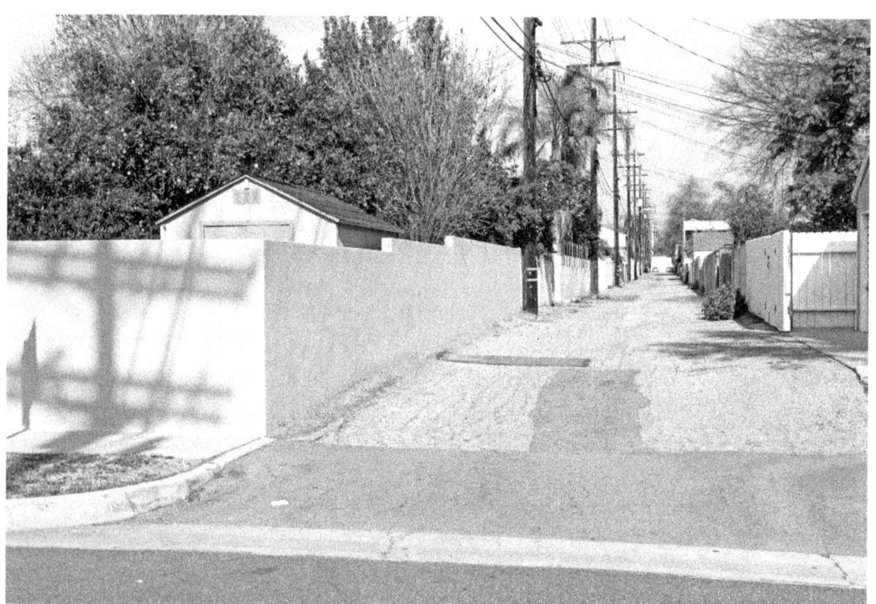

Hotsie Alley, where fearsomely defiant teenage girls gathered in the 1960s. *Wes Clark.*

much makeup, ratted hair, provocative blouses and cigarettes held between fingers would loudly demand, "Are you *hassling* me? Ya wanna *hassle*?"

"Hotsie?" This is what Wes Clark's mother (born in 1921) called the drugs she was certain were being distributed at the site. But what self-respecting teen in the late 1960s would ever call a drug a "hotsie?"

CITY HALL AND THE BALLIN MURALS

Groundbreaking for the current city hall building took place on February 17, 1941. The edifice was designed by architects William Allen and W. George Lutzi, and the project was funded by the Federal Works Agency, Works Project Administration (WPA). It was completed in 1943 at a total cost of $409,000. On our website Burbankia, pictures of city hall are as numerous as fleas on a junkyard dog; it seems that the city could not take enough photographs of the place, and it was a constant subject for city photographer Paul E. Wolfe. Old photos turn up all the time. Granted, it is an architecturally striking building, a fine example of Art Deco design. But the authors have always maintained that it's what's inside that is especially interesting: the Hugo Ballin mural. Ballin (1879–1956), a muralist, film producer and author, was quite active in the 1930s. He did work for the *Los Angeles Times*, the Wilshire Boulevard Jewish Temple and the Los Angeles City Hall chambers.

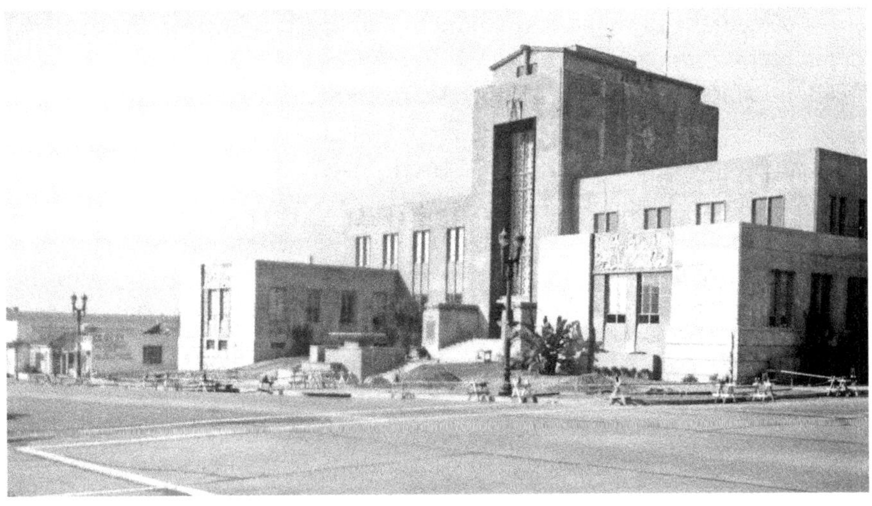

City hall nearing the end of construction in 1942/1943. *City of Burbank.*

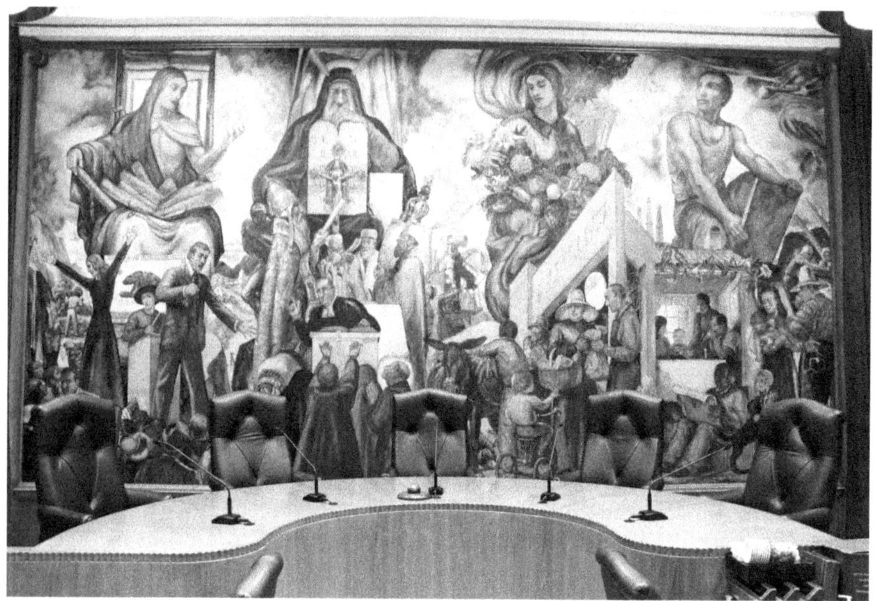

Hugo Ballin's *Four Freedoms* mural in the council chamber of city hall, depicting the themes of a famous January 6, 1941 speech by Franklin Delano Roosevelt. *Left to right:* Freedom of Speech, Freedom of Religion, Freedom from Want and Freedom from Fear. *Wes Clark.*

If you've ever visited the Griffith Park Observatory in Los Angeles, you are acquainted with Ballin's work. Look up. Those impressive and striking paintings of Greek gods, the Zodiac and other celestial figures are by Hugo Ballin. But he also designed the impressive mural *The Four Freedoms,* which can be seen in the Burbank City Council chamber. It refers to basic freedoms identified by President Franklin D. Roosevelt in 1941: Freedom of Speech, Freedom of Religion, Freedom from Want and Freedom from Fear. It really is impressive. The next time you're in the building, ask to see it.

What about city hall can be considered "lost"? In the early 1960s, before the construction of suitable facilities, it also served as the city jail—the bars and cells are still easily recognizable in the basement on the west side. But where criminals and scofflaws once glumly spent their evenings is now the domain of paperwork, records and other official impedimenta. The city clerk uses the area—now called the Records Center—for storage. Another room in the jail still has the huge iron door that once protected the Burbank police weapons cache. Now the door protects used office supplies for redistribution within the city departments and records due to be shredded. Of additional historical interest is that this room holds a collection of all the portraits of the Burbank mayors that hung in the council chamber during their tenure.

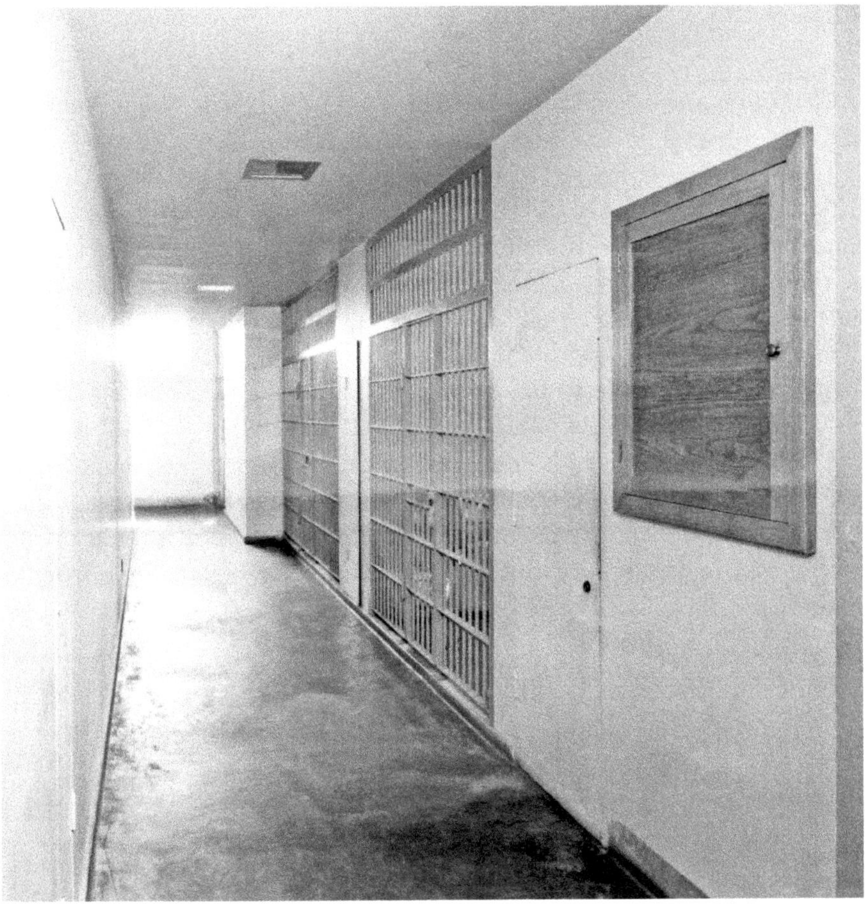

The jail in the basement of Burbank City Hall, 1950s. Rumor is, the ghost of convicted murderer Barbara Graham haunts this place. Over the years her image has appeared to various city and custodial workers. That's what we're told, folks! *Burbank Historical Society.*

A final item of interest in the old jail is the wall where police department employees took accused persons' photographs and formed lineups for identification by witnesses.

Also now lost is the original courtroom that was above the jail on the main floor of city hall, now the city attorney's offices. The original portrait of "Justice" that hung in the court is in the main entrance to the attorney's office. The stairs by which perps were led from the basement up to the courtroom to have the book thrown at them remain intact.

The basement of the building is also the domain of Mike McDaniel, who works in the print shop there.

CABRINI CHAPEL

It used to be a small white structure on the Burbank side of the Verdugo Hills, seen by all in the valley—a spiritual landmark for fifty-six years. Cabrini Chapel was ordered built in 1917 by Saint Francesa Saveria Cabrini (1815–1917), aka Mother Cabrini. She was the first American citizen to be canonized a saint by the Roman Catholic Church, in 1946. The site used to be the focal point for devotional processions and pilgrimages sponsored by the Italian Catholic Federation, and in covering the news of such processions, the hard-bitten and worldwise newsmen of the *Los Angeles Times* also called the site charmed, as it somehow escaped damage during the occasional brushfires in the area.

The humble little white chapel couldn't evade progress, population and the march of time, however, and as the building of the Cabrini Villas housing development in the early 1970s threatened the site, the building was moved to the grounds of St. Francis Xavier School in Burbank,

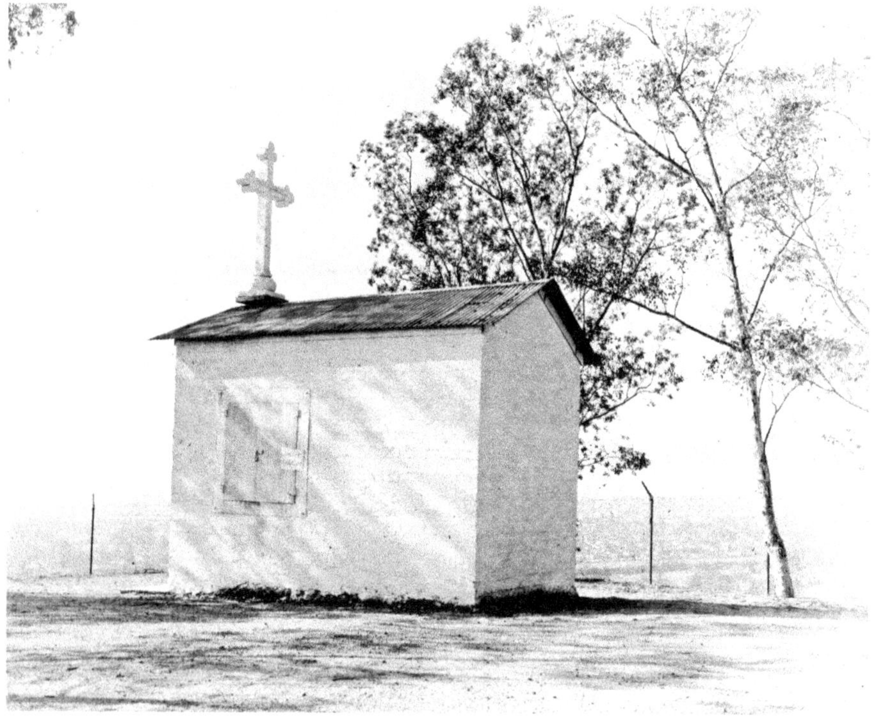

Undated image of Mother Cabrini's little chapel on the Verdugo Hills, a landmark for miles around. *Collection of Michael B. McDaniel.*

at 3801 Scott Road. The authors are happy to report that the housing developers moved the building at their own expense and that the chapel was restored and can today be seen on the grounds of the school, where a library has been added to it. A pretty mosaic of Mother Cabrini was subsequently placed above the door.

VERDUGO FAULT

Ever since the authors read that the Verdugo Fault, which runs more or less along the Burbank side of the Verdugo Hills, is visible from the cul-de-sac at Churchs Court off North Sunset Canyon Drive, we've wanted to highlight this relatively unknown spot. If you go there you can see where the land and the rocks lift a bit; when the celebrated Southern California Big One finally hits, this will perhaps be new shoreline and increase immeasurably in property value—of scant interest to the people living there, as their homes will be in the Pacific Ocean.

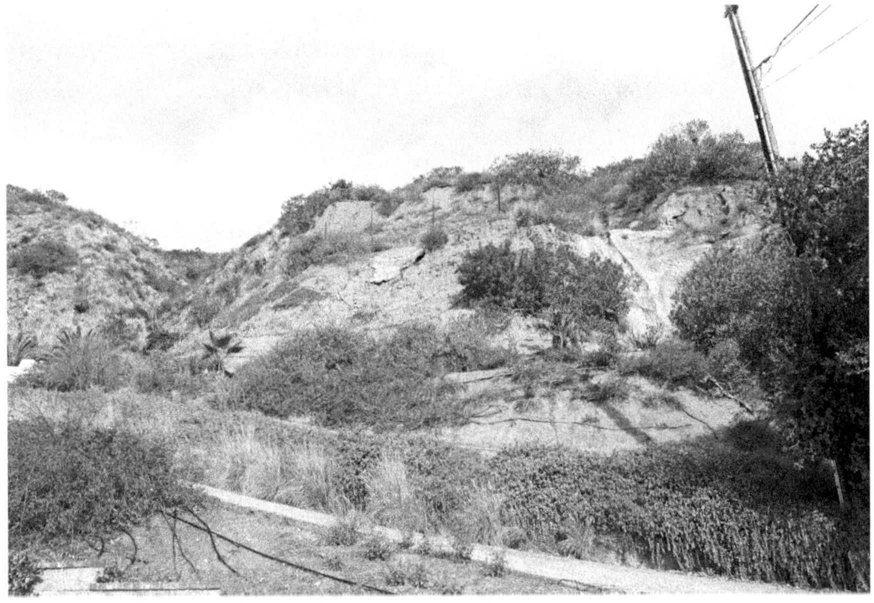

The Verdugo Fault at the end of Churchs Court. Will this be beachfront property in the future? *Wes Clark.*

PNEUMONIA ALLEY

With the disappearance of the Lockheed Aircraft Corporation came the disappearance of a location in the plant known to employees as Pneumonia Alley. It was one of the interesting aspects of working in Lockheed's B-1 plant. Pneumonia Alley was a breezeway formed by two closely adjacent buildings that shared a common roof at some point in its life—at least, that's how it seemed. The name came from the fact that both ends were open, and a constant breeze flowed through the place. It was pleasant in the summer but foul and objectionable on very cold days. No less a photographer than Ansel Adams once took a photograph showing it from one exterior end.

Wes Clark used to work at Lockheed in plant maintenance, which meant that he was required to shuttle around B-1 in a small Cushman scooter, picking up trash, moving things and so on. Driving through Pneumonia Alley gave the distinct impression that one was not in a plant where cutting-edge airplanes were built but rather a Disney dark-house ride, specifically the Snow White ride, where the dwarves were working in the mine and singing "Heigh Ho." Pneumonia Alley was always rather poorly lit. Looking to the left and the right while driving through it, one could see the various cutting machines used to manufacture parts, with machinists walking around, tending big pieces of aluminum and pushing what looked like mine cars. It was actually rather picturesque in an industrial fashion.

BURBANK VILLA/THE SANTA ROSA HOTEL/ DOWNTOWN POST OFFICE

The Santa Rosa Hotel, originally the Burbank Villa, was built in 1887 by none other than Dr. David Burbank, from whom the city gets its name. It was a focal point for social celebrations by Burbankers and hosted parties and weddings. By 1927 it had been torn down, and in 1938 the site was used for a new post office, which still stands at 125 East Olive Avenue and is on the National Register of Historic Places. Lost lore? One of the Santa Rosa Hotel's most faithful early guests was Hollywood star Billie Burke—none other than Glinda the Good Witch of the North in *The Wizard of Oz* (1939).

THE LOVEJOY CASTLE

If one drives on East Providencia Avenue past South Sunset Canyon Drive to the end of the street, an interesting sight can be seen against the Verdugo Hills—a white, stucco-covered tower, complete with a crenellated roofline. It looks impressive, almost like a castle. What is this place? Brian Schneider, whose family owns the property, told Wes Clark in a June 8, 2012 e-mail message:

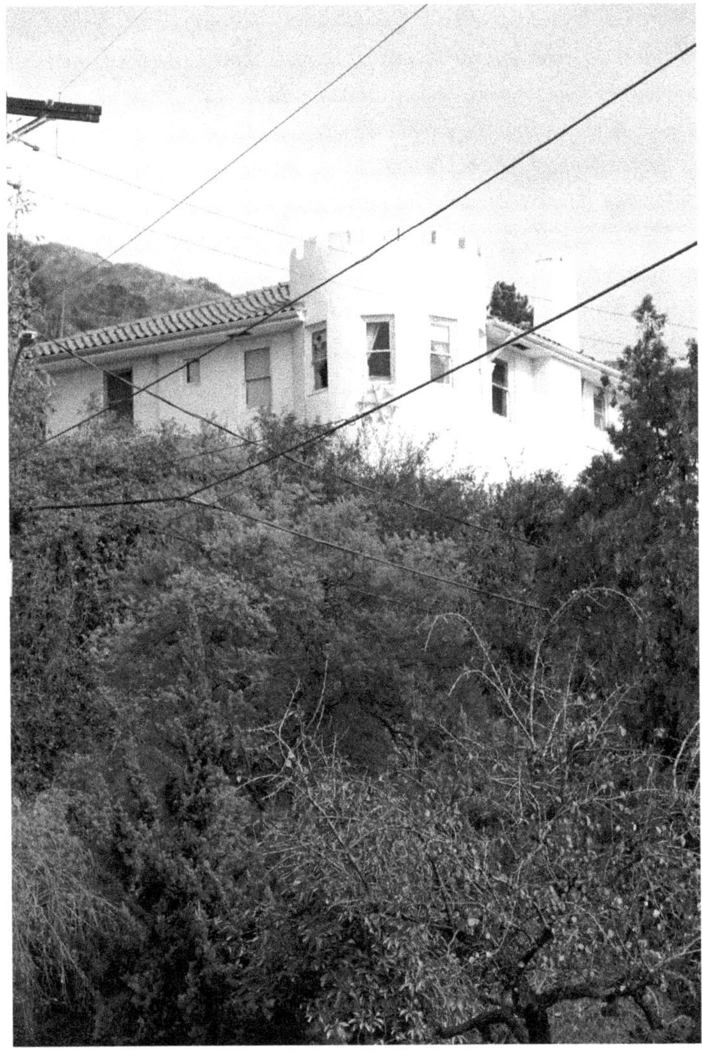

The Lovejoy Castle, atop East Providencia Avenue. The warlord living therein can station archers on the roof! *Wes Clark.*

> *It is a Moorish castle built in 1926 by a man named Lovejoy, who was a railroad tycoon and the son of a Confederate who owned the Lovejoy plantation in Atlanta, now known as the Crawford-Talmadge House. The property is on eleven acres and was purchased by Lovejoy. Over the years it was used as an orphanage and a sanitarium. Lovejoy went bankrupt in 1929, and the purchasers felt sorry for him, so they took a shack on the property, moved it to a corner and gave it to him. His relatives owned Lovejoy's Antiques in Toluca Lake for years. One cool thing about it is that for some reason, the property has been adopted by a herd of deer. There are usually between five and fifteen deer just hanging around on it, under trees in the front lawn or in what we call "the meadow" below the house. In the 1980s my parents rented the house to Olivia Newton-John's production company. She had her musicians stay there when they were in town and I believe they filmed a music video there. At least that's what they said. But I never saw it.*

Fun fact: "Burbank" is both a common place-name in English-speaking countries and a fairly common surname. It is of English origin and means "lives on the castle's hill." Sounds like the Lovejoy property.

THE PUMPKIN BUILDING

As has been endlessly noted, Southern California is a different kind of place. The architecture can be odd, too, and for at least thirty years a building in the shape of a giant pumpkin stood on 3611 Magnolia Boulevard. It was known variously as the Pumpkin Inn ("ballroom dance and prizes!"), the Pumpkin Palace, the Studio Club (one of the owners was Ed "Strangler" Lewis, a wrestler), the Valley Gospel Center, Stan Summeril Real Estate and Magnolia Park Hardware ("Fine Old Colony paints"). In 1938, a *Los Angeles Times* columnist noted:

> *An extraordinary edifice, shaped like a pumpkin, is yours for the seeing in Magnolia Park, a suburb. Upon it are painted three legends. One reads, "The World's Largest Pumpkin," another, "Valley Gospel Center," and the third, "For Sale by Owner."*

It appears that the building's distinctiveness did not necessarily endear it to owners. Another 1938 article noted that there was an opening-night fire,

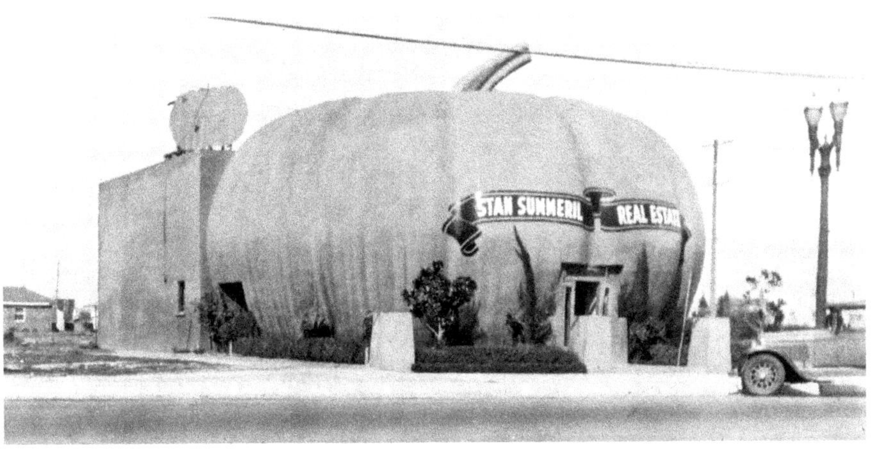

Burbank's celebrated Pumpkin Building on Magnolia Boulevard, seen here in its incarnation as a real estate business, 1930s. *Collection of Michael B. McDaniel.*

which was put out without much fuss. But it cast an ill omen. The owner later gave up the business, stating, "Heck, I ought to have had more sense than to fool around with a pumpkin!"

By 1956 the *Los Angeles Times* reported that a "hard luck gal" named Mae Williams bought a part ownership in the Pumpkin; later on in the year she began wearing her earrings on the top of her head.

MUSHROOMS EATERY

The Pumpkin Building wasn't alone; in the late 1920s at 3500 West Olive Avenue stood a walkup eatery called The Mushrooms—yes, it was built in the shape of a giant fungus. We have no other information about it, save that a sign in the front said (perhaps ominously), "Won't Be Long Now."

THE GOLDEN MALL

You have to give the city planners credit. The Burbank Golden Mall was a bold exercise in forward thinking: six city blocks long, it incorporated futuristic, hexagonal designs with restroom facilities, fountains and pedestrian-only access to the stores along San Fernando Road. No dirty,

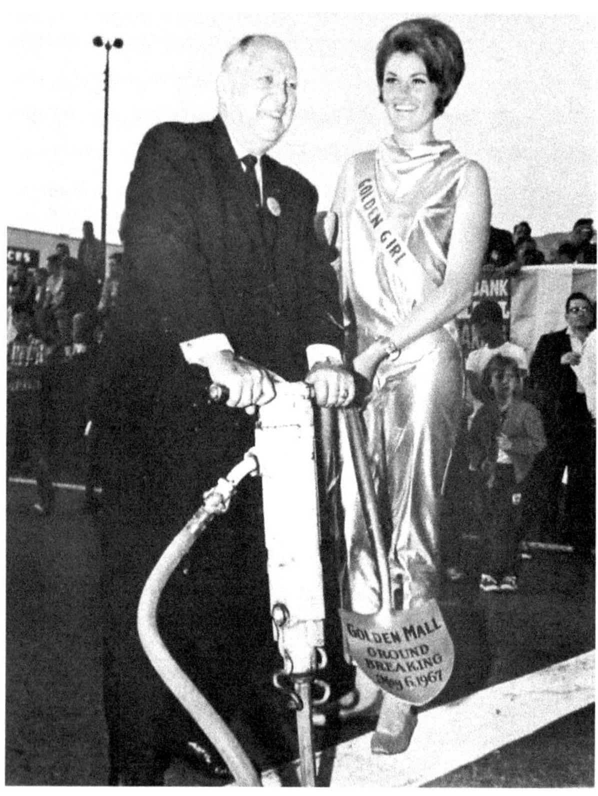

Left: Jan Chronert, the Golden Girl, and the mayor of Burbank at the groundbreaking for the Golden Mall on May 6, 1967. *City of Burbank.*

Below: The construction of the Golden Mall on San Fernando Road, circa 1967. *City of Burbank.*

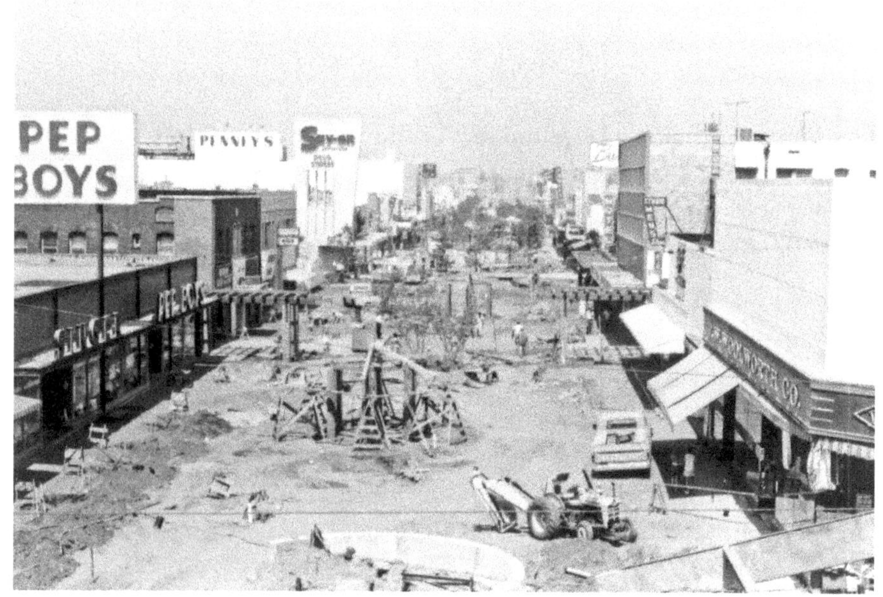

noisy cars would ruin the Burbank shopping experience. The promotional text that Burbank supplied said it all: "A six-block, traffic-free 'Golden' Mall has been scheduled for construction during 1967. The area will encompass the present downtown Burbank on San Fernando Road from Tujunga Avenue to San Jose Avenue. This undertaking has been intelligently designed for pleasurable shopping and browsing in a relaxed and attractive atmosphere."

It didn't take long, however, for the dream to sour. Shoppers complained about having to park far away from the stores they wanted to visit, rather than right in front, as they were used to doing in the pre-Golden days. Shoppers increasingly drove to Glendale to buy. Also, the quality of the stores began to decline, and then they failed entirely. Bur-Cal (a store name that deserves to be revived), Thrifty Drug Store, Sav-On, Newberry Co., Woolworth's, J.C. Penney, good jewelers and banks—they disappeared one by one. Shabby used bookstores began to open in the large spaces where, previously, impressive department stores could be found. Even the water in the fountains became dirty, when there was water in them at all. The worst became apparent in the late 1970s, when the city opened a job-assistance office across from Ed's Town Shoppe; shabby-looking men ambling around the office was hardly the sort of thing one expected from the futurists. Conceding defeat, in 1989 the City of Burbank removed the mall entirely and once again opened up San Fernando Road to vehicular traffic.

The authors are happy to report that business is once again thriving along a revived San Fernando Road.

THE SMOKE HOUSE RESTAURANT

Established in 1946 by two Lockheed engineers, the Smoke House is beloved by Burbankers for its garlic bread (you must really try it when in town). After a start elsewhere in Burbank, in 1948 the business moved to its present site, Danny Kaye's planned but never opened Red Coach Inn. The restaurant benefited from its location on the banks of the Los Angeles River, across the street from the Warner Bros. Studios; Kaye had chosen well. Bing Crosby, Bob Hope, Judy Garland, Errol Flynn, Humphrey Bogart, Cary Grant, Milton Berle, Robert Redford and anyone who was on staff or onscreen at the studios during Warner's "golden" (and present) years ate there. In fact, according to the Smoke House's website, George Clooney was such a fan of the place that he named his production company Smokehouse Pictures, Inc.

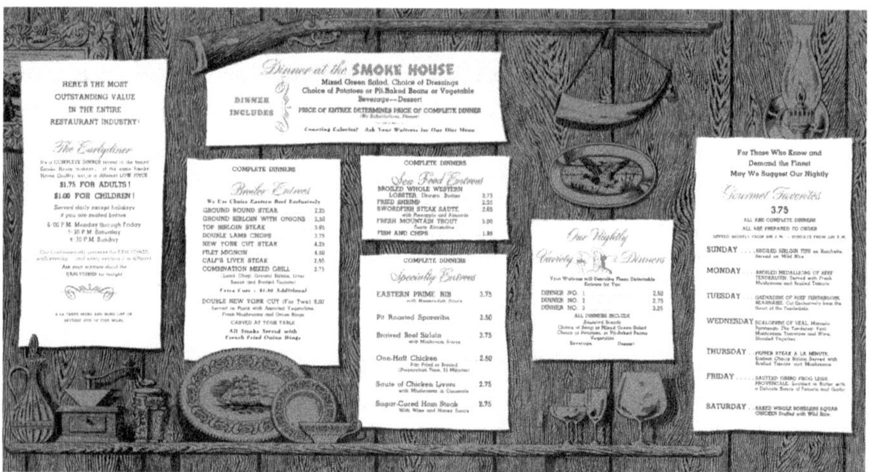

A Smoke House menu, circa 1960. Look at those prices! The garlic bread is, of course, legendary. *Collection of Michael B. McDaniel.*

The Smoke House has impeccable Burbank credentials in addition to the garlic bread: George Schlatter, the producer of *Rowan and Martin's Laugh-In*, cast Gary Owens—the man who popularized the phrase "beautiful downtown Burbank"—on the spot upon hearing him say, "My, the acoustics are good in here!" in the men's room in his impressive announcer's voice.

(Fun fact: Johnny Carson was not the only entertainment industry figure who enjoyed skewering Burbank. George Schlatter did as well. Some of his zingers: "Burbank is a lot like Paris—with chickens." "Beautiful downtown Burbank is nestled on the banks of the Los Angeles River: a cement canal." "If you've seen Tijuana, you'll love Burbank.")

The Burbank–St. Louis Connection

At the intersection of West Olive Avenue and South Virginia Avenue is a modern athletic facility called the Olive Recreation Center; it features play areas for children and no less than four baseball fields. On the same site once stood Olive Memorial Stadium, built in 1947 and dedicated to the memory of American war veterans. It was deemed unsafe and demolished in 1995. Once, Burbankers were proud that it was the spring training site of Major League Baseball's St. Louis Browns. But the history of the Browns at Burbank is lost.

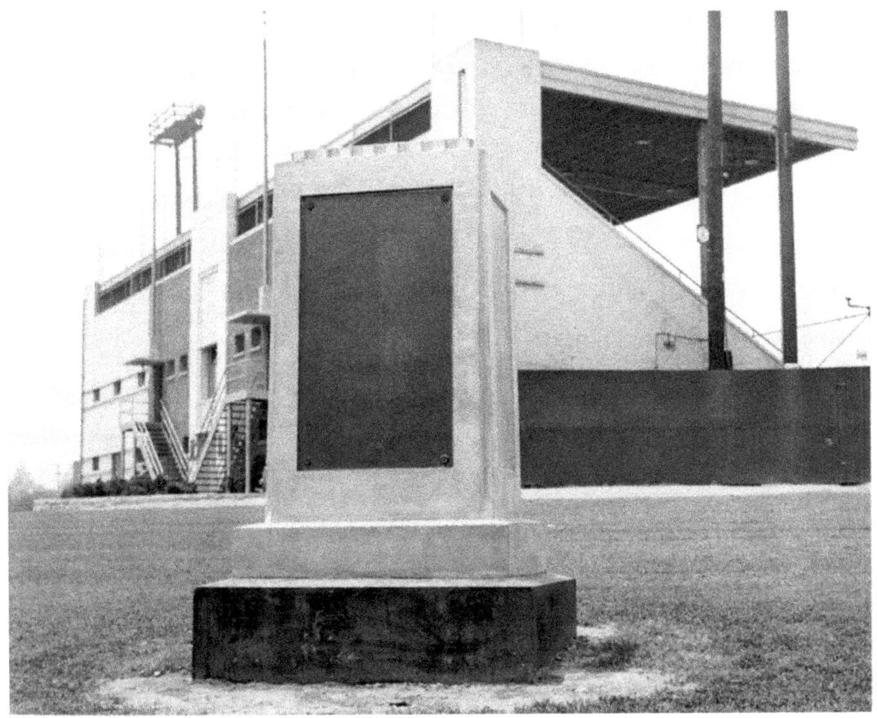

Olive Avenue Recreation Center Stadium, almost completed in 1946. *Collection of Michael B. McDaniel.*

A *Los Angeles Times* article, "Burbank's Big Leagues: At Olive Memorial Stadium, Hapless St. Louis Browns Got Some Respect," from October 2, 1994, by Vivien Lou Chen describes the importance of the place:

> *Burbank, where the feckless baseball team conducted spring training from 1949 to 1952 at Olive Memorial Stadium. Hundreds of spectators, among them Bing Crosby, Bob Hope, Dinah Shore and Nat King Cole, eagerly piled into the stadium to see the likes of pitcher Satchel Paige and Manager Rogers Hornsby in 1952, despite the fact that the Browns were arguably the worst team to ever play the game.*
>
> *"We were not all that good a team, but Burbank was just happy to have a major league team and the guys we had playing were just happy to be in the major leagues," said former Browns infielder John Beradino, now a television actor who plays the chief of staff on General Hospital. Forerunners of the Baltimore Orioles, the Browns will always be remembered by baseball buffs as the team that sent a midget to bat, used a*

one-armed outfielder and once finished 64 1/2 games out of first place. The Browns' proudest moment—the 1944 World Series against the St. Louis Cardinals—ended in embarrassing defeat, with a team batting average of .183.

THE *WONDER YEARS* HOUSE

The authors are fans of this ABC television series, which ran from 1988 to 1993, for a number of reasons: (1) The protagonist, Kevin Arnold (played by Fred Savage), was described as being sixteen in 1972, which means that he was born in the same year as the authors and experienced the 1960s and 1970s at the same ages we did; (2) The production company used Mike McDaniel's junior high school in Burbank, John Muir, for filming. In fact, Kevin's locker is just five spaces away from Mike's and appeared in the interior shots on the show;[25] (3) The teleplays are easily as good as anything that was ever on television; and (4) The home shown in the series as being that of the Arnold family is in Burbank, at 516 North University Avenue.

PORTAL OF THE FOLDED WINGS, SHRINE TO AVIATION (AKA DOME OF THE AVIATOR)

Burbank has its very own nifty little aviation industry spots in the shade of this venerable and artistic structure, located in a cemetery (Pierce Brothers Valhalla Memorial Park and Mortuary, 10621 Victory Boulevard), within sound of the planes taking off and landing at the nearby airport. By visiting and looking at the various plaques, you can learn a thing or two about aviators in the early days of flight. The structure, built in 1924, was originally the entrance to the cemetery, but that was changed so that the park entrance appeared on the much more heavily traveled Victory Boulevard, a main east–west route in the San Fernando Valley. Fourteen of the United States' most famous and accomplished aviators are buried within or near the structure;[26] Charles E. Taylor, the man who hand-built the first aircraft engine used by the Wright brothers, is buried here.

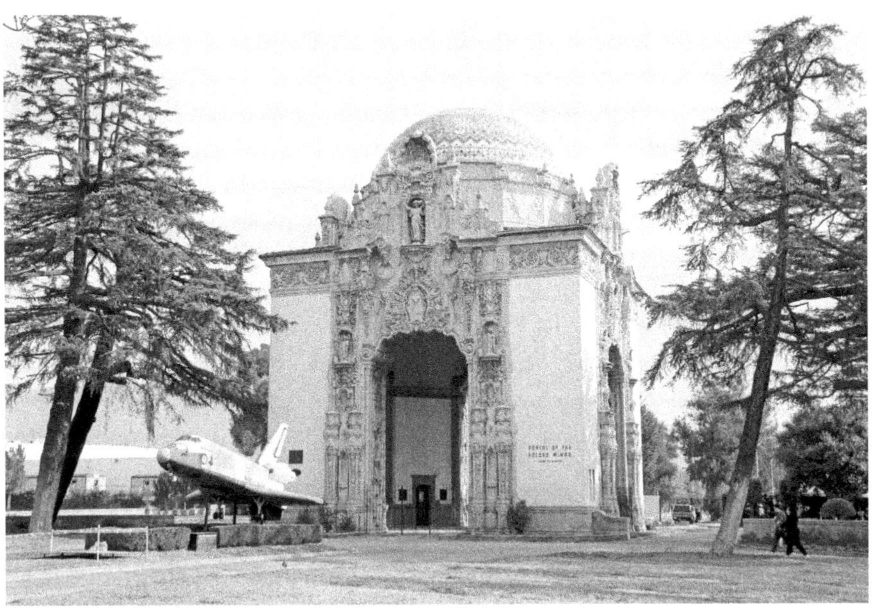

A modern image of the Portal of the Folded Wings. *Wes Clark.*

BOB'S BIG BOY

The Toluca Lake Bob's on 4211 Riverside Drive was built in 1948 and is the oldest remaining Bob's Big Boy restaurant in the United States. It has long been a gathering place for car enthusiasts on Friday nights. The well-attended, informal car show is truly something to see and is so reflective of the Southern California culture: swaying palm trees, a western sunset, warm weather and 1956 Chevys. According to the restaurant chain, this particular location also has a claim to Beatlemania. In August 1965, while on tour in the United States, John, Paul, George and Ringo, reportedly seeking an authentic American diner experience, ate there. A plaque is mounted on the wall near the booth where the Fab Four allegedly sat. It gets stolen from time to time, but Bob's management always replaces it. However, it seems odd that, as fully documented as the Beatles were in that mad summer, there are no photographs of the visit. Their biographer, Barry Miles, described them as being trapped in their house during the tour, a result of fans watching their every move. But it's a good story, and it sells burgers.

THE MOST ACCIDENT-PRONE HOUSE IN THE COUNTY

Called that by the reporters of the *Los Angeles Times*, the house sits at a Burbank "T" where North Buena Vista and Vanowen Streets intersect, nestled in a depression behind protective guard rails and flashing red lights. But that doesn't stop motorists from flying into the property of the Espinoza family—and this has been going on for five decades. The problem, according to reporters in articles from 1975 to 1985, is that neglectful, intoxicated or even sleeping motorists fail to realize that Vanowen Street ends—drivers must turn right or left onto Buena Vista Street—and they plow into the property's trees, garage, kitchen, front yard and porch. (The count in 1975 was seven garage doors, several automobiles, two retaining walls and dozens of shrubs.) The site has seen at least five traffic deaths and an untold number of nonfatal crashes.

When Wes Clark was a child, he noted the many accidents that seemed to happen there (the Clark home was less than a half mile away from where the family lived) and asked his father why this was. "Lockheed drunks," was the laconic reply.

THE THREE G DISTILLERY

As noted earlier, Burbank used to have many vineyards. It also had a nationally advertised whiskey distillery. McDaniel family lore was that Burbank was once also known as "Beer-tank," in recognition of the city's output of alcoholic beverages. The Three G whiskey distillery (producers of Rock and Rye, "conceded the world's finest all-around drink") was located just north of San Fernando Road. In order to gain more floor space to design and produce the famous P-38 Lightning, the distillery was purchased by Lockheed in June 1939. Lockheed workers vividly recall coming to work on Monday mornings, the factory redolent of the scent of bonded whiskey in oak barrels in the converted facility. The distillery turned aircraft factory is gone, as is Lockheed. It only turns up in Three G Whiskey bottles or advertisements sold on eBay.

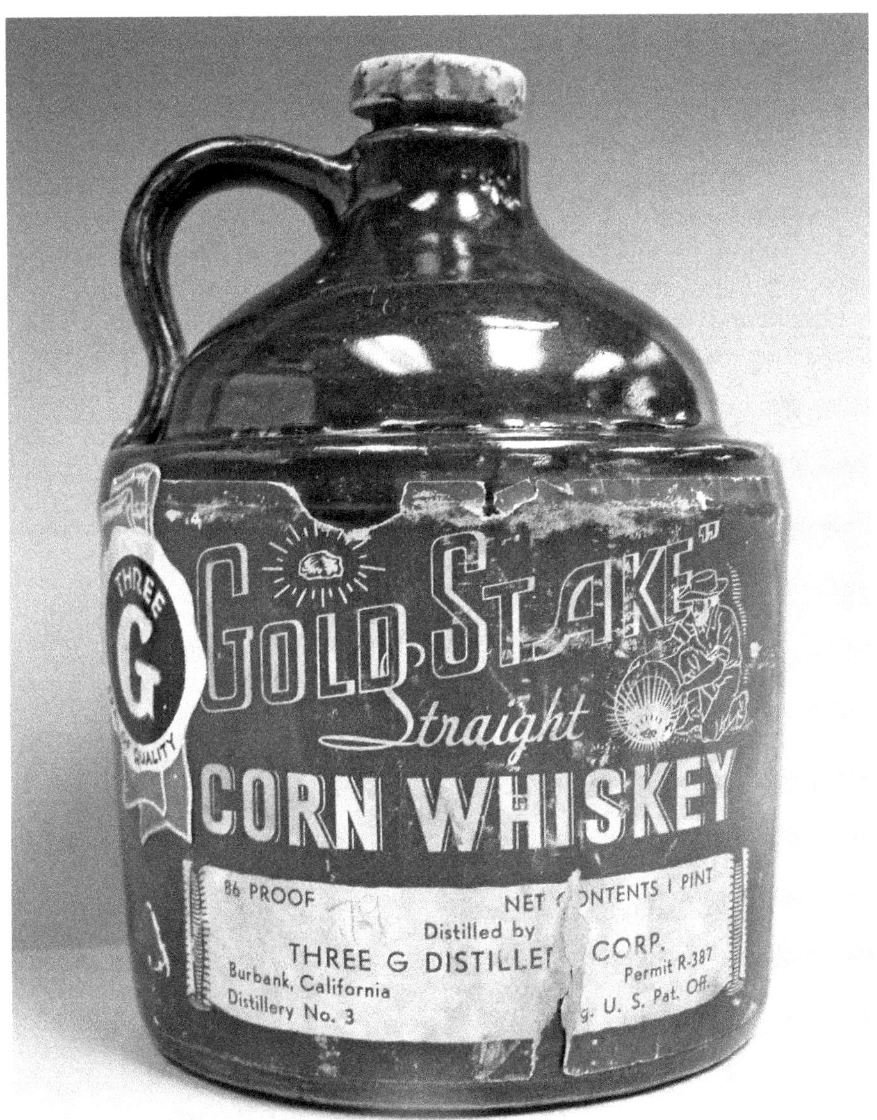

Gold Stake Corn Whiskey, a proud product of the Three G Distillery in Burbank. *Collection of Michael B. McDaniel.*

Where the Postman Always Rang Twice

It's not commemorated, but it's true: the unassuming home on 616 South Bel Aire Drive was once the residence of pulp novelist James M. Cain (1892–1977). He wrote *The Postman Always Rings Twice* while renting this property for forty-five dollars a month in 1934. In 1949 his book was turned into a famous film noir starring John Garfield and Lana Turner. Cain also wrote the noir classics *Double Indemnity* and *Mildred Pierce*.

Cain found Burbank's Depression-era hoboes inspiring. In *Packed and Loaded: Conversations with James M. Cain*, he writes:

> *Take a book of mine that was about something somewhat off beat, The Moth, which was about a young, ex-football player and singer who I put through the depression of the early 1930s. Well, I came to that book honest. I was living in Burbank briefly at the time and I'd drive out past Warner Brothers' Studio and be held up to enter the Town of Burbank. A freight train parked on the side there. This would happen quite a few times. The freight would seem to arrive right about the same time. Maybe I'd been in Hollywood to some picture show or something. This would be*

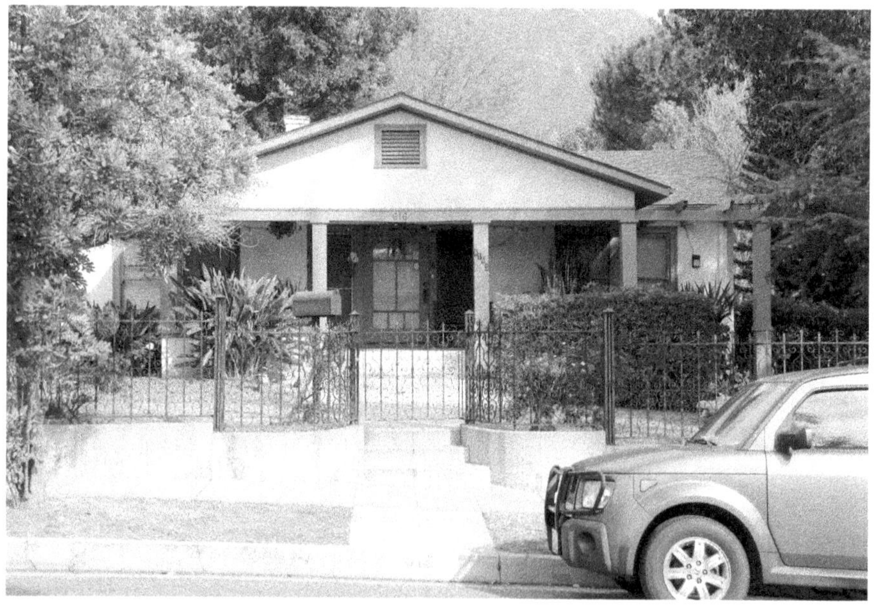

The little home on 616 South Bel Aire Drive that James M. Cain rented in the 1930s. Here, Cain developed the plot by Frank and Cora to murder husband Nick in *The Postman Always Rings Twice*. *Wes Clark.*

> *my* [sic] *11:15 every night and silhouetted against the dark of Burbank itself would be these heads on the top of these freight cars. Not just two or three of them, or three or four dozen—three or four hundred of 'em! And it seemed so terrible a thing that these boys—most of them just boys—couldn't stay home anymore. Had no place to go but the top of this horrible freight car…"*

There are probably other notable places involving lost lore in Burbank; the more the authors do research, the more we find out about these. It seems that just when we think we have the last word in odd, quirky or unusual Burbank things, something else turns up—fodder for a future book or website updates, perhaps.

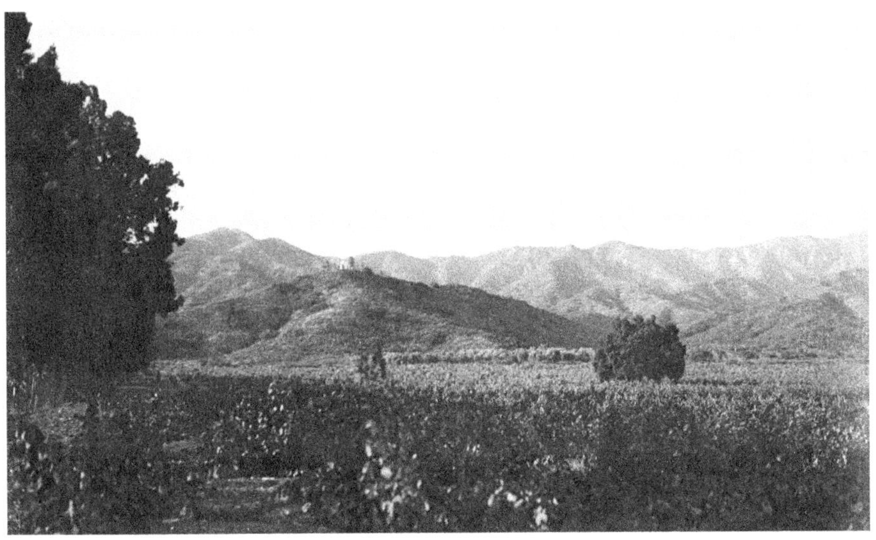

The McClure Winery. Burbank used to be this rural. The little Cabrini Chapel is seen atop the hill. *Burbank Historical Society.*

5
MUSICAL BURBANK

Where you have people, you have music. Where you have a media capital, you have unusual and even extraordinary music. This chapter examines musical Burbank; there are some interesting tales and lost lore therein.

Burbank's Official Song I

The authors know of no official Burbank theme song, that is, one that is presented as such at civic occasions or has been designated as such by the city council or mayor. But there are a couple of contenders for the title. The first, "In Burbank," was written in 1924 by Code Morgan, author of "The Old Apache Trail," "Under the Spreading Antlers" and, best of all, "I've Got the Giggles." The sheet music shows a hillside view of Burbank with the caption, "Burbank is as delightful as this song. For any information address Chamber of Commerce." Morgan was reportedly a Burbank High School graduate. Both the music and the words are by Morgan, and the song is described as being in a foxtrot rhythm.

There used to be a clever arrangement of it on YouTube, but that has unaccountably disappeared. Nevertheless, one of the features of our

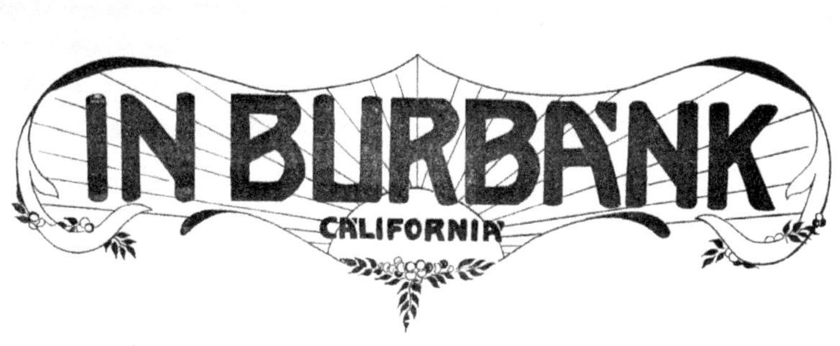

Song--Fox Trot

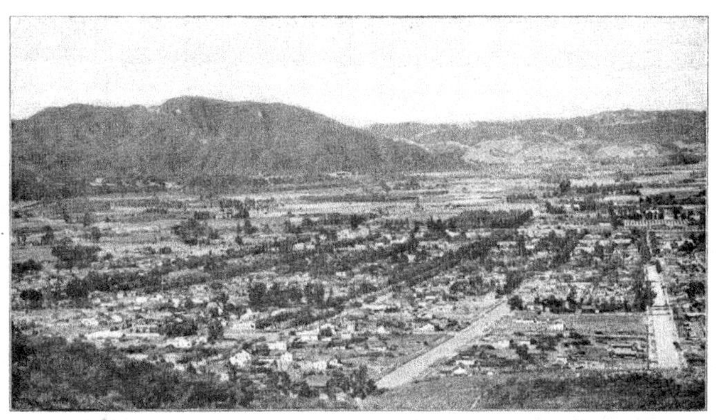

Burbank is as delightful as this song. For any information address Chamber of Commerce.

Words and Music by

Code Morgan

AUTHOR OF

"KATIE DEAR" "MY YANKEE GIRL" "CHEROKEE ROSE"

"THAT'S WHERE MY HEART IS TONIGHT" "UNDER THE SPREADING ANTLERS"

"THE OLD APACHE TRAIL" "I'VE GOT THE GIGGLES"

The sheet music to Code Morgan's magnum opus. *Collection of Michael B. McDaniel.*

occasional Burbankia slide shows held in Burbank libraries is a sing-along of this tune. After you've heard it about 427 times, it begins to grow on you.

In Burbank
By Code Morgan

Way out west, I've built a nest,
In a spot that Nature surely blessed,
'Tis the place I love the best,
Everywhere sunbeams rest,
In the Valley 'neath the mountain crest.
I'll never stray far away,
For there's peace and rest both night and day,
Soft breezes sway,
Flowers by the way,
And even all the songbirds seem to say:

Chorus
In Burbank, In Burbank,
Way out in Burbank, California,
I want to warn you,
Don't let your footsteps stray,
When you start to come this way,
For you will surely stay,
Until the Judgment Day.

In Burbank, In Burbank,
There's no place on earth that could be fairer,
That's no error.
There's a happy throng,
Just ten thousands strong,
And in Burbank Town you can't go wrong.

Burbank's Official Song II

The invaluable 1944 *Burbank Community Book* by George Lynn Monroe contains the following candidate as an official Burbank anthem:

It fell to the lot of W.P. Coffman, at one time Postmaster, former owner and publisher of the Review, and still holding down an important position on that paper, to write what might be called the community's official song. It was originally intended for the Kiwanis Club, is sung to the tune of "Tramp! Tramp! Tramp! (The Prisoner's Hope)" composed in 1863 by George F. Root.

BURBANK'S OFFICIAL SONG
By W.P. Coffman

There's a town in Southern Cal
That we love just like a pal,
Where we work, and boost, and sing, and dance, and play.
There's no other place in sight
That can give us more delight,
And we're full of pep and ginger
When we say:

Chorus
Bank, Bank, Bank, we bank on Burbank—
Bank on Burbank every day.
Nestled up against the hills
All our hearts with pride she fills—
Yes, we bank on Burbank and we're here to stay.

When this whole Kiwanis bunch
Gets the right and proper hunch
Everybody gets behind us with a swing.
All for one, and one for all.
[Possibly missing line]
That's what makes us want to get
Right up and sing.

Chorus
Bank, Bank, Bank, we bank on Burbank—
Bank on Burbank every day.
Nestled up against the hills
All our hearts with pride she fills—
Yes, we bank on Burbank and we're here to stay.

BE TRUE TO YOUR SCHOOL

The Burbank High School 2008 centennial commemorative book *The Blue and White Wave High* gives an interesting story of an instance when an enthusiastic BHS co-ed inspired the legendary Beach Boys songwriter Brian Wilson to pen the hit song "Be True to Your School":

> *As a child growing up in Burbank, Jodi Gable (Class of 1965) fondly remembers the grape arbors that filled the hillside above her house and describes her life as living in "a Norman Rockwell painting." When Jodi was 13 she met the Beach Boys at an Olive Rec Center dance and was amazed at their sound. After talking with them she was asked to head up*

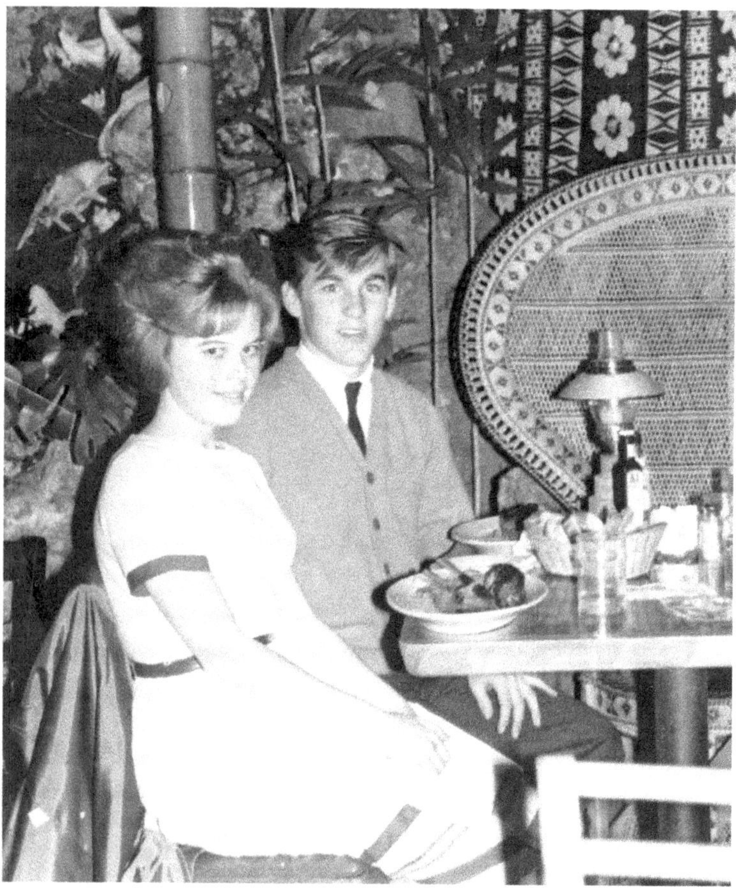

Jodi Gable, the girl who drove Brian Wilson crazy with her Burbank High School spirit, on her first date with Beach Boy Dennis Wilson, circa 1962. *Jodi Gable Firgens.*

> *their fan club. After her parents met the Wilsons (parents of Brian, Dennis and Carl), Jodi began hanging out with the boys, who treated her like a sister, and building fan support.*
>
> *"I loved BHS and couldn't wait to get to school each day," she recalls. "I called Dr. Leland, 'Unc,' and I had teachers who really seemed to care." Jodi was an active member of the Drill Team, and her loyalty to BHS became the genesis of one of their hits. Jodi recalls, "Brian Wilson was a genius and could come up with lyrics on the spot. We were eating chili fries one day at an A&W in Hawthorne and he penned, 'Fun, Fun, Fun.'" Jodi was driving the guys crazy with her drill team stories and Wilson came up with "Be True to Your School" (which coincidently contains part of "On Wisconsin," Burbank's fight song). On her 16th birthday, the Beach Boys threw a party and performed in her back yard.*

The book ends with the reassuring information that Jodi "has stayed connected to her classmates and has always remained true to her school." As do all good Burbank High School Bulldogs!

BURBANK POLICE BOYS BAND

Burbank has the reputation of being a socially conservative community; whether this is still true or not is open to speculation. At one time the community had a musical ensemble for boys that was associated with the Burbank Police Department, called the Burbank Police Boys Band. It was sponsored by the city's Parks and Recreation Department. Members, numbering from forty to one hundred, dressed in uniforms reminiscent of police officers. In fact, they looked like small-scale policemen. The black uniforms were reportedly hot and uncomfortable in the summer months.

The band began in 1953, founded by Ben Porter. The very first members gathered in a building at McCambridge Park for Monday evening rehearsals. Marching practice took place in a local parking lot. Not surprisingly, the band drew its membership largely from Burbank junior and senior high schools. Parents did what parents always do: formed a group of supporters and kept track of sheet music, scheduled concerts and parades, maintained the uniforms and performed the other usual functions of a booster organization.

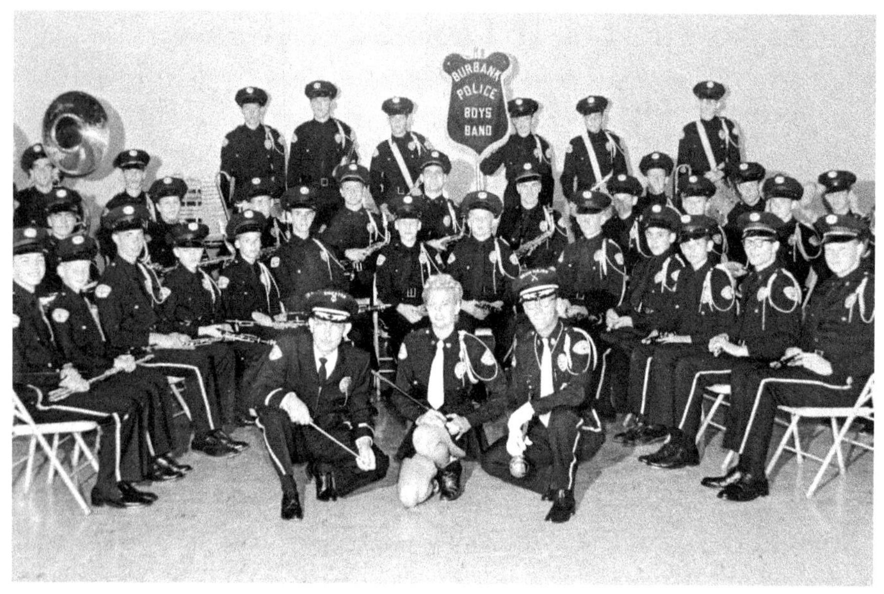

An undated image of the Burbank Police Boys Band. During the anti-establishment 1960s, it was known as the Fuzz Band. *Burbank Historical Society.*

The band was initially an all-boys ensemble (girls were admitted in the 1970s). But girls served as majorettes and members of the color guard. Fierce competition soon erupted among the boys to seek the attention of the girls. In the 1960s the band humorously referred to itself as "the Fuzz Band," an allusion to a dismissive and uncomplimentary countercultural slang term for police officer.

Bill Kuzma, a former director of the band as well as a former band member and drum major, reports that the famous film director Tim Burton was a clarinet and sax player in the Boys Police Band in the early 1970s and was elected leader of the officer group. Another well-known member of the band was Anson Williams, known as "Potsie" in *Happy Days*. He, too, played the clarinet.

An anniversary concert was staged every spring, when alumni were invited to play. Some of these were professionally recorded and appear on vinyl LPs. (One of these appeared in an art show of personal items owned by Tim Burton.) The band also participated in the annual Tournament of Roses Parade, sometimes by itself and sometimes with the two Burbank high school bands. The band's main tunes were "The South Rampart Street Parade" (its signature piece), "Strike Up the Band/I Love a Parade," "Horns A-Plenty," "High Society" and "The Soaring Eagle."

The Burbank Police Boys Band was discontinued in the 1970s and is now but a fond memory for its past members.

RANDY RHOADS

Sometimes what is lost from a community is a promise of what could have been. Such a loss was legendary rock guitarist Randall William "Randy" Rhoads (Burbank High School, class of 1975). He lost his life in an airplane crash in 1982 at age twenty-five. Rhoads, a founder of the influential rock group Quiet Riot along with original member Drew Forsyth (BHS class of 1974), was a different sort of rock guitarist. His mother, Delores, was a music teacher and managed a music store; Rhoads began with classical training on the guitar and, as a sixteen-year-old, taught the instrument at his mother's store. When he played at home, he played loud. As a result, he got to know many of the Burbank policemen by name. By the time he was in his twenties he was considered one of the best guitar teachers in the Los Angeles area. While at Burbank High, Rhoads was a casual sports participant. He often ran remedial laps and wore two softball mitts to preserve the touch in his hands and fingers. His rise to fame with Ozzy Osbourne is the stuff of rock legend.

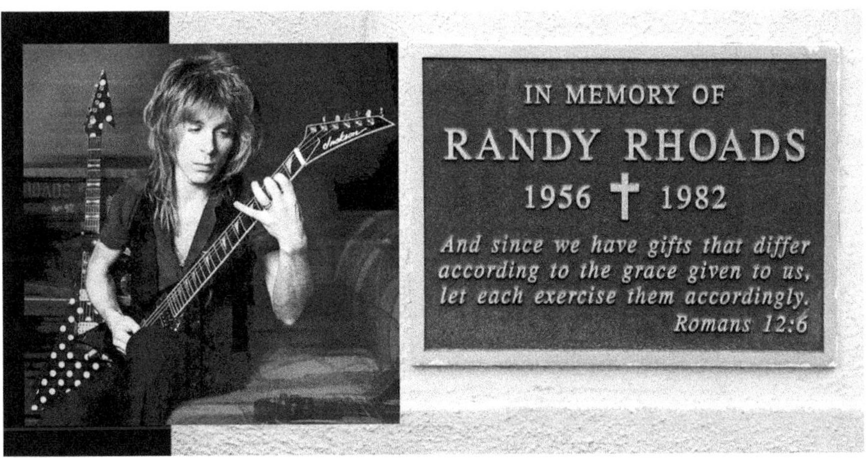

Randy Rhoads and the memorial plaque at the First Lutheran Church. *www.randy-rhoads-online.com/Wes Clark.*

The Rhoads family worshipped at the First Lutheran Church at 1001 South Glenoaks Boulevard. Within the church grounds is a memorial plaque to Rhoads. To honor his memory there are also music scholarships in his name at UCLA and Cal State Northridge.

Theresa/Athena

Burbanker Theresa Russell was born Theresa Paup in San Diego, California; she attended Burbank High School and appears in the 1973 yearbook, but she did not graduate. She married English film director Nicolas Roeg in 1982.

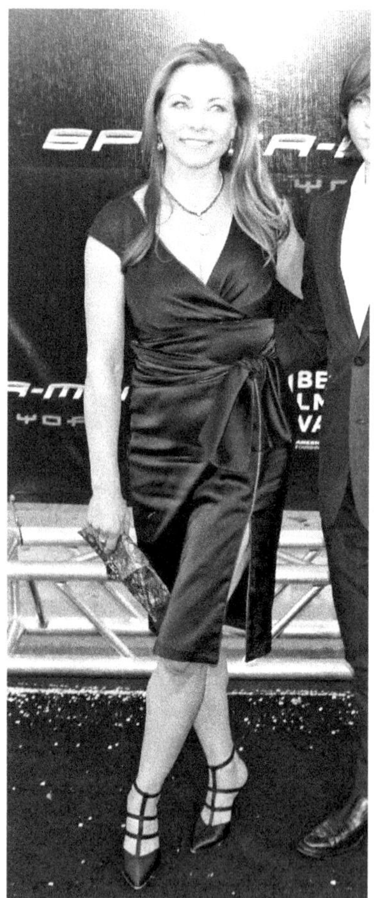

Burbanker Theresa Russell (Theresa Paup), jilter of rock stars, in 2007. *David Shankbone/wikipedia Creative Commons.*

Pete Townshend of The Who says that Russell was the inspiration for his song "Athena," which was first called "Theresa." From the Wikipedia entry for the song:

Pete Townshend wrote this song after an encounter with actress Theresa Russell. He promptly fell in love with her, and his frustration of being rejected is contained in this song. In this context, associated with an issue with a film director, it became a subplot of the much later The Lifehouse Chronicles. Townshend initially changed the title to "Athena" to disguise who the song was really about.

Some Burbank girls are girls—others, as Townshend's song insists, are bombs.

THE LAST LENNON AND McCARTNEY GIG

It's a fun question the authors ask at Burbankia slide shows: "Where was the last John Lennon–Paul McCartney gig held?" Since a roomful of people are assembled to hear fun facts about Burbank, the answer is obvious: Burbank. Wikipedia gives the details:

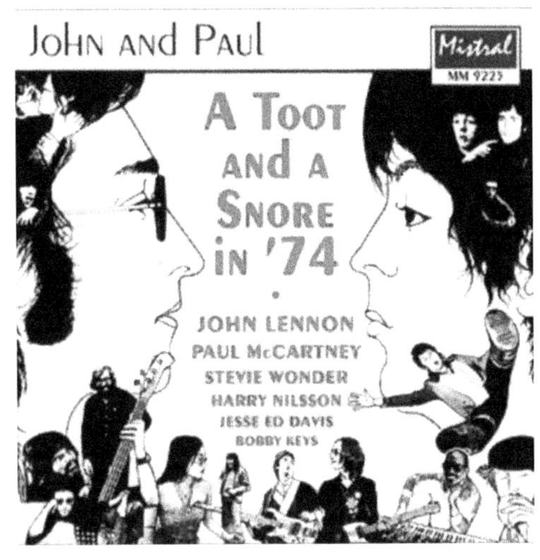

A Toot and a Snore in '74, a recording of the last time Paul McCartney and John Lennon jammed with each other. *Wikipedia.*

> A Toot and a Snore in '74 *is a bootleg album of the only known recording session in which John Lennon and Paul McCartney played together after the break-up of the Beatles. First mentioned by Lennon in a 1975 interview, more details were brought to light in May Pang's 1983 book,* Loving John, *and it gained wider prominence when McCartney made reference to the session in a 1997 interview. Discussing it with Australian writer Sean Sennett in his Soho office, McCartney claimed the "session was hazy...for a number of reasons."*
>
> *Lennon was producing Harry Nilsson's latest album,* Pussy Cats, *when Paul and Linda McCartney dropped in after the first night of the sessions, aka "the Jim Keltner Fan Club Hour" at the Burbank Studios on 28 March 1974. They were joined by Stevie Wonder, Harry Nilsson, Jesse Ed Davis, May Pang, Bobby Keys and producer Ed Freeman for an impromptu jam session.*
>
> *Lennon was in his "lost weekend," separated from Yoko Ono and living in Los Angeles with Pang. Although he and McCartney hadn't seen each other in three years and had lashed out at each other in the press, according to Pang they resumed their friendship as if nothing had happened. The jam session proved not very productive musically. Lennon sounds to be on cocaine and is heard offering Wonder a snort on the first track, and on the fifth, asks someone to give him a snort. This is also the origin of the album name, where John Lennon clearly asks: "You wanna snort, Steve? A toot? It's goin' round." In addition, Lennon seems to be having trouble with his microphone and headphones.... The*

events of this night are intriguing to Beatle fans as it is the only known instance of the former songwriting team playing together between their 1970 formal breakup and Lennon's murder in 1980. Aside from informal, special occasions such as weddings, collaborations of more than two ex-Beatles were rare after the band's bitter 1969–70 split, especially between Lennon and McCartney, whose conflict was the most pronounced and long-lasting.

101 STRINGS

There were many contenders for the title of most ubiquitous Beautiful Music performers of the 1960s and the 1970s—the Anita Kerr singers and the San Sebastian Strings come to mind. But based on appearances in record bins in grocery stores across America, the king must have been the 101 Strings espousing "The Sound of Magnificence." Their records were everywhere, and included such titles as *The Emotion of 101 Strings at Gypsy Campfires*, *A Mediterranean Cruise to The Rivieras—Spain, France, and Italy* and *Concertos for Lovers*. The ensemble also recorded the popular *The Soul of* series (Spain, Mexico and Poland were a few of the nations having their souls explored). The 101 Strings' violins, violas, cellos and basses could be heard dramatically cascading through the scales on turntables, FM dials and in elevators across the country.

While the 101 Strings was, in reality, the Orchester des Nordwestdeutschen Rundfunks Hamburg (the Northwest German Radio Orchestra of Hamburg), with recordings made in Europe, the pressing plant for all of that vinyl was in Burbank, at the Alshire facility at 1015 Isabel Street. Alshire Records is now defunct. To confirm the location, the authors once stopped by the business currently at that address and asked around. While nobody there had ever heard of the 101 Strings (you'd have to seek out somebody at least fifty or sixty years old for that), the twenty-something at the front counter did confirm that, yes, an organization named Alshire had once pressed vinyl at the location.

DEL CASHER, FATHER OF THE WAH PEDAL

The name of guitar session man Del Casher is perhaps not as well known as that of Les Paul or Leo Fender, but this fleet-fingered musician has performed and recorded with the likes of Elvis Presley, Les Paul, Eddy Arnold, Connie

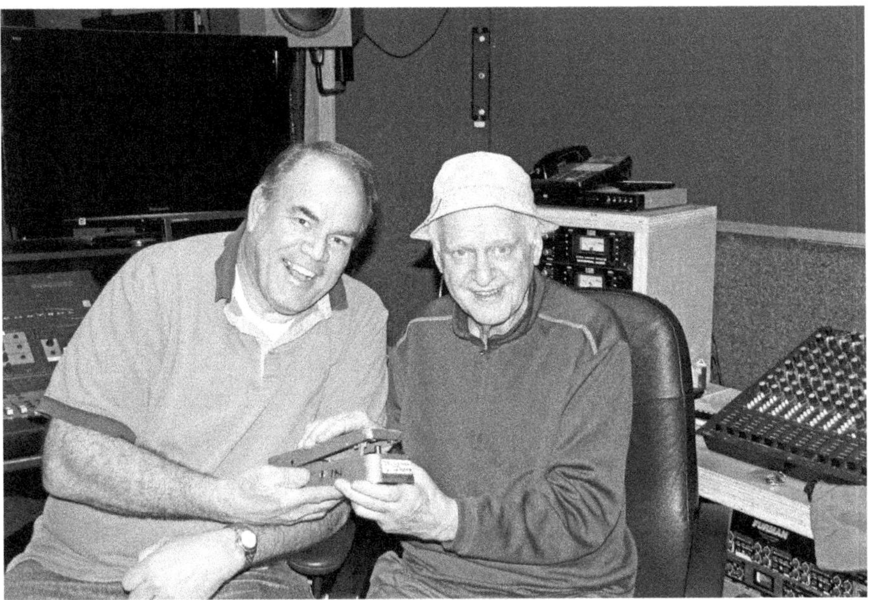

Wes Clark (left) and guitar legend Del Casher in his recording studio in Burbank. They're holding a wah pedal prototype from the early 1960s. *Michael B. McDaniel.*

Francis, Bobby Vinton, Julie London, Bobby Troup, Buddy Rogers, Bob Hope, Peggy Lee, Buddy Ebsen, Donald O'Connor, Danny Thomas, Sammy Fain, Bob Russell, Paul Francis Webster, Burt Bacharach, the Ray Conniff Orchestra, Sonny and Cher and Frank Zappa. Casher has appeared as a guest soloist on the *Lawrence Welk Show*[27] and is regarded as the father of the guitar wah pedal, later used so flamboyantly by Jimi Hendrix and Isaac Hayes. The latter's "Theme from *Shaft*" is practically a wah pedal anthem.

In the early 1970s, when the nation was traumatized by evening news reports about Vietnam and Watergate, Casher composed a soothing guitar instrumental that was in stark contrast to the forceful news show music. It was used for the closing credits of the *NBC Evening News*. It played for an amazing eighteen years.

The Burbank connection? Del owns the California Digital Post, Inc. recording studio on 2700 West Magnolia Boulevard. Stop by and say "Hi!" to a guitar legend!

(Note: When Del was a twenty-something musician in the early 1960s, he lodged in a converted garage in a house rented by Wes Clark's family in Los Angeles; Del became a family friend. It was fun listening to him fiddle around with electronics and various guitar sound devices.)

It's worth mentioning that the Tel-Ray Electronics Manufacturing Company, Inc., which built the Morley Wah pedal, was located at 2301 West Victory Boulevard, right at the corner of the street where Wes Clark lived.

BURBANK'S TWO SYMPHONIC ENSEMBLES

The Burbank Symphony Orchestra began in 1943, when it was founded by Leo G. Damiani. The orchestra made its concert debut at the Olive Avenue Recreational Center; it was sponsored by the Parks and Recreation Department. In 1953, the orchestra, under Damiani's leadership, performed a Christmas program on NBC, which represented the first time a West Coast orchestra had been televised by a major network. A similar program was produced the following year.

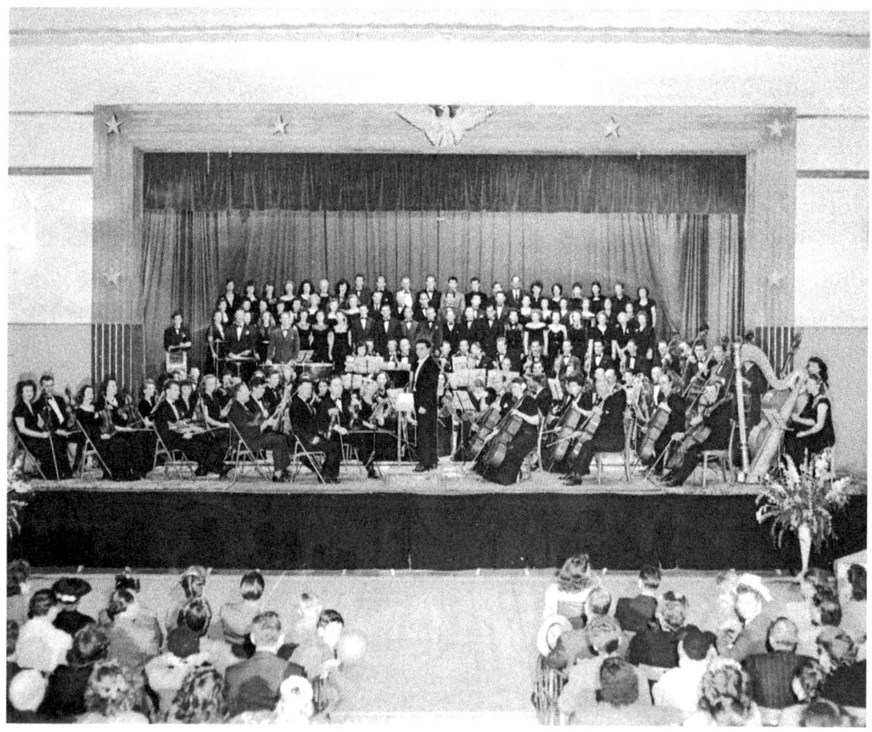

The Burbank Symphony Orchestra, conducted by Leo Damiani, in the Olive Recreational Center, 1940s. The center was the orchestra's home before it moved to the Starlight Bowl. *Collection of Michael B. McDaniel.*

Leo Damiani resigned in 1959 and was replaced by Constantin Bakaleinikoff, who had a long and successful career as a Hollywood film composer before his tenure in Burbank.[28] Dr. Leo Arnaud replaced Bakaleinikoff in 1964 as conductor of the Burbank Symphony Orchestra. Arnaud, another successful film composer, is primarily known for his fanfare "The Bugler's Dream," used as the theme for the Olympics as broadcast by American networks.

In the 1960s Burbank supported no fewer than five musical ensembles: the Burbank Symphony, the Youth Symphony, the Choral Club, the Civic Light Opera and the Police Boys Band. The city budgeted $37,000 for the support of these groups, and more support was gathered from contributions by the public. But by the early 1980s the Burbank Symphony Orchestra was reporting money woes, and at some point in the 1990s it discontinued its active musical seasons.

Happily, not all was lost in the symphonic life of the city. The Burbank Chamber Orchestra, founded in 1991 under the direction of Steven Kerstein, who served as the conductor and music director, debuted in 1992. Ten years later it became the Burbank Philharmonic Orchestra. A donor- and grant-supported 501(c)(3) organization, the Burbank Philharmonic now brings world-class concert music free of charge to Burbank and Southern California. Since 1992 the philharmonic has performed for more than 115,000 attendees.

The Burbank Community Band

Lockheed's wartime employees were an outgoing bunch who spent long hours at the plant; that being the case, recreation was important. One of the many pursuits for employees was the Lockheed Concert Band.[29] The first corporate mention of this ensemble was in a Lockheed Employees Recreational Club (LERC) calendar for Monday, April 22, 1940. It mentioned that band practice was held at the John Muir Junior High School cafeteria at 7:30 p.m. The band entertained employees at various locations at noon breaks.[30] By the early 1980s, the band rehearsed at the Robert E. Gross Park (owned by Lockheed) on Friday mornings. The band was led by Domenic Schieffo and managed by Anne Boscke, who worked in the Lockheed Planning Department and was also the band vocalist.

When Lockheed moved from Burbank to Palmdale, California, in February 1993, the band remained in Burbank. Eventually, Lockheed

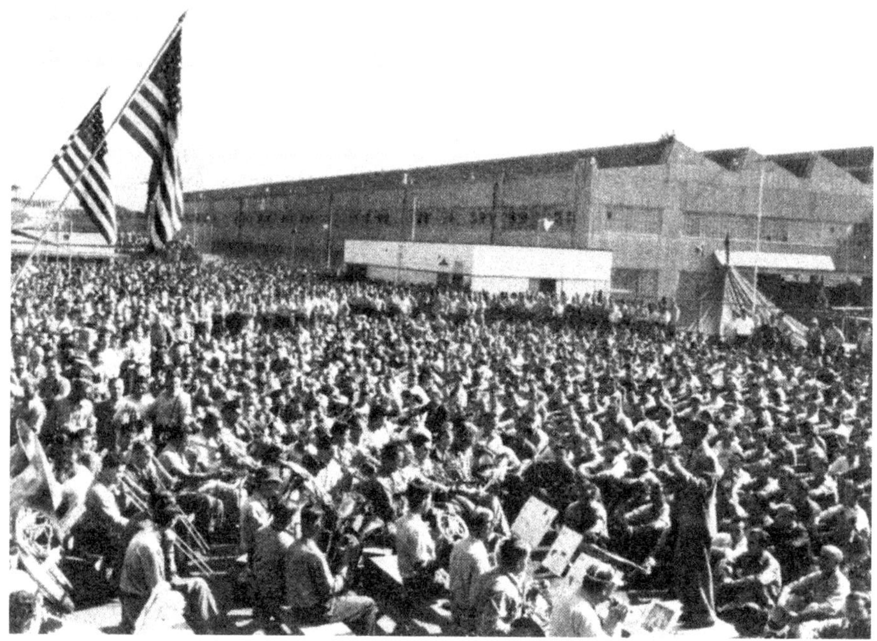

Lockheed employees listen to a lunchtime performance by the Lockheed Band, 1940s. *Collection of Michael B. McDaniel.*

donated Gross Park to the City of Burbank, with the stipulation that the city continue to support the band by providing rehearsal space free of charge. The band continues to rehearse there. The present name of the ensemble, the Burbank Community Band, was adopted on November 14, 1997. While Lockheed is gone, the band still exists. In fact, in 2012 a board of directors was formed, and the band was incorporated as a 501(c)3 charitable organization. The band performs at various occasions, as well as at events sponsored by the Burbank Veterans Committee.

The Burbank Chorale

The original name and the women-only membership rules are lost, but the singers continue to perform. The present-day organization is known as the Burbank Chorale, but it was formerly known as the Burbank Choral Club. Founded in 1920, it has the distinction of being the oldest continuously performing arts organization in the San Fernando Valley and one of the oldest musical organizations in the state of California. It was originally made up only of feminine voices; men were barred from membership. That changed later. In 1932, the Burbank Choral Club was represented in the Olympic Chorus, which performed during the Olympic Games in Los Angeles. It also performed at the World's Fair expositions in San Diego (1935) and San Francisco (1939).

Disney Music

You may have never stepped into the boundaries of the city of Burbank and you may be entirely unfamiliar with the city or its inhabitants, but it's a sure bet that you are very familiar with music created and/or recorded in Burbank by the Disney organization. Reflect that every song appearing in nearly every Disney film released after *Snow White and the Seven Dwarfs* in 1939 was likely arranged, performed and recorded in Burbank. Disney used the proceeds from *Snow White* to build the campus in Burbank.

In fact, the (infamously) most performed and translated song of all time, "It's a Small World," is a product of the studios on the Burbank campus. While the song has some competition for ubiquity and performance with the Beatles' "Yesterday" and the Righteous Brothers' "You've Lost that Lovin' Feeling," the song's composer, Robert Sherman Jr., pointed out in a songfact.com article that "the thing to remember is that 'It's A Small World' is not a radio song and the 'Most performed or translated' assertion does not necessarily apply to radio performances or internet downloads for that matter....It is not limited to one venue or another (i.e. ringtones or radio plays). For example, neither 'Yesterday' nor 'Lovin' Feeling' are featured on an amusement park ride which plays non-stop, 16 hours a day on an endless loop in four (soon to be five) locations worldwide."

Sherman's point is valid: it might be that there is not a moment when "It's a Small World" is not playing somewhere on Earth. Consider *that* when you're trying to get the tune out of your head; you carry the ultimate earworm courtesy of the fine folks in Burbank, California.

STARLIGHT AMPHITHEATRE

The origins of what later came to be the Burbank Starlight Amphitheatre center on Maestro Leo Damiani's outdoor rehearsals with his musicians in a naturally shaped ravine in the foothills above Burbank. Damiani founded the Burbank Symphony Orchestra in 1943 and the Burbank Youth Symphony in 1948. Something of a musical sensation began at the site, which came to the attention of the Burbank City Council. With Damiani's enthusiastic urging, the city began work on a formal structure with formal seating (listeners originally sat on logs). Built in 1950, the Starlight today seats three thousand people in chairs and two thousand more on the lawn.[31]

The facility hit a financial rough spot in the early 1980s. The Starlight was described as "perennially troubled" and "years away from financial stability" in a September 27, 1984 *Los Angeles Times* article. The article also described problems with city officials affronting artists like Bette Midler and

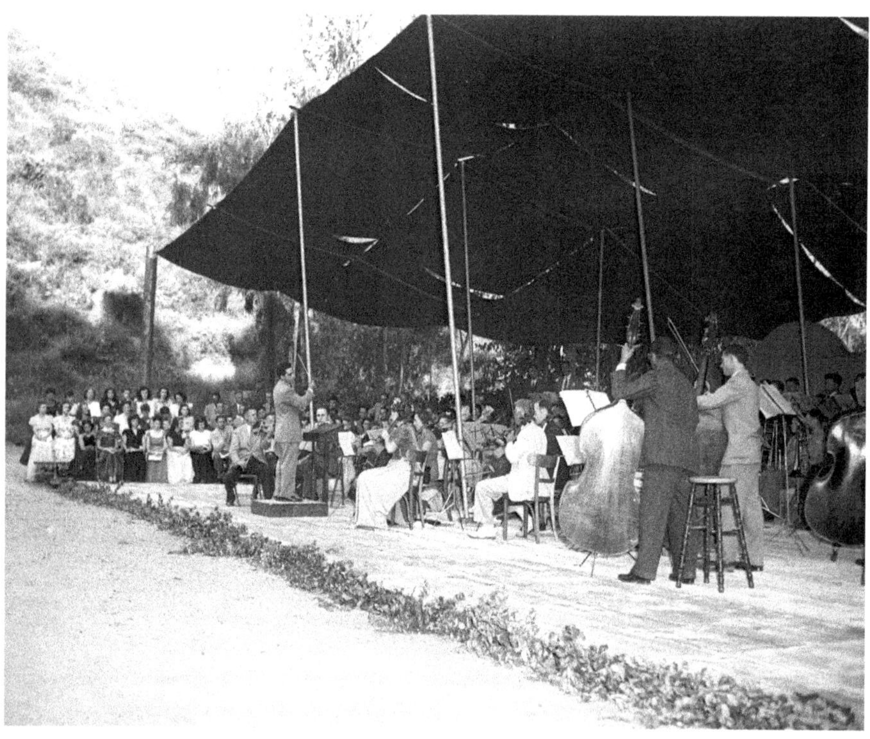

Leo Damiani conducts the Burbank Symphony Orchestra in its rough-and-ready facility in the Verdugo Hills where the Starlight Bowl would later be built, 1946. *Collection of Michael B. McDaniel.*

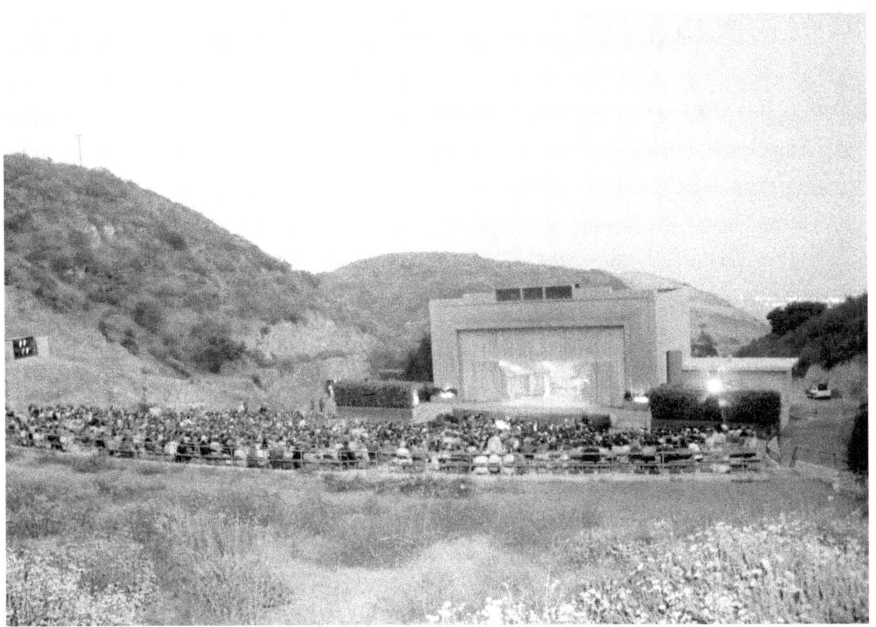

A production of Rodgers and Hammerstein's *Oklahoma!* is the fare at the Starlight Bowl, 1965. *Collection of Michael B. McDaniel.*

Toto by describing them as "disruptive." On evenings with other acts, the Burbank police criticized the facility for drug and alcohol abuse, parking shortages and inadequate security.

Nevertheless, during the decades since its 1950 start, the Starlight Amphitheatre has seen many of popular music's greats perform there: "Weird Al" Yankovic, Bob Marley, Jethro Tull, Nazareth, Black Sabbath, the Kingston Trio, Eric Clapton, Smash Mouth, Flock of Seagulls, Iron Butterfly, Quiet Riot, Berlin, the Outlaws, .38 Special, the Marshall Tucker Band, Lynyrd Skynyrd, Johnny Winter, the Commodores, Rick Springfield, Todd Rundgren, Deep Purple, Don McLean and Genesis. While past financial troubles seem to have been overcome, the problem exists of an outdated infrastructure in need of replacement; plans exist on the Internet showing proposed remodelings. It may be that in coming years the old Starlight Amphitheatre will also be lost.

A bit of present-day lost lore and irony is contained in the Starlight's address: 1249 Lockheed View Drive. Lockheed is no longer in town to view.

Bill "Suntan Charlie" Miller

Bill "Suntan Charlie" Miller was Frank Sinatra's pianist and musical associate for decades. He got his ironic nickname from Sinatra, who made fun of his pale skin. From a July 16, 2006 *Boston Globe* obituary:

> *Bill Miller, Frank Sinatra's longtime pianist and closest musical adviser, who accompanied the legendary singer from 1951 until his last performance in 1995, died Tuesday at a Montreal hospital of complications of a heart attack. He was 91. Mr. Miller, who lived in Burbank, CA for more than 50 years, was performing in Montreal with Frank Sinatra Jr. when he broke his hip two weeks ago. He subsequently had a heart attack and died after heart bypass surgery, according to his daughter, Meredith, of Berkeley, Calif.*

It should also be pointed out that Bill Miller lived on 949 Country Club Drive, a part of Burbank occasionally subject to floods and mudslides. His house was destroyed, and his wife, Aimee, was tragically killed in a 1964 mudslide when they were swept from their home and carried to a catch basin in a torrent of mud and water. She was forty-seven. Their seventeen-year-old daughter escaped by scrambling up the hill behind the house.

Don't Rock It too Hard

We close this musical chapter with our favorite artifact of rock-and-roll from that lost, charmed decade of the 1950s. It's a piece from the *Los Angeles Times* that ran on July 12, 1956, entitled, "Teen-agers in Burbank May Rock, but Softly." The city fathers had to decide how to weigh in when the Parks and Recreation Department turned down a request to permit the Platters to sing at a Saturday night dance in the Olive Recreation Center. (The Platters, of course, are known for their classic mellow hits "Only You," "The Great Pretender" and "Smoke Gets in Your Eyes.") A fifteen-year-old named David Friedlander took his record player to city hall and had some officials listen to various Platters hits. Despite reservations, the police chief thought that the songs weren't too inflammatory, and the decision was made to allow the youngsters to go ahead with the dance. Harmon Bennett, the city manager, had the best quote: "Tell the Platters not to rock it too hard."

We'd like to be able to report that the Platters did indeed appear, but a *Times* article the next day reported that the group had a previous engagement in San Diego and couldn't do the Burbank gig after all.

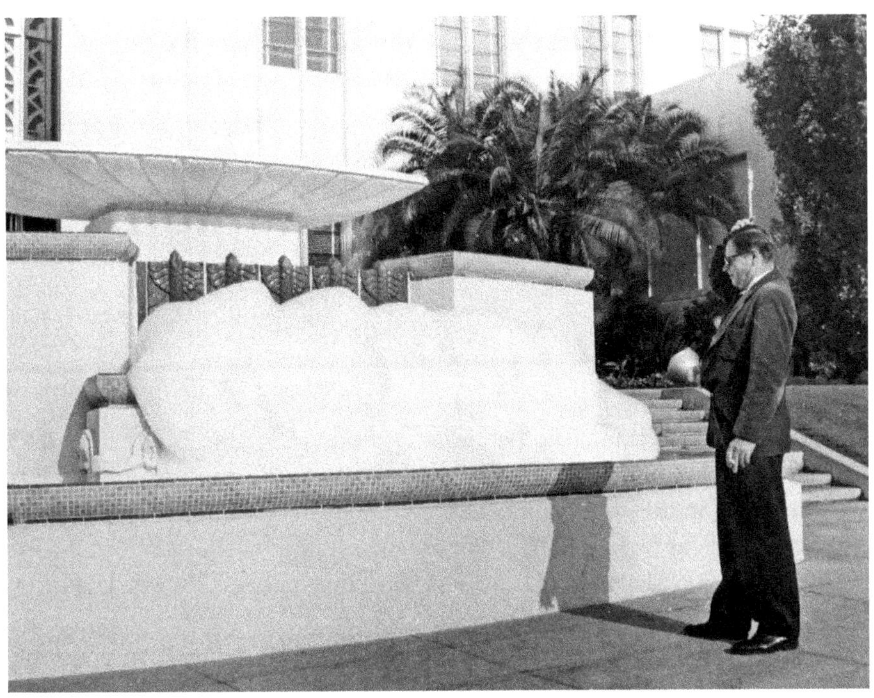

A Burbank city councilman looks at the result of a youthful prank: soap suds in the fountain in front of city hall. And these darn kids want the Platters to rock out here? *Collection of Michael B. McDaniel.*

6
BURBANK INVENTORS

Is Burbank, California, a hotbed of invention? Using the U.S. Patent and Trademark Office's online search tool returns 2,337 patents on a search for "Burbank" in the inventor city field. A quick search returns 6,872 patents for "Lockheed" as a search term. We are uncertain how many of these date before the 1990s, when Lockheed left Burbank, but the answer is almost certainly thousands.

We begin with historical Burbank's most celebrated and, it must be admitted, quaint inventions and inventor.

Fawkes's Folly and Joseph Wesley Fawkes

Let us consider the invention before the inventor.

Most accounts of Burbank's famous "Aerial Swallow" (as inventor J.W. Fawkes called it) describe his innovative transportation scheme as a monorail, but this is only accurate in a loose sense. The system involved a passenger transportation vehicle, driven by a huge fan (an enormous potential safety concern) suspended from what appears to be a tube or pipe. U.S. Patent number 1,020,010 (granted May 28, 1912) describes an "aerial trolley" suspended from a "trolley line." There was no rail. However, patent number 1,051,093 (granted January 21, 1913) describes a "strong wire or angle bar"; Fawkes's creation was probably undergoing refinement.[32] Without belaboring the technical

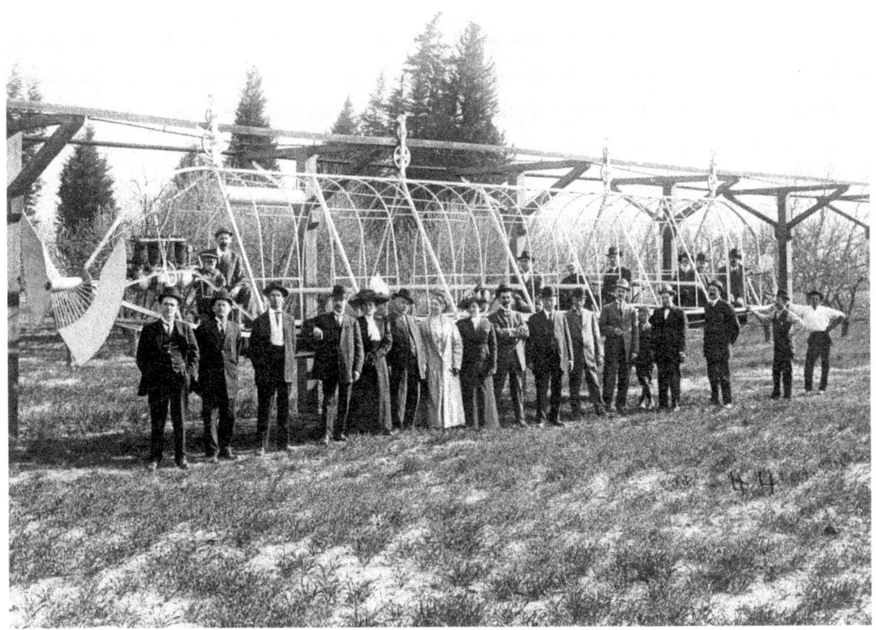

Fawkes's Folly, aka the Aerial Swallow, Burbank's famous monorail, circa 1911. *Burbank Historical Society.*

matters, the occasional claim to Fawkes's Aerial Swallow being "America's First Monorail" needs some elaboration or, perhaps, an asterisk. The aerial trolley car was tested on a six-hundred-foot line on Fawkes's farm at 110 West Olive Avenue, roughly the area where the Bormann Steel Corporation and a recreational vehicle business are located today.

You can't fault Joseph Fawkes for not presenting his invention with a sense of occasion. On July 4, 1911, he opened his farm to the public, hired a musical ensemble (it looks like a jazz trio) and hung streamers and American flags on the Aerial Swallow. Men in bowler hats and women with parasols clustered about as Fawkes presumably made a speech on a platform. People then boarded the system, and the enormous propeller was made to spin. A photograph shows the thing apparently in motion, with somebody running alongside. (But why was he running? The Swallow reportedly had a top speed of three miles per hour—walking pace.)

Fawkes's idea didn't take off, mainly because mass-transportation schemes of the day faded in favor of individually owned, gasoline-powered automobiles. And when it came down to actually deciding on a scheme to get people from Burbank to Los Angeles and back, a conventional electric trolley was the chosen solution.

Fawkes's trolley, abandoned and rusting, was dismantled in the early 1920s, probably when he sold off his property as an industrial tract in 1923.

What sort of man was Joseph W. Fawkes? To answer that question, we proceed to the next section of this chapter.

The Fawkes Family Follies

You can imagine the glee and anticipation experienced by reporters for the *Los Angeles Times* whenever news came in about the troubled Fawkes family of Burbank. The fuss began in 1895, when an August 25 piece entitled "Brotherly Love—Conspicuous Its Absence in a Recent Case" describes how Jacob Fawkes and a firm called Cairns & Company vied for a contract to maintain street signs for free. (The value was in the fact that the winner of the contract was able to use the signs for advertising.) The board of public works denied the offer, and it came out that Cairns & Company was an unnamed brother of Jacob Fawkes (Joseph?). The two were described as "deadly enemies anxious to cut out each other's throats in business." In addition, one of the brothers claimed to be the inventor of the street sign who then lost the patent when the other brother learned of the invention.

The article concludes with a mention of the Fawkes brothers' father, Joseph Walker Fawkes ("J.W. Fawkes, Sr." as styled in the papers), described as the inventor of the famous Fawkes steam plow, which made a fortune for the family.

A subsequent *Times* article from December 29, 1895, describes the "Fawkes fraternity" having a "social session" in court. J.W. Fawkes Jr. (the Aerial Swallow inventor) initiated a suit against his father, J.W. Fawkes Sr., over some property. (J.W. Sr. is an old man at this time, over seventy-two years of age.) J.W. Jr. is described as being the black sheep of the family, at loggerheads with all the rest save his brother H.B., who served at the time as a deputy constable in town. There is some discussion of J.W. Fawkes's wife, of whom the rest of the family did not approve. One Fawkes brother offered J.W. twenty-five dollars to tell him where the valid marriage license was issued. An accusation was made, serious in those strict times, that the two were living together. Feelings ran high in Burbank against "Joe" Fawkes, the piece claims. The article ends with the surprising revelation that Joe Fawkes once mixed some sort of "dope" in front of his mother's window, chanting, "Dynamite blow you up tonight!"

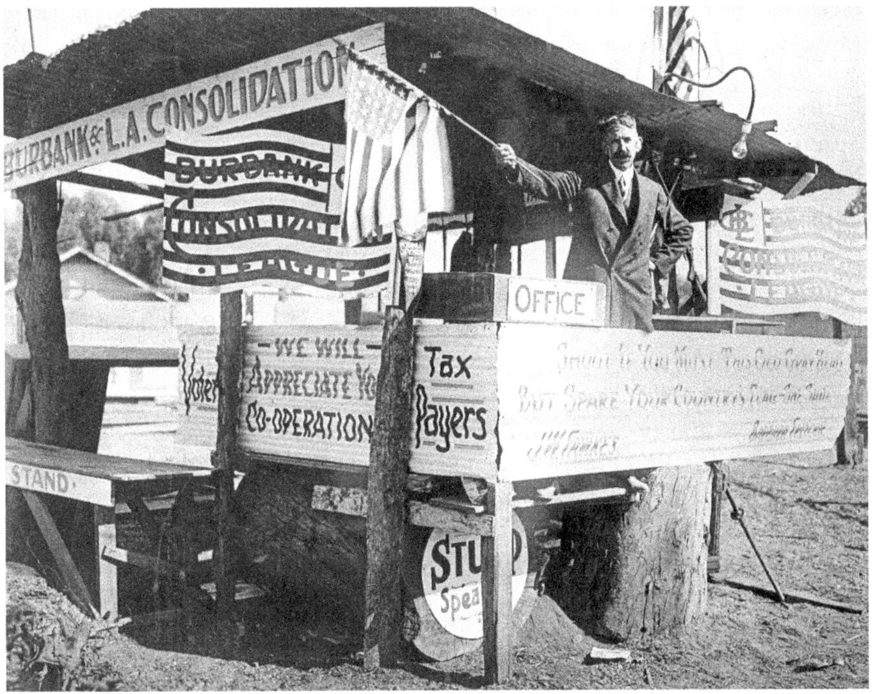

J.W. Fawkes doing some flag-waving at his Burbank–Los Angeles Consolidation booth around 1922. Note the shotgun behind Fawkes's left elbow. Was he expecting trouble? *Burbank Historical Society.*

A *Times* article dated August 9, 1896, describes a search warrant filed by J.W. Sr. against his son J.W. Jr. (henceforth "Joe" for clarity). The issue involved 325 feet of iron water pipe.

The Fawkes family's *annus horribilis* seems to have been 1898. A January 29 piece entitled "House Divided Against Itself" describes how "time and again one member of the family has been dragged into court by the other." In 1898 Joe Fawkes swore out a warrant for the arrest of his brother H.B. Fawkes for petty larceny involving a load of lumber. Joe also filed a suit in civil proceedings against his brother to have him evicted from the premises and require reimbursement for the destruction of a barn, a hen house and a pig pen.

On March 23, 1898, an over-the-top article entitled "An Infernal Machine" described allegations by J.W. Fawkes Sr. that Joe had deliberately planned to blow up Fawkes Sr. and his wife by means of a bomb placed under the house, connected to a detonator by means of an electric wire. There is also some discussion of property lines and the erection of a shed built spitefully by Joe to be within inches of his father's house; when the shed was completed, it completely shut out the light in the kitchen so that the mother had to use a candle any time of the day to see. Burbankers familiar with the situation would have none of this, however. One night, they banded together as vigilantes and mounted the structure on skids, hauled it away and burned it!

Getting back to the infernal machine, the Fawkes mother reportedly heard her son say to a carpenter, who was in cahoots, things like, "It must be arranged to blow the old man up first," "I want to scatter their bones all over the orchard" and "It'll be hard work to find any of the pieces after this thing explodes." Murderous, indeed. The Fawkes mother told her husband what was up, and he investigated a second shed placed near his home. He found an object about a foot high, eight inches in diameter and wrapped in paper, with five wires running from it. J.W. Sr. went to the district attorney and had his son and the carpenter arrested and hauled before the justice of the peace. The article ends at this point.

Was it really an explosive device? No. An April 16, 1898 article revealed that the bomb was just sand in a tin can with wires running therefrom, created in an attempt to prevent indignant Burbankers from hauling another structure away. An April 19 article describes the release of Joe and the carpenter on a writ of habeas corpus, and a piece in May describes the carpenter attempting to sue Fawkes Sr. for $10,000 in damages. In June the carpenter swore a complaint against a Fawkes brother, H.B., for perjury in court. Another suit between T.W. Fawkes and H.B. Fawkes is mentioned. Is this getting confusing?

In late November, a Judge Van Dyke attempted to get the Fawkes family members to reconcile and to go home and enjoy Thanksgiving. After a recess, Joe Jr. and Joe Sr. agreed to bury the hatchet and dismiss their suits. But Joe's brother Howard, not feeling the love, refused to be placated, and his case continued. December 1898 rolled around, and the *Times* reporters noted that "the drear monotony of surburban life has been relieved, and the courts of the county have been prevented from stagnating by having the Fawkes cases to adjudicate." In the same month a Solomonic judgement was issued that resulted in a moral victory for Howard Fawkes and a cash settlement for his brother Joe. Has family peace finally settled in?

Apparently. In 1899 Joe Fawkes Jr. and Sr. settled over a matter concerning possession of a home and a barrel of vinegar. (One cannot help but see the vinegar as metaphorical.) But Joseph Fawkes Jr. wasn't finished with the media, nor were they finished with him.

In a 1922 letter to the *Los Angeles Times* editor, Fawkes complains about high taxes in Burbank and describes why consolidation with Los Angeles would be beneficial. (In the 1920s he led a failed annexation drive.)[33] Also in 1922, Fawkes wrote a letter to the editor seeking to calm the populace about a rabid dog and about rabies in general. In September he is thrown in the Burbank City Jail for disturbing the peace. In 1925 he pleads innocent to firing a shotgun at some anti-annexation boys who threw red flares on his lawn. The animus might be understandable, as earlier anti-annexation celebrants hanged him in effigy near a bonfire on San Fernando Road; a placard read, "Here lies the body of Consolidation Joe." In June 1928 J.W. Fawkes Jr. died at age sixty-six.

The last time Joe Fawkes is mentioned in the pages of the *Los Angeles Times* was on February 10, 1929, in a piece describing how Howard, William and Leslie Fawkes (brothers of the deceased) claimed that Joe's will was "unnatural" because it didn't mention them. The three also asserted that the woman he names as sole heir of his $29,000 estate, his wife, Emma, was married as a result of an illegality. The situation never seems to end.

Let us quit there. So, what kind of man was Joseph W. "Joe" Fawkes? The authors must conclude, something of a nut.

MAURICE POIRIER, THE TEN IDEAS PER MINUTE MAN

Monsieur Maurice Poirier looked like a movie star, with a boyishly handsome face and smooth dark hair. He always dressed in a well-tailored suit. Sometimes he wore a natty moustache, sometimes a white yachtsman's cap. An appealing and dapper figure, one can see why the newspapermen and magazine editors liked him and reported on his various inventions. He was apparently of a brilliant turn of mind; a *Los Angeles Times* reporter called him the "Ten Ideas per Minute Man."

Maurice Poirier was a French or French-Canadian naturalized American who settled in Burbank at the close of World War I; he resided at 324 East Tujunga Avenue. Sources variously describe him as a watchmaker, jeweler, inventor and, later on, aircraft worker. He was described as working out of a "mountain laboratory" in the "back of Burbank," where he invented things, dreamed great technological innovations and patented useful devices. (He held at least five patents that we could find.)

Some of his inventions seem quaint, now that technology has passed him by. Or were they prophetic? A 1928 press caption shows him standing with a

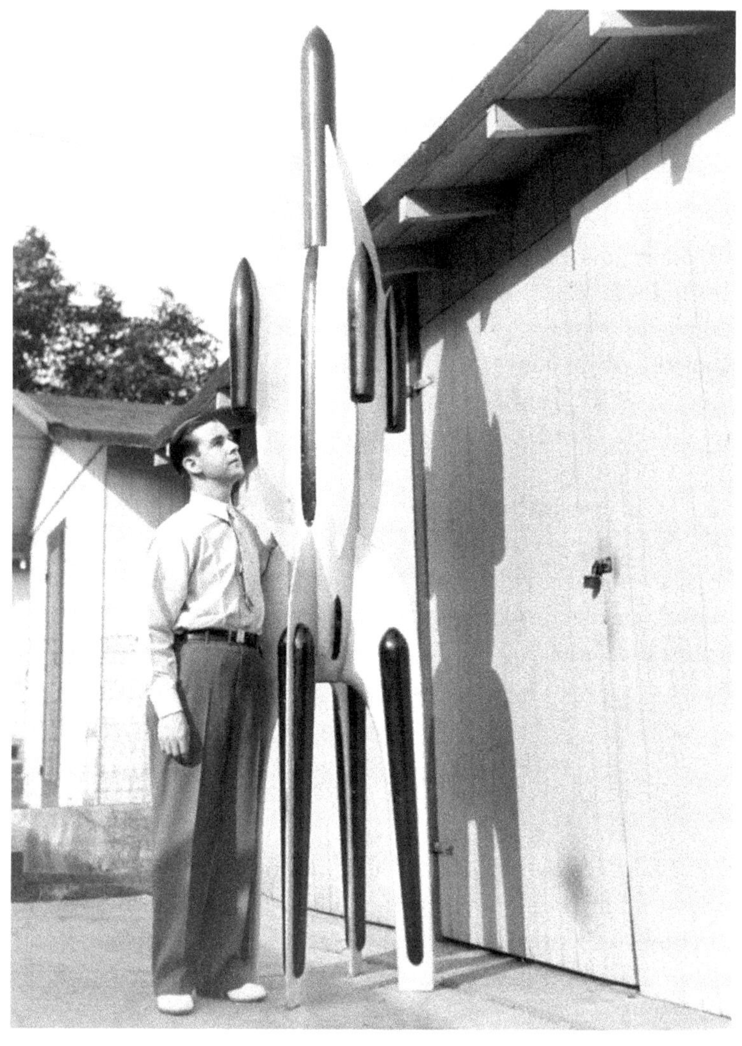

Inventor Maurice Poirier with his futuristic-looking rocket ship in his Burbank backyard, June 26, 1937. *Collection of Wes Clark.*

"radio power plant." Whether this one-thousand-foot device was meant to power airplanes over a distance or merely direct them is not made clear. In 1929, *Modern Mechanics* included a photograph of his rocket plane, a standard gasoline-powered craft augmented with rocket motors and eighty-six gun barrels; the thrust from the rockets propelled the plane to as much as four hundred miles per hour. In a 1930 photograph from the *Cumberland Evening News*, Poirier is shown with his assistant Franklin Wallace examining a plane with no fewer than fifteen rocket tubes on the tail. Poirier hopes that such a plane might achieve a speed of six hundred miles per hour. The cover of a 1930 *Popular Aviation* magazine shows a rocket plane described as able to reach one thousand miles an hour. Clearly, Poirier had a need for speed.

Was there anything too audacious for Poirier? A 1939 photograph shows him, hand casually placed in pocket, standing next to a fantastically shaped rocket that would be at home in a 1950s science-fiction thriller. As war approached, a 1936 piece in *Popular Science* showed his war rocket that could, it was claimed, rain bullets over a mile-wide area. With one technology, he was on the right track: liquid rocket propellants in place of explosives. In another area, he was all wrong: the ingredients for the liquid propellant were extracted from weeds found only in Europe—Germany, in fact! In other articles, Poirier claims altitude targets, to cross the barrier of Earth's gravitational pull with a rocket that can exceed 500,000 feet.

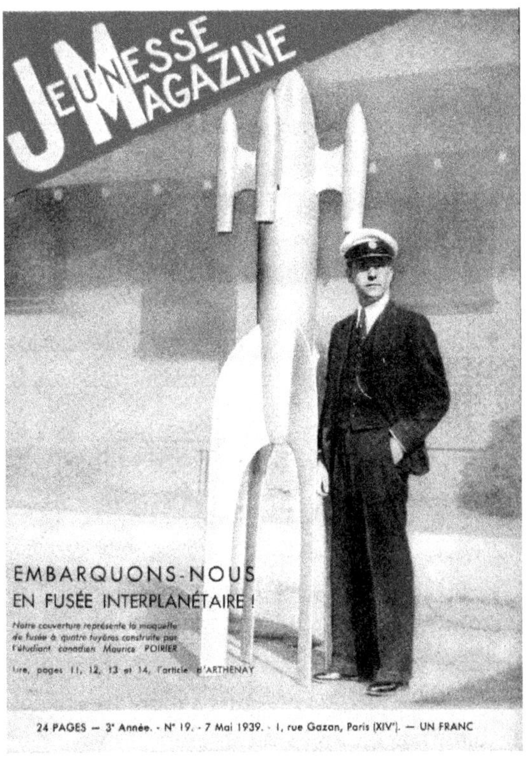

Maurice Poirier on the cover of *Jeunesse (Youth) Magazine*, May 7, 1939. "Let's board the interplanetary rocket!" says the caption. *Jean-Jacques Serra.*

Poirier was probably better off with his inventions concerning time and special-purpose clocks and watches. One such watch, developed in 1937, featured a twelve-minute dial to aid in the use of following navigational radio beams. In 1941 his attention was fully focused on the war; he developed an "arc and time clock" useful for navigating long-range bombing runs.

It is, sadly, the lot of many visionary men to suffer the slights of the public and the media. A 1931 British Pathe film clip entitled "Another Good Idea Goes Wrong!"[34] shows Poirier launching a plane powered by twenty-eight rockets; it quickly crashes. "Inventor Poirier's novel craft goes like a rocket—but comes down like a stick," says the title card, crushingly.

So, was Maurice Poirier another J.W. Fawkes Jr., a somewhat crazed man with an overactive imagination? No. We can find five patents for him (1936, two in 1938, 1951 and 1956), all dealing with providing suspension of each wheel in a vehicle physically separate from the others—what we now call independent suspension. Poirier may have been the father of it, as least as far as transportation vehicles and trucks are concerned, which were the subjects of his patents. It perhaps goes without saying, in our off-road and utility vehicle society, that independent suspension is an important automotive development. Poirier played his part in making our car rides a bit smoother.

CLARENCE B. "KELLY" JOHNSON

Like Willis Haviland Carrier, the father of modern air-conditioning,[35] Kelly Johnson was a man who might be termed an engineer's engineer. A famous aeronautical genius and two-time Collier Trophy winner, Johnson, the head of Lockheed's celebrated Skunk Works, was involved in the design and production of many groundbreaking and innovative aircraft: the Model 9D Orion, various Electra models, the Model 18 Lodestar, the PV-1 Ventura, the P-38 Lightning, the multitudinous Constellation family of aircraft, the F-80 Shooting Star, the P2V Neptune, the XF-90, the F-94 Starfire, the X-7, the F-104 Starfighter, the F-117A Nighthawk, the C-130 Hercules, the U-2, the Blackbird family and the JetStar/C-140. What an incredible résumé!

Johnson, musclebound from his early days as a hod carrier,[36] was able to use the same golf club for all his shots. But he was also a gifted mathematician, reportedly able to do accurate estimates involving lengthy sequences of calculus in his head. In fact, he performed calculus the way other people doodled.

Why was his Lockheed organization called the Skunk Works? As a teenager, Wes Clark asked his father that question and got the response that there used to be a lot of skunks around the plant in that part of Burbank. The Wikipedia article on Kelly Johnson has the real answer:

> *Johnson became Vice President of Advanced Development Projects (ADP) in 1958. The first ADP offices were nearly uninhabitable; the stench from a nearby plastic factory was so vile that Irv Culver, one of the engineers,*

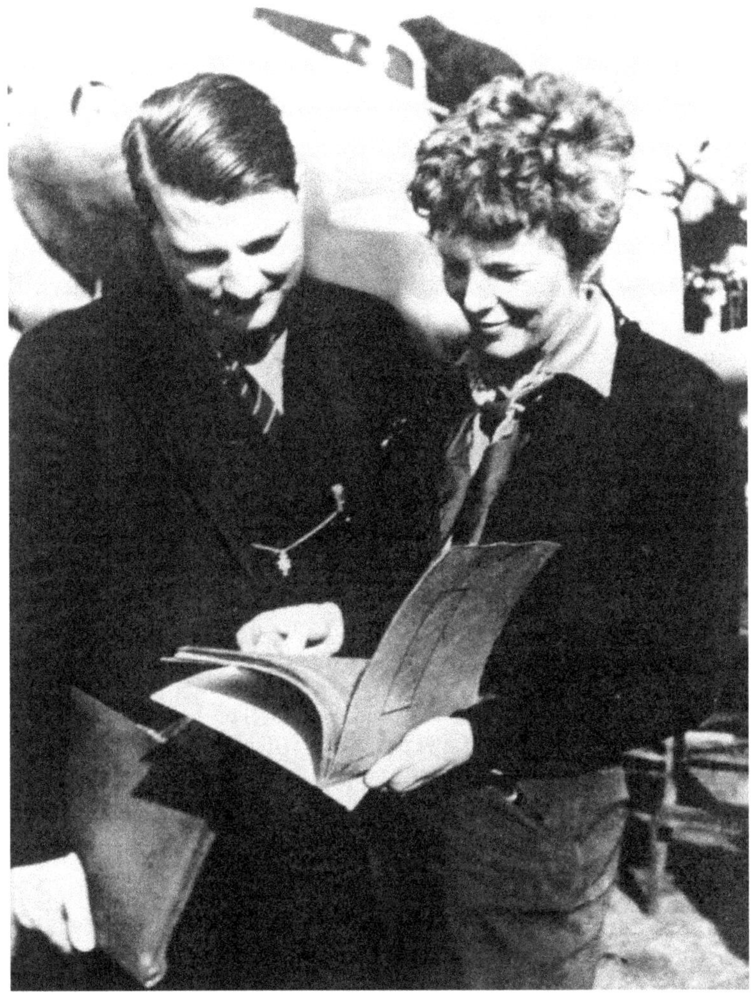

Clarence Kelly Johnson and Amelia Earhart inspect airplane specifications at Lockheed, 1930s. *Burbank Historical Society.*

began answering the intra-Lockheed "house" phone, "Skonk Works!" In Al Capp's comic strip Li'l Abner, *Big Barnsmell's Skonk Works—spelled with an "o"—was where Kickapoo Joy Juice was brewed. When the name "leaked" out, Lockheed ordered it changed to "Skunk Works" to avoid potential legal trouble over use of a copyrighted term. The term rapidly circulated throughout the aerospace community, and became a common nickname for research and development offices; however, reference to "The Skunk Works" means the Lockheed ADP department.*

Ben Rich's book *Skunk Works* contains a lot of interesting Kelly Johnson lore. There's an amusing chapter entitled "Blowing Up Burbank" that describes Johnson's development of what became the famous U-2 spy plane, powered by jets burning liquid hydrogen (necessary for the extremely high operating altitude of the aircraft). One day in late 1959 there was a fire in the Skunk Works near containers, holding seven hundred gallons of extremely volatile liquid hydrogen. The Burbank Airport came very close to being blown up. Rich describes the scene with the Burbank firemen:

> *The fire department noisily arrived at our hangar door and the next problem was that security didn't want to let them in. The firemen weren't cleared and this was a project above top secret.... "What is inside?" the fire chief asked me. "National security stuff. Can't tell you," I replied. The firemen saw the fog and went running for their gas masks. Had they known they were playing around with liquid hydrogen so close to Burbank Airport, I'm sure they would have had my scalp, but they put out the fire in two minutes and went away, no questions asked.*

How is Kelly Johnson a Burbanker? He worked long hours at Lockheed from 1933 to his retirement in 1975, and the 1940 Federal Census shows him living at 1027 Country Club Drive—coincidentally, a few houses away from Burbank's aviation legend and Nazi agent Laura Ingalls (whom we cover in the next chapter). While he lived elsewhere during much of his time at Lockheed, the city proudly claims him.

VOLMER JENSEN

While his creations didn't fly as high or as fast as those of Kelly Johnson, Volmer Jensen nonetheless made his mark in the world of personal aviation, creating small aircraft that were safer and more affordable than those previously available.

As a young man in Seattle, he learned to fly a hang glider, the design for which appeared in an issue of *Popular Mechanics*. He then began to build other hang gliders, and by 1930, he had a worldwide reputation as a sailplane (glider) pilot. Beginning in 1937, when he moved to Glendale, California, he began to build light craft of his own design. One such, the VJ-10 high-performance sailplane, was purchased by the military for its assault glider training program. Jensen spent the war years as an instructor; when the war ended, he began to envision an affordable airplane. This became the VJ-21, which, sadly, never got to the marketplace due to economic factors out of his control.

By the 1950s Jensen had developed an interest in scuba diving, and in 1958 he marketed the VJ-22 Sportsman, a two-seat, high-winged, amphibious plane. Interest in this aircraft took Jensen into the light airplane business, and today VJ-22s are found on every continent save Antarctica. In the late 1960s, when hang gliders became popular, Jensen introduced the safe and sturdy VJ-23 Swingwing, which evolved into the VJ-24E SunFun. Dave Cook flew one across the English Channel in 1972.

Volmer Jensen was a master craftsman who had the reputation of being able to build anything. He founded the Production Model Company on East Providencia Avenue in Burbank, where, in December 1964, he rolled out his most instantly recognizable product, the original USS *Enterprise* from the 1966–69 *Star Trek* series. The piece is now in the Smithsonian Institution. (A photograph of Jensen and his *Enterprise* appear later on in this book.)

Burbank's Lost Language

We conclude our survey of Burbank inventors with this curious gentleman. Your authors are aware of a photograph of a barefooted gentleman, long of hair and beard, dressed in what looks like some kind of white institutional shirt and trousers (a 1924 *Los Angeles Times* article claimed he wore "picturesque garb"). His arms are crossed, and he stands gazing at the viewer with a morose expression on his face that almost says, "What of me?"[37] He is Harper B. Henry, described as living on a Burbank hill in the style of a hermit. The piece acknowledges that he looks like a fanatic of some kind but isn't. What has he invented? A new breakfast food (the art on the cover of the box was done by him), a vehicle of some kind that was described as a sort of pink zeppelin on wheels and his own language, "Azonic" (a language of ideas independent of emotion, not of words). Why did he invent Azonic? "I am doing it purely for my own amusement!"

There are twelve characters in Azonic and six punctuation marks. The twelve characters describe not sounds, but twelve basic principles of nature. It will be appreciated that with basic principles of nature such as "unit substance" and "unit force," trying to parse an object in Azonic is not for

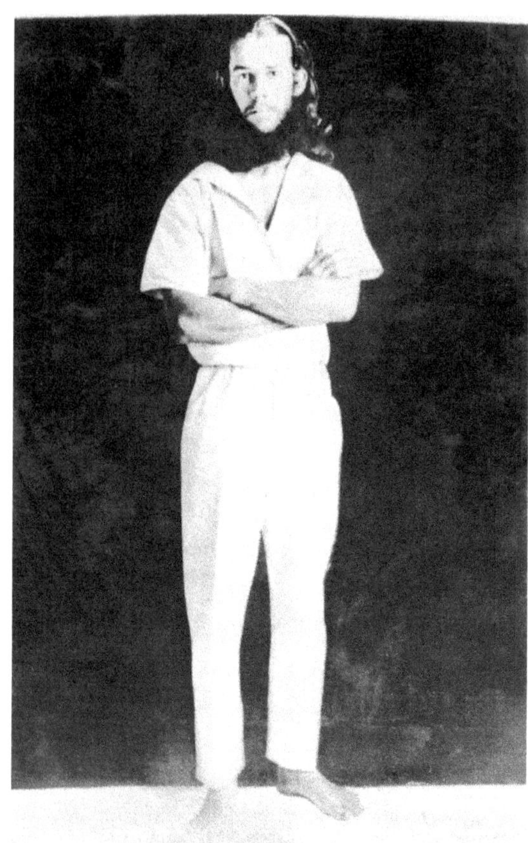

Left: Harper B. Henry, inventor of the Azonic language, in picturesque garb, circa 1924. *Collection of Michael B. McDaniel.*

Below: Eat your heart out, Mattel! This clever wooden airplane was built by the Seaver Toy Company in Burbank. *Collection of Michael B. McDaniel.*

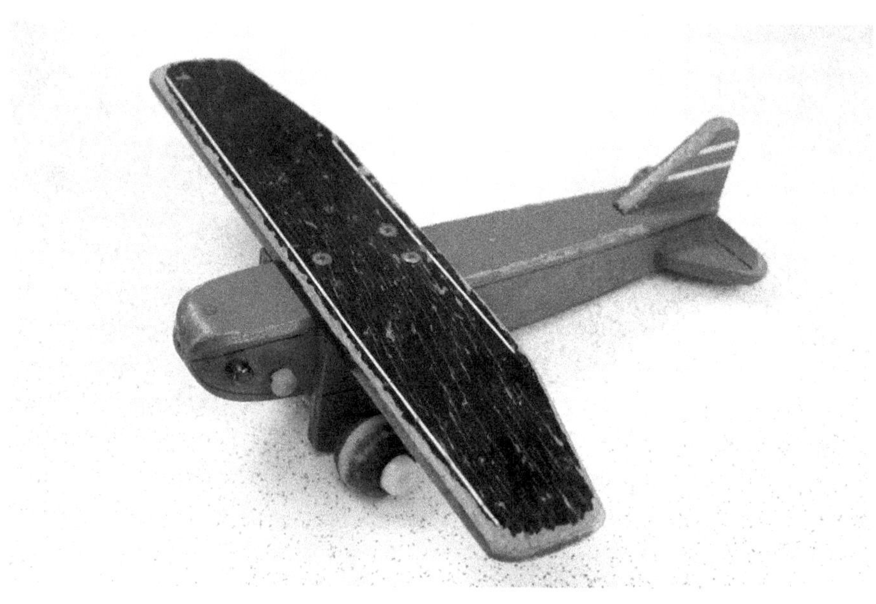

the faint of heart. A sheet of paper, for instance, is rendered in Azonic as "a plane of dead vegetable matter." (A cynical observer notes that the same could be applied to a garbage can run over by a truck.) Azonic also has within it a time-reckoning system, the base of which is, of course, the day Azonic was founded.

As an invented language, Azonic stands with Tolkien's Elvish, *Star Trek*'s Klingon and Zamenhof's Esperanto—just far less successful, as fewer people write in it. (We guess that back in the 1920s, that number was exactly one.) Not even Burbankers have heard of Azonic. Later in life, after rediscovering a long-lost daughter, Henry led a Utopian community on an island off the coast of Panama.

Harper B. Henry's father was an unusual fellow, too. From 1913 to about 1930, Leroy "Freedom Hill" Henry lived in what is today the Shadow Hills section of Sunland (then Roscoe) and issued philosophical pamphlets from a Burbank address (back then, the Burbank post office served this part of Roscoe). His musings included "Freedom from Fond Friends," "The Divinity of the Devil," "The Usefulness of Useless Husbands" and "Henry's Glass Eye." That last one was actually about Henry's real glass eye.

An interesting family!

7
THOSE AMAZING BURBANKERS!

This chapter celebrates people living or working in Burbank: Burbankers. These can be ordinary citizens whom you do not know, celebrities you do know or celebrities from the past who are now forgotten. But each has his or her story.

JAMES J. JEFFRIES

In Burbank history books, James J. Jeffries is always cited as the town's first national and international celebrity—and so he is. But these books never look at his career as a boxer, other than to cite his heavyweight championship of the world. Let us look a bit more into the lost lore of the amazing physicality of Burbanker James J. Jeffries.

At six feet, one and a half inches and 225 pounds in his prime, he was called "Big Jim." Look at that physique! Jeffries had a build any man in any era would envy. His upper-leg development was unique for his time, too. He could sprint one hundred yards in just over ten seconds—still impressive in our day and age—and he could high-jump over six feet. Gilbert Odd, an author on boxing, wrote, "According to those in Jeffries training camp, Jeff, a lover of hunting, once killed a large deer and carried it on his shoulders nine miles to camp without stopping to rest. Friends who accompanied him had difficulty keeping up with him on the jaunt home."

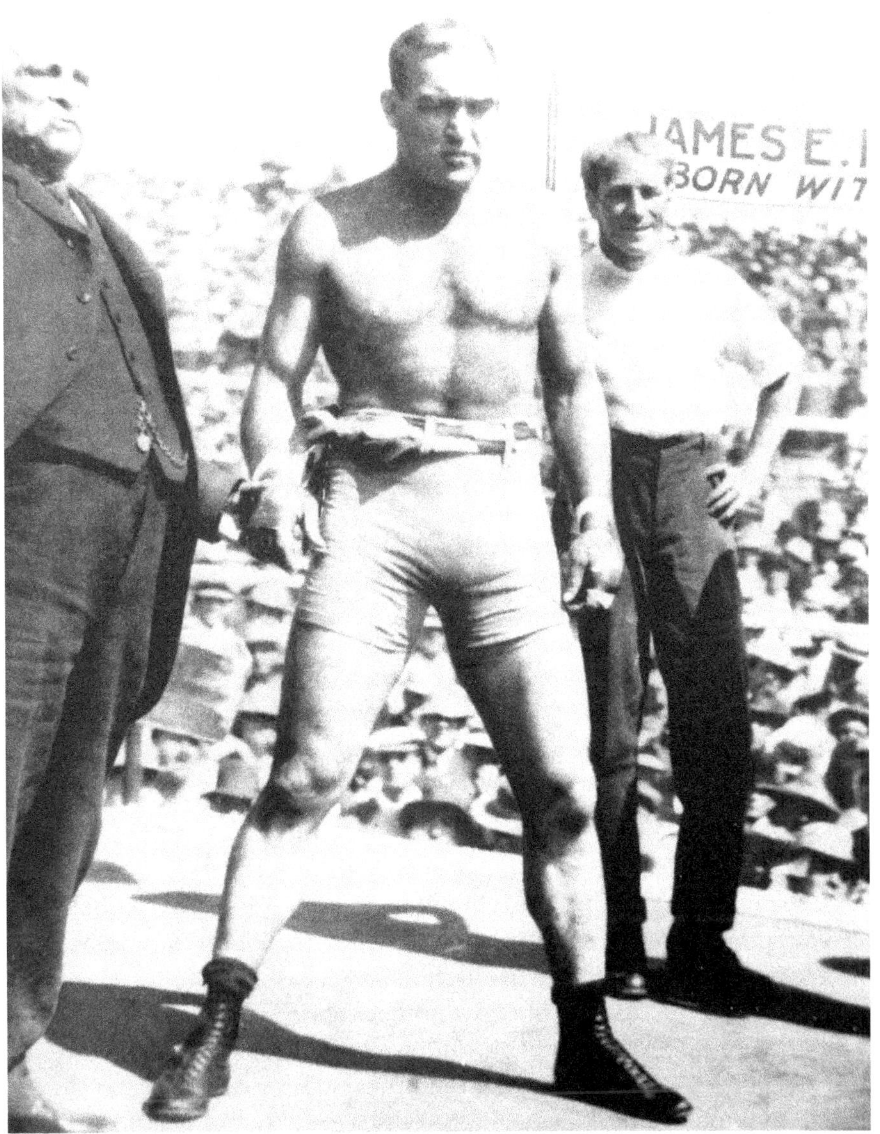

Big Jim: James Jackson Jeffries, heavyweight champion of the world, in his prime.
Library of Congress.

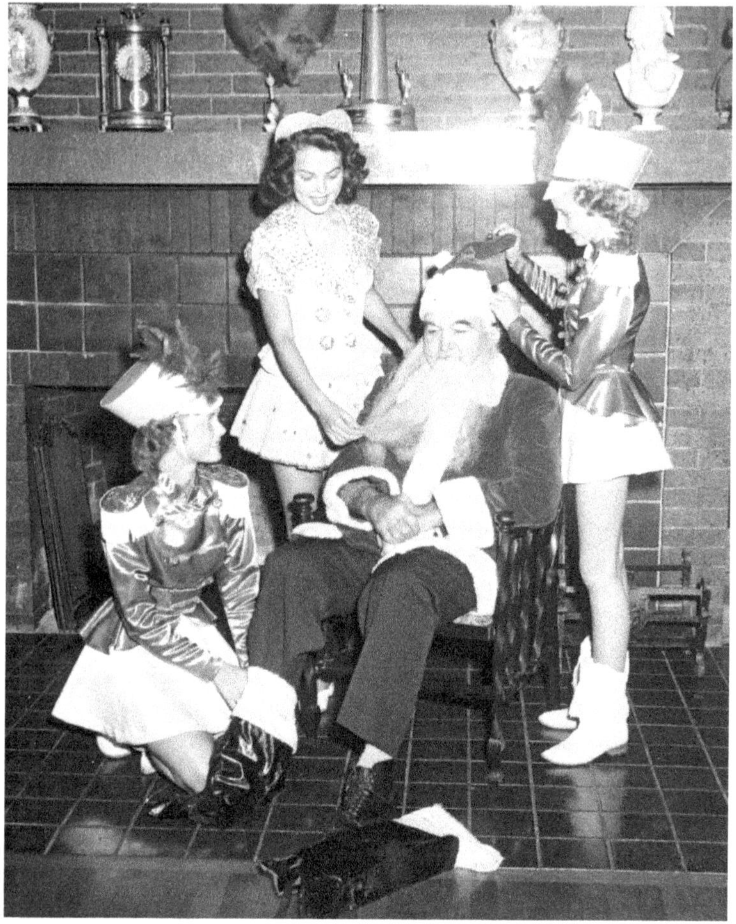

Big Jim in later days, playing Santa for Debbie Reynolds (left), Alice Kelly (center) and an unknown lass, 1948. *Burbank Historical Society.*

Jeffries was well known for being able to absorb great punishment in the ring. In his 1902 bout with Bob Fitzsimmons, one of boxing's hardest punchers, he was viciously battered for eight rounds, with a broken nose, his cheeks cut to the bone and gashes over his eyes. Just as it appeared the fight would have to be stopped, Jeffries threw a hard right to Fitzsimmons's stomach, followed by a knockout left hook to the jaw. Jeffries retired undefeated in 1905.[38] His accolades were many: "Champion of Champions," "the greatest Heavyweight Champion that ever lived," "the greatest fighter of all time." Such was the boxing legacy of the man who established a ranch, a boxing ring in his barn and alfalfa fields at the intersection of Buena Vista Road and Victory Boulevard in Burbank.

For a macho man who lived by his fists, one is impressed by the soundness of James Jeffries's holdings and investments. His acquisition of real estate in Burbank was canny: with 107 acres, he had enough land to become a rancher and maintain his interest in boxing, training new fighters and staging bouts in his barn. He also held rodeos on his property, and the Jeffries Ranch became the site of many civic and philanthropic activities. When the alfalfa market declined, he raised cattle on his property, eventually establishing a herd of thoroughbred bulls for export to Mexico and South America. In the business world, that's called a diversified portfolio.

James J. Jeffries died an honored and respected Burbanker in 1953.[39] A plaque was placed on Buena Vista Street in his memory. The lore is that Jeffries collapsed on the sidewalk running alongside Buena Vista Street, and the plaque was placed at the spot.

LAURA HOUGHTALING INGALLS

Let us state immediately that in this section we are not talking about Laura Ingalls Wilder, the author of the Little House books. As far as we know, the two are not related.

In today's parlance, Laura Ingalls had it all. She was a celebrated lady flyer in the early years of aviation who held a number of records, including the longest solo flight ever made by a woman (seventeen thousand miles), the first solo flight by a woman from North to South America, the first solo flight around South America by man or woman, the first complete flight by a land plane around South America by a man or woman and was the first American woman to fly solo over the Andes mountain range. Obviously, four of these, being "firsts," still apply, ensuring her fame.

She had important and influential friends, with whom she posed for a photograph near her Lockheed Air Express plane in the Lockheed plant in Burbank: Amelia Earhart and Roscoe Turner (a barnstormer and personal friend of Howard Hughes). In 1934 Ingalls won the Harmon Trophy for her aeronautical skills and achievements. She had great publicity: a 1935 Universal newsreel, seen by millions, described the occasion of her being granted her transport pilot's license. A 1938 article in the *New Haven (CT) Sunday Register,* entitled "Woman's Place Is in the Air," was highly laudatory:

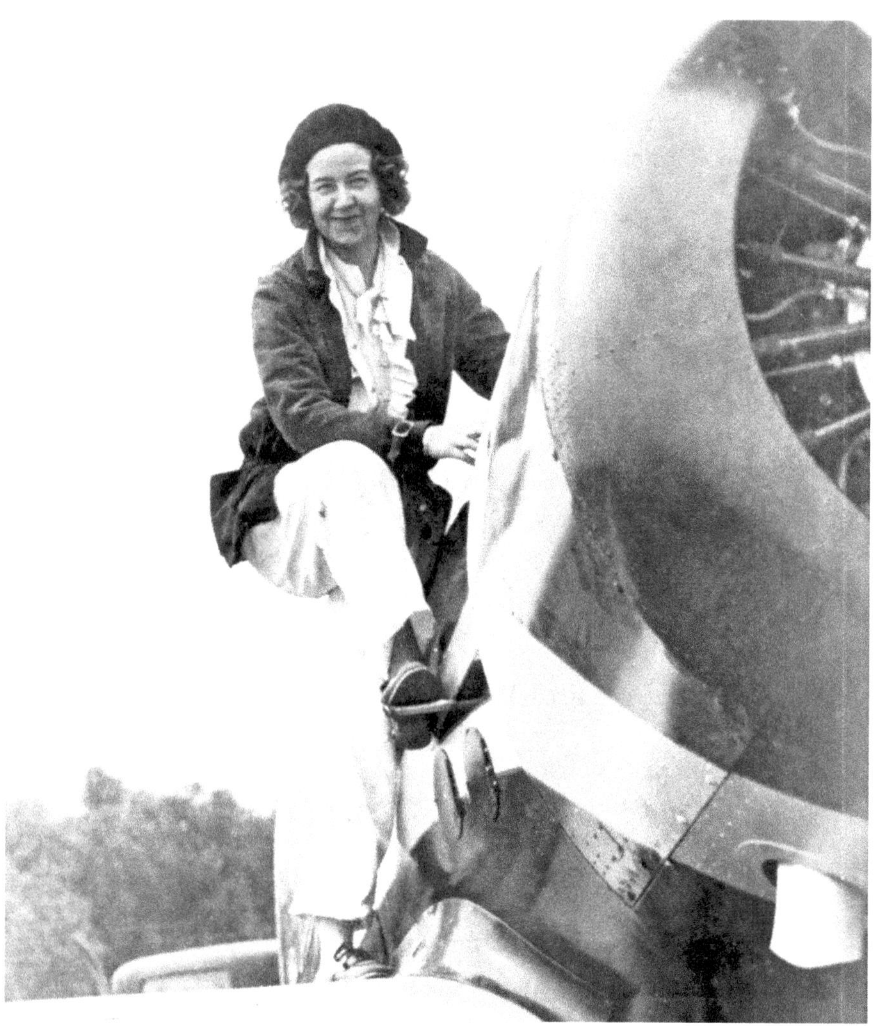

Laura Houghtaling Ingalls, pioneer female aviator and Nazi spy, 1935. *Burbank Historical Society.*

"A girl flier, with no time for love, would lift her sisters from the kitchen to a cloud…flying is their field as much as man's—and the sky's the only limit to their latent aeronautical abilities."

Laura Ingalls was a daring new role model for young women; she was flying high, figuratively and literally, as an early feminist heroine. It makes her subsequent activities and publicity puzzling in the extreme.

The website Pardonpower.com gives an account of an interesting 1939 flight:

On September 26, 1939, Ingalls took the flight that doomed her legacy of extraordinary flight to scorn, if not general obscurity. Serving the interests of the Womens' National Committee to Keep the United States Out of War, Ingalls flew over the nation's capital for two hours and dropped red-white-and-blue "peace pamphlets" addressed to "All Members of Congress." Officials of the Civil Aeronautic Authority (CAA) greeted Ingalls when she arrived at Washington Airport. They abruptly informed the aviatrix that her leaflet dropping was unacceptable given the fact that she had not been granted permission to do so by the CAA or the municipality of Washington. She was also informed that her flight had violated a restricted zone (including the White House). Ingalls was ordered to show cause why her license should not be revoked.

Three days before Christmas, the CAA suspended Ingalls's pilot certificate for this ill-considered activity.

The trouble, as reported by the *Los Angeles Times*, really began in January 1942, when she was indicted in a Federal District Court for being an unregistered paid agent of the German Reich, in violation of the Foreign Agents Registration Act. She was charged with attempting to influence public opinion via isolationist speeches and distribution of printed matter. She pled not guilty but was tried and convicted as a Nazi agent in February. Details that came out in court didn't help her cause: she wore a swastika pendant, called Hitler a "marvelous man," berated President Roosevelt for helping England instead of Germany, received money from a German contact and concluded letters with "Heil Hitler!" She was quoted as saying, "This country needs somebody like Hitler," "Democracy is the bunk" and "The H.M.S. *Hood* was sunk today. Seig Heil!" In her defense, her lawyer stated that Ingalls had offered her services to J. Edgar Hoover and the FBI as a Mata Hari but was rebuffed, which angered her.

Ingalls was sent to prison in Washington, D.C., where inmates, not amused with her Nazi racial beliefs, beat her as the culmination of a series of near riots she reportedly started. She was moved to a facility in West Virginia, and in October 1943, she was released. Eventually Ingalls moved back to Burbank and resided in a home on Country Club Drive.

Laura Ingalls died on January 10, 1967, in Burbank, aged seventy-three, and was buried in Kingston, New York. Her obituary in the *Burbank Daily Review* doesn't mention her Nazi affiliation or her prison sentence. To the end of her days, she told friends that she had not said or held opinions different than those of American hero Charles Lindbergh (who was accused of being a Nazi sympathizer), but that she unfairly paid a penalty for them, whereas he had not.

DeLos Dickson Wilbur

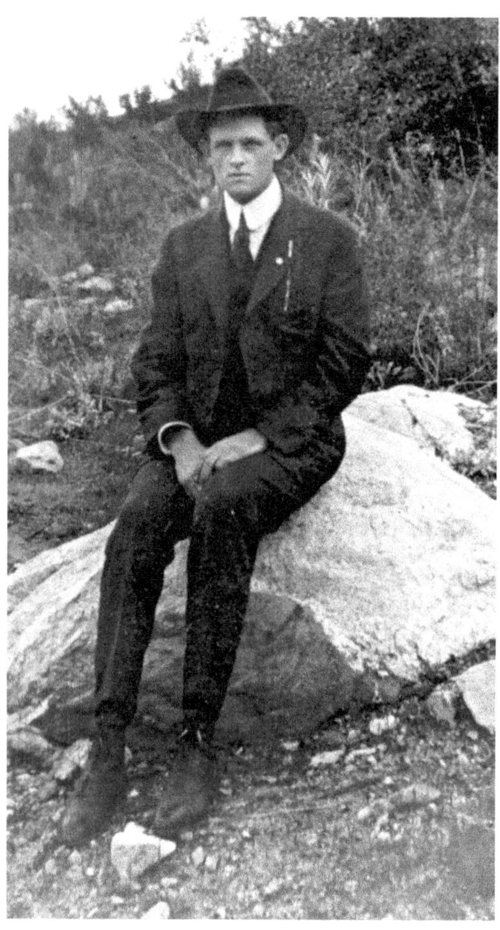

DeLos Dickson Wilbur somewhere in the Verdugo Hills, 1917. He took this image of himself while on a postal delivery run. Apparently he used a pneumatic bulb to close the camera shutter. You can barely see the tube at his feet. *Collection of Michael B. McDaniel.*

A few years back Mike McDaniel came across an interesting and important collection of early Burbank photographic history, loose pages from the scrapbook of DeLos (pronounced "day-*loss*") D. Wilbur, an early resident. DeLos Dickson Wilbur was born on March 31, 1893, in Illinois, the son of Andrew L. and Hattie C. Wilbur. He had a younger brother named DeWitt Wilbur, born in 1896. In 1900 the family was still in Warren, Lake County, Illinois, but sometime between then and 1910 they moved to Burbank and took up residence in a house at 810 East Angeleno Street. DeLos graduated from Burbank High School on June 16, 1911. At some point he became a rural mail route carrier in town; it is unclear what his route was, but it appeared to have taken him well out of town.

He registered for the draft in 1917 and went to

Washington State for training. He was assigned to the 185th Aero Squadron in France, working as an airplane mechanic. He returned to Burbank after the war (he is named in the 1944 *Burbank Community Book* as a World War I veteran) and resumed work as a mail carrier in Burbank.

At some point he seems to have struck up a friendship with members of the Luttge family, a prominent family in Burbank who owned a grocery store on San Fernando Road. In DeLos's photos they are shown in front of their store in Burbank and at a beach.

DeLos and his wife, Lucile, had three kids, Doris (born in 1919), Wesley (born in 1921) and Lynn (born in 1926). The Wilbur family moved to Oceanside, California, between 1938 and 1940 (he and his wife living with their daughter Doris), where he is listed on the voter registry. Little is known beyond that. He died in August 1978, aged eighty-five. He was mentioned in an Oceanside, California paper as being a member of a local photo club and gave a slide presentation in 1956.

Wilbur's enthusiastic amateur photography captured a charmingly rural Burbank that has long since vanished and been replaced by the thoroughly modern city we know now. Some of the photographs of San Fernando Road show buildings and locations that, to our knowledge, appear in no other known photographs. The great majority of the images are from early 1917, an era when the motorcar was beginning to replace the horse and buggy. Burbankers owe Delos Wilbur thanks not only for his service in World War I but also for his photographic documentation. (These may be viewed on the Burbankia website.)

DEBBIE "FRANNIE" REYNOLDS

Debbie Reynolds is, of course, a film legend and has been for decades. But in the beginning—and by that we mean May 1948—she was just Mary Frances "Frannie" Reynolds of 1934 Evergreen Street in Burbank, a sixteen-year-old Burbank High School student and Miss Burbank contestant. The contest was sponsored by Lockheed, and every girl who entered was guaranteed a blouse and a scarf. In her autobiography *Debbie, My Life*, she describes herself as not especially pretty or glamorous (she didn't even wear lipstick) and doubtful of the outcome. After all, her bathing suit had a hole in it (stitched up by her mother.) But she wanted the blouse and scarf.

What Mary Frances had in spades, however, was a winsome personality and charm. When asked on stage why she wanted to be Miss Burbank, she

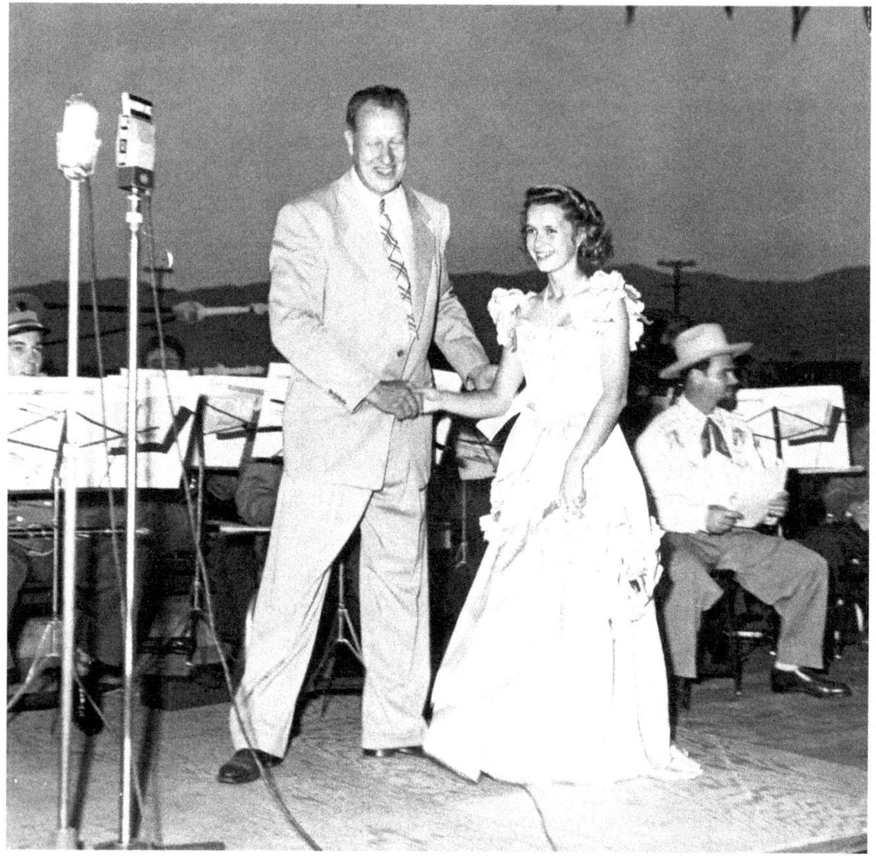

A very young Debbie Frannie Reynolds comes to the microphone, circa 1948. The man is unknown. *Burbank Historical Society.*

readily admitted that she really didn't—she was in it simply because she lived in Burbank. During the talent portion of the pageant, she won over the audience by lugging a record player and nearly tripping in her high heels, which, after permission was gained from the audience, she removed. She then sang a tune, "I'm a Square in the Social Circle." After that, she attempted to simply go home but was prevented by a contest official. When it came time to announce the three winners, in the beauty, talent and personality categories, Mary Frances was called out as the winner in the latter category, and the crowd went nuts.

The rest, as they say, is history. After winning the Miss Burbank contest, Mary Frances got a seven-year contract from Warner Bros., for which she worked while attending John Burroughs Senior High School, where she transferred from Burbank High. (For years her photograph was part of a student montage above the Burroughs auditorium doors.) While at Warner's, she also worked for a time in the women's clothing section of the downtown Burbank J.C. Penney. With her earnings from Warner Bros. she bought her parents a swimming pool for the house on Evergreen Street. After Mary Frances became Debbie and moved out, however, her father had it filled in with dirt—a situation that was only reversed when the house was sold in the early 1970s. (Her father felt that he alone should be responsible for improvements to the home.)

A *Los Angeles Times* piece from December 29, 1949, is worth noting: Miss Debbie Reynolds and another girl, two of Burbank's civic queens, served as honorary timekeepers in a wrestling match[40] held in the Jeffries Barn to raise funds for the Burbank float in the Tournament of Roses competition. Debbie Reynolds, the Jeffries Barn and the Burbank float: it doesn't get much more Burbank than that!

Jay Leno

Readers will know that comedian Jay Leno was the host of *The Tonight Show* on NBC from 1992 to 2009. Burbank is the site of Jay's automobile garage, located near the airport. Leno owns approximately 286 vehicles—169 automobiles and 117 motorcycles. A television and web show, *Jay Leno's Garage*, is based on his collection. The show includes lots of footage of Burbank streets. Leno can be seen occasionally driving around Burbank in some fantastic old or classic car; Mike McDaniel once saw Leno at the wheel of a Stanley Steamer on one occasion and in a 1966 Ford Galaxie on another. Fun fact: Jay Leno's stated favorite employee at the Ralph's grocery store on Buena Vista Street and Victory Boulevard is Mike's son Nate.

Johnny Weissmuller

Johnny Weissmuller was the star of the Tarzan films (1932 to 1948) and the Jungle Jim films (1948 to 1954) and an actor who was billed by MGM as being "the only man in Hollywood who's natural in the flesh and can act without clothes." Weissmuller, six feet, three inches tall and 190 pounds,

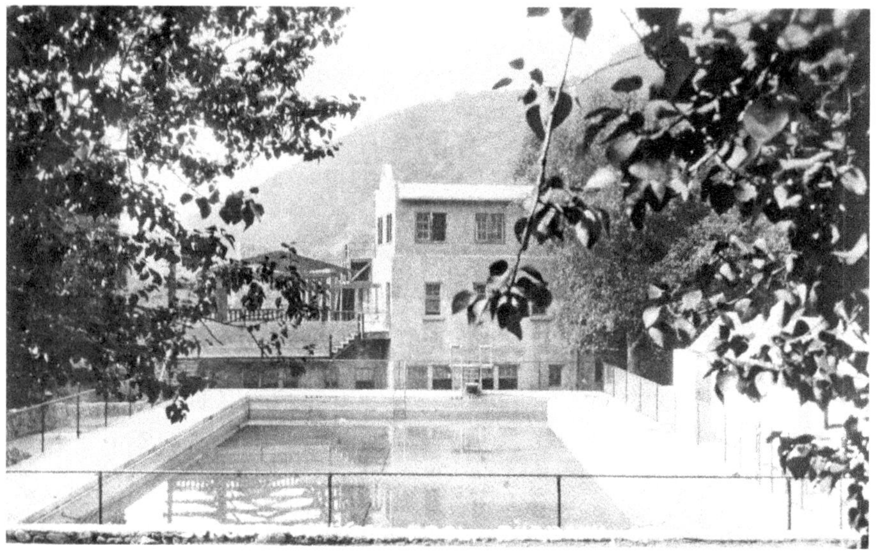

A 1920s photograph of the pool at the old Country Club building, later Johnny Weismuller's. *Collection of Michael B. McDaniel.*

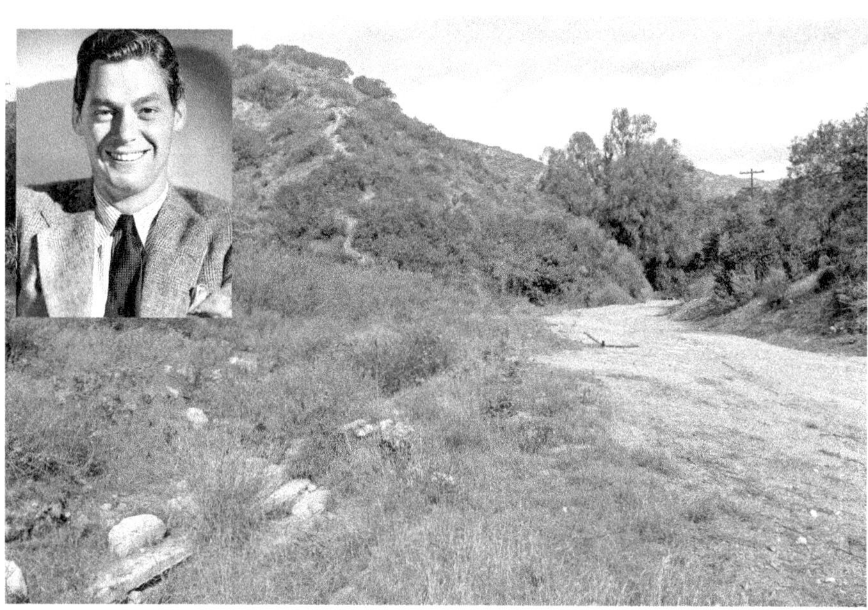

The Country Club/Weismuller pool site today. Johnny Weismuller is shown in the inset. *Wes Clark/Wikipedia.*

was a champion swimmer and winner of five Olympic gold medals, sixty-seven world titles and fifty-two national titles. He held every freestyle record, from one hundred yards to the half-mile. Swimming being important to him throughout his life, it was natural that, when the original Burbank Country Club, with its large pool, came up for sale, he purchased it. According to Country Club Drive authority Doris Vick, Weissmuller made a home of the facility from at least 1960, when Vick took up residence in the canyon, to 1962, when he sold the country club to the family from whom the City of Burbank purchased the property in order to build a spillway dam.

Billy Barty

Barty was a physically small actor with an outsized talent, reputation, sense of humor and style. The authors are happy to credit him as a Burbanker. Billy Barty was born William John Bertanzetti in 1924; the Internet Movie Database lists him with no fewer than 189 films and television appearances. Known for his enthusiasm and energy, in 1975 he founded the Burbank-based Billy Barty Foundation (first in North Hollywood, later on 929 West Olive Avenue), an advocacy group for little people, helping them integrate into mainstream society. Wes Clark was delighted to once chat with Billy at a Washington, D.C., function, discussing Burbank, his participation in a softball team for little people in town he named the "Short Ribs" and his role as Mickey Rooney's "kid brudder" in the Mickey McGuire film series (1927 to 1934). Barty was a member

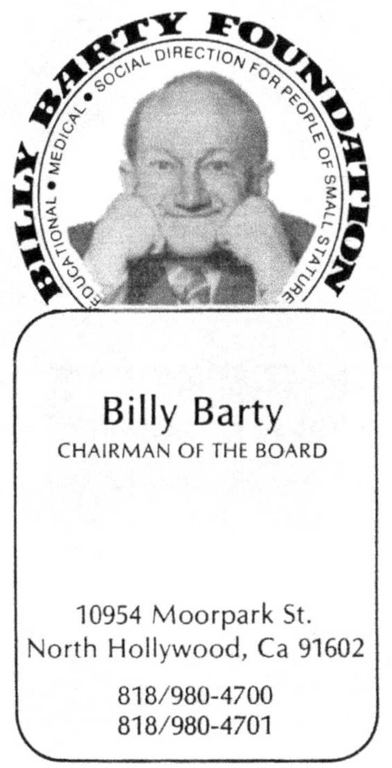

Billy Barty's business card, given to Wes Clark at a 1988 party. *Collection of Wes Clark.*

of the Church of Jesus Christ of Latter-day Saints and worshiped in nearby Studio City. He can be seen in a YouTube video from 1989 singing "The Sheik of Araby" and other tunes in a now-defunct Irish pub in Burbank.

HENRY M. MINGAY

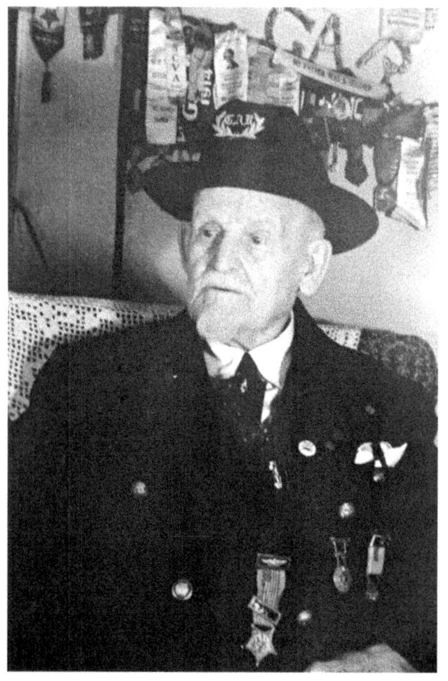

Civil War veteran Henry Mingay, for whom Mingay Elementary School in Burbank is named. A frequent speaker in city schools, he is shown here in his Grand Army of the Republic (GAR) uniform. The Burbank Historical Society has his hat and many of his medals. *Burbank Historical Society.*

Wes Clark, a Civil War buff, listened with interest when his father-in-law, Don Bilyeu (Burbank High class of 1945), spoke of seeing the Burbank school presentations of a Civil War veteran who lived nearby. Who was this person? He was Captain Henry M. Mingay, U.S. Army (Company D, Sixty-ninth New York Infantry Regiment, a part of the famous Union army "Irish Brigade"). The honorific obituary of the *Burbank Daily Review* (April 24, 1947) gives the details:

Passing of Capt. Henry Mingay, 100, Civil War Veteran, Mourned—Thousands of school youngsters and the city today mourned the passing of Capt. Henry M. Mingay, 100-year-old Civil War veteran, last survivor of the 69th New York Infantry and of the Glendale N.T. Banks post. He died yesterday at Sawtelle Veterans Hospital.

He was one of eight surviving Civil War vets left in the state....The Board of Education, in a statement issued today, said it "recognized again the tremendous influence of this soldier" on school children and expressed its sympathies to members of the family. In public ceremonies Dec. 5 1946, the city had officially dedicated the elementary school at Allan and Maple in Capt. Mingay's honor. The student body, representatives from the various veteran organizations and school officials had participated in the fete. Three oak trees, symbolic of the old soldier's strength and stamina, were planted and youngsters gave him gifts. The aged veteran had urged the youngsters to "be good."

Capt. Mingay had appeared before countless school assemblies for over a quarter of a century, contributing much to instill in youth of this community an appreciation for true democratic principles and love of country, the board's resolution read. Capt. Mingay, although failing in sight for the past several years, had enjoyed good health until recently when he broke a hip and was confined to his bed at the family home, 804 E. Elk, Glendale.

Born on Dec. 3, 1846 in Filby, England, the fourth son of Richard and Ruth Mingay, the boy and his family left for New York four years later in August, 1850. It took them six weeks to span the Atlantic in the old sailing vessel, America. He left school in 1860 to become a bootblack and printer's devil on the Saratogian, Saratoga Springs, N.Y. When the Civil War broke out, he was refused enlistment because the "army is not signing up children." But he got by on his second attempt and was sworn into the 69th Regiment. He saw action in all the regiment's many battles and was mustered out as a sergeant. He was wounded in the right arm. Later he was commissioned a first lieutenant and was advanced to captain.

In a 1973 article on Henry Mingay, the *Burbank Daily Review* noted that when Warner Bros. filmed *The Fighting 69th* with James Cagney in 1939, the studio employed Mingay as a technical consultant. A studio limousine picked him up each day at his Tujunga home and whisked him out on location.

Henry Mingay was buried at Grand View Memorial Park in Glendale. He was described as living in, at various times, Inglewood, Monrovia, Tujunga and finally Glendale. Burbank, naming a school after him, claims him.

Edward W. Spencer

The Wisconsin Historical Archive at Wisconsinhistory.org records a heroic tale that happened far from Burbank:

Around 2 A.M. on September 8, 1860, the steamship Lady Elgin collided with the schooner Augusta in the waters of Lake Michigan near Waukegan,

Illinois. The Lady Elgin was carrying more than 300 passengers and crew on a round-trip sightseeing tour from Milwaukee to Chicago. Its return trip was never completed. The captain, not realizing how badly the ship was damaged, continued toward Milwaukee in the dark. About a half-hour later, the heavy boilers and steam engine broke through the weakened hull and the ship quickly tore apart. Most of the passengers and crew died. Only a handful reached the lifeboats. "Just when the Elgin took her final plunge," the captain recalled, "a heavy sea took off the upper works, the cabin floated, and several hundred people got onto this." . . . Seventeen people were saved that night by a Northwestern University student named Edward W. Spencer, who battled the breakers for six hours. An experienced swimmer, he had a rope tied to his body, and time after time swam through the waves to grab exhausted passengers. His associates on the other end of the rope then pulled him and the victim to shore. Finally, having reached the limits of his strength, his body covered with scrapes and bruises, Spencer passed out. He woke up in his room in Evanston where his brother, William, waited on his recovery. Edward's first words were, "Will, did I do my full duty—did I do my best?"

Although he tried to resume his studies, the physical and emotional toll on Spencer had been severe. Newspapers around the nation praised his deeds but he was never completely comfortable with the attention. The faces and cries of the victims he had not been able to save forever haunted him. Spencer never completed his education, and it was almost fifty years before he returned to Evanston to talk about the wreck of the Lady Elgin. After his death, his brother described Edward's private torment: "His face would turn ashen pale, and he would fasten his great hungry eyes on me and say, 'Tell me the truth. Did I fail to do my best?'"

This maritime hero ended his days in Burbank; his February 8, 1917 obituary in the *Los Angeles Times* records that he lived at 220 San Jose Avenue.

There's a footnote: In 1924 hymn writer Ensign Edwin Young heard the tale of Spencer's heroism and was inspired to publish a song with lyrics that drew from Edward W. Spencer's searching question. "Have I Done My Best for Jesus?" became quite well known.

OCTAVIA LESUEUR

The authors are fond of Miss Octavia Lesueur, who, in her obituary, was called Burbank's "Grand Little Lady." As children we played in Burbank's parks, and we feel she's owed some recognition. The best account of her contributions to Burbank is contained in a passage from the 1944 *Burbank Community Book*:

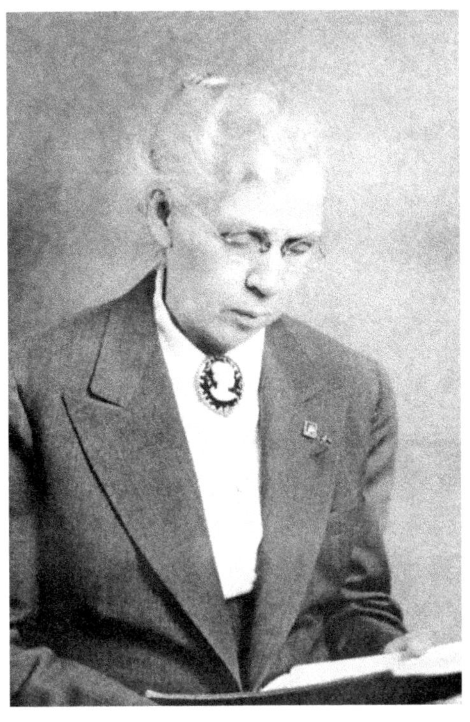

Burbank's "Grand Little Lady," Octavia Lesueur. Without her, Burbank parks wouldn't be the same. *Burbank Historical Society.*

> *If a man can be designated as the "Father" of any worthwhile community movement, it is assumed that when the person happens to be a woman, she can be designated as the "Mother" of such a movement. On this assumption it is quite befitting to designate Miss Octavia Lesueur as the "Mother" of the park movement in the Burbank Community.*
>
> *Before Miss Lesueur came to the aid of the trees, anybody who took a notion assumed the privilege of yanking out a tree whenever and wherever the spirit moved him. It was in a controversy over whether or not a certain group of trees should be removed that the Burbank Park system came into being. The uncertainty as to who should have the say on occasions of this kind brought forward the proposition of some kind of a system to protect the trees....As a member of the Commission of Freeholders which drafted the City Charter, Miss Lesueur became an ardent champion of Parks and Playgrounds, and had an important part in mapping it out and establishing the Parks and Playgrounds Department. At first the two were operated separately, but later were joined together as Parks and Recreation Department. The Park Board during Miss Lesueur's regime centered largely on planting trees in the parkways throughout the city. The more than 30,000 trees planted in*

those days are well matured and make an important contribution to the attractiveness of the city.

It should also be mentioned that in addition to being the owner of an insurance company, which she founded in 1919, and the first president of the Park and Forestry Commission, Octavia Lesueur helped to write the Burbank City Charter. She was a founding member of St. Jude's Episcopal Church and the Zonta Club for women executives. This noble Burbank lady died on January 22, 1948.

PAUL E. WOLFE

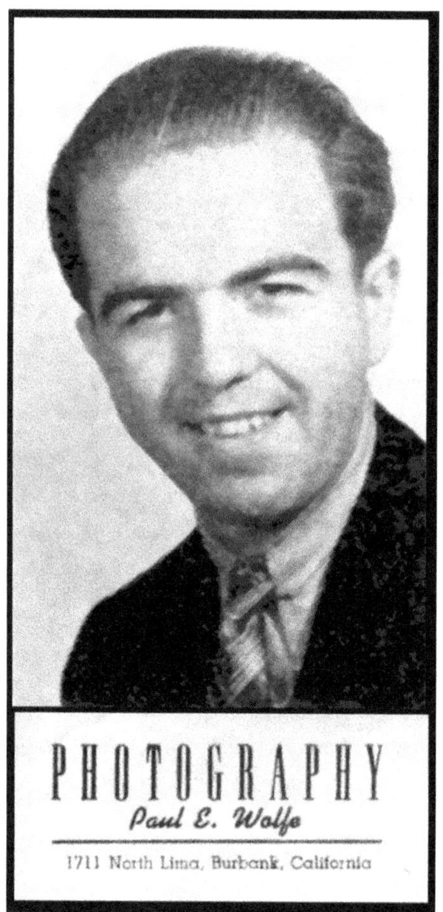

Doing Burbank research, one cannot help but encounter the many city photographs credited to Paul E. Wolfe; they are ubiquitous. Biographical information about him, in contrast, is scant. He was born in 1912 in Wilkes Barre, Pennsylvania, and died in 1997 in Lancaster, California. He apparently moved into Burbank or Glendale about 1940. By 1946, however, he's listed at 711 North Lima Street in Burbank. In 1963 he registered a business: Paul E. Wolfe and Associates, located on Victory Boulevard. He was cited as an official City of Burbank

City photographer Paul E. Wolfe. His photos are everywhere, but finding an actual image of the man is much harder! *Collection of Michael B. McDaniel.*

photographer in 1950; he also had a business taking baby photos at St. Joseph's Hospital. We owe this gentleman a debt of thanks for so thoroughly documenting the city in midcentury.

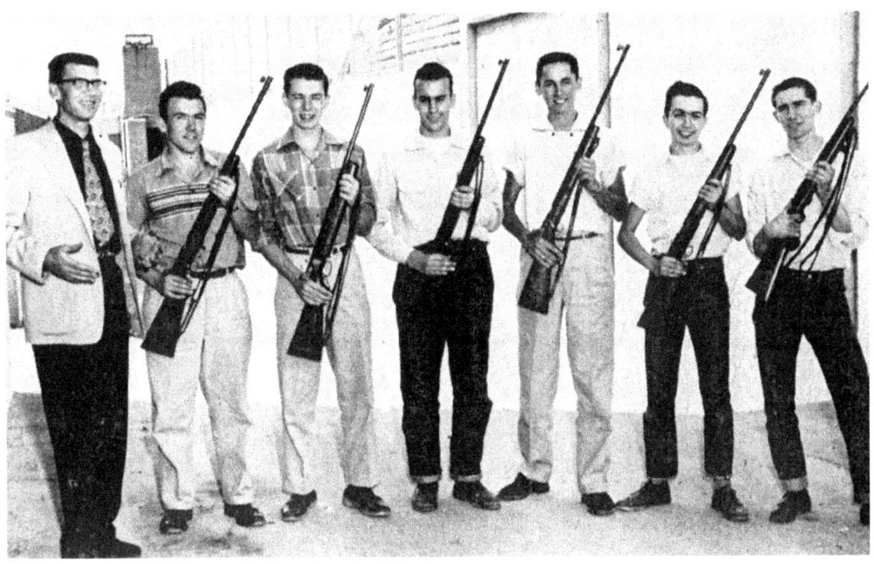

It's difficult to believe today, but back in 1955, high schools had rifle and gun clubs. Here's the Burbank High Rifle Club, armed and on campus! *1955* Ceralbus *yearbook.*

8

MURDER AND HIGH CRIMES IN BURBANK!

Burbank is no stranger to murder, malfeasance, crime, suicide and death by misadventure. A search of the *Los Angeles Times*'s online database using the terms "Burbank" and "death" turned up a staggering number of articles. Occasionally, in Burbank, what's lost are lives. Here are a few of the notable, more well-known criminal cases.

Burbank's Red Light of Danger

In 1925 everyone in town knew when something was up, due to Burbank's version of the Bat Signal: a large, two-thousand-watt red light placed above the reservoir in the Verdugo Hills between Palm and Magnolia Boulevard. It was easily seen in all parts of the valley. The police installed it as a signal for all patrolmen to get in contact with headquarters. Was it lit on the following occasions?

The 1933 William "Tom" T. Bay Murder: Death of a Cowboy Star

Texan William T. Bay (1901–1933) was an actor, rider and stuntman in silent films in the 1920s and, later, in early talkies. He starred with western

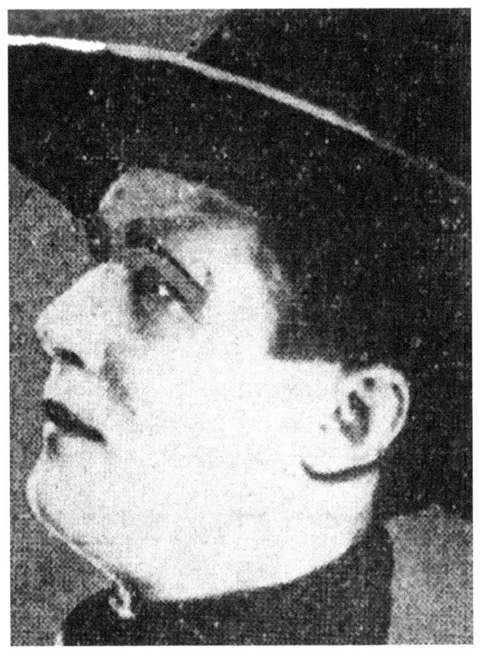
Murdered cowboy star Tom Bay from an unknown newspaper, October 12, 1933. *Burbank Historical Society.*

heroes Bob Custer, Buddy Roosevelt, Wally Wales, Buck Jones, Ken Maynard, Tom Keene, Tim McCoy (for whom he served as a stunt double) and, once, John Wayne.

In the 1988 book *Tim McCoy Remembers the West* by Tim McCoy and Ronald McCoy, Tim mentioned Tom Bay and a 1925 shooting incident: "Tom Bay, my double in many pictures, cooled a mean hombre named Yakima Jim with a slug from his pistol when Yakima had the gall to pull a knife on him in a Gower Gulch saloon." What Tim is referring to is a Hollywood drunken brawl that turned fatal in 1925; the victim was James "Yakima Jim" Anson. Period newspapers described Bay exiting from a second-story window and leading the police on a chase. Bay claimed that Anson shot himself in a struggle; when the incident came to trial, Tom Bay was acquitted by a jury. Bay lived for another eight years.

On October 11, 1933, Tom Bay was shot and killed by his lover and companion, Alta Lessert, in the home they shared on 602 North Lincoln Street;[41] the house still stands. A *Los Angeles Times* piece from October 12, 1933, gives the basic story:

> *The colorful and daring career of Tom Bay, actor and who as a film stuntman had "doubled" for many of Hollywood's Western stars in breath-taking episodes, was ended last night by a bullet wound. The asserted slayer, Mrs. Alta Lessert, 36, was in the prison ward of the general hospital today, suffering from two self-inflicted bullet wounds. She was expected to recover. Police reported the shooting followed a quarrel between Bay and Mrs. Lessert, both of whom resided in the same house. Another woman, whose name was not revealed by police, was present when the shots were fired and was reported to have been the target of one shot. She was uninjured.*

The woman who was present was Mary F. Miles, known on the screen as Frances Martin; she was summoned by Bay and Lessert and attempted to play the part of peacemaker during the argument, which centered on Lessert's jealousy of another woman who entered Bay's life. (Whether or not this was Miles, who seems to be the obvious candidate, is unknown.) The case went to trial, and the *Times* noted that in court Lessert testified that Bay had beaten and abused her on numerous occasions and that on the day of the shooting, October 11, he said that he was going to kill her. She seized the pistol lying on a table and shot him first. On March 10, 1934, the *Times* reported that, after eight hours, the jury was unable to reach a verdict; six stood for conviction and six for acquittal. The case was dismissed on April 13, and Lessert was freed after Deputy District Attorney Paul Palmer advised the judge there was insufficient evidence to obtain a conviction.

Lessert walked; her name does not appear in any subsequent newspaper articles. She died in 1951.

The 1934 Eric D. Madison Murder: The Rise of the Spousal Battery Defense

Nellie May Madison, who lived from 1895 to 1953, holds the distinction of being the first woman to be sentenced to death in the state of California. (Two earlier condemned women in California history had their sentences overturned.) Madison was tried and convicted for the murder of her fifth husband, Danish immigrant Eric D. Madison, in 1934 and was slated to hang. However, she was not executed. In what may be regarded as an early victory for the feminist movement, her sentence was commuted to life in prison. Madison was eventually released when it came out that she was a battered wife. The case helped to legitimize the abuse defense in criminal cases, which was a legal concept almost entirely unknown at the time.

The murder took place on March 24, 1934, in their home on 3516 Riverside Drive in Burbank, across from the Warner Bros. Studios back lot; both worked as cashiers in the studio commissary. (Eric Madison would be fired by studio boss Jack Warner for shouting at and shoving director Alfred Green and for overcharging Green for cigars.) After a number of spousal abuse episodes, Nellie Madison pointed a gun at her husband while he was lying in bed. He reached under the bed for a box of butcher knives and hurled two at her, which missed. As he bent down to reach for more knives,

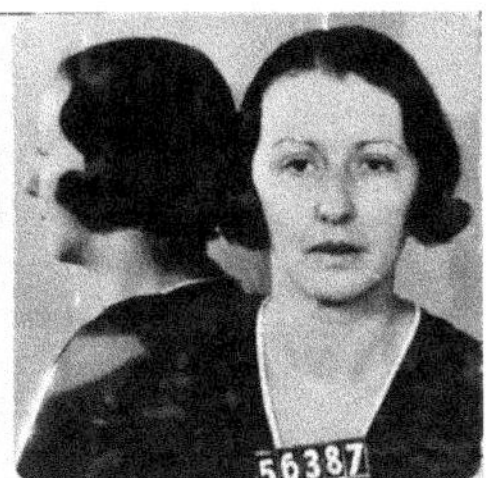

Nellie Madison, the first woman to be sentenced to death in the state of California, 1934. *Burbank Historical Society.*

Nellie fired five times and hit Eric in the back, killing him. (As a teen, she was known as a crack shot with a revolver.)

The California Supreme Court opinion contains an interesting glimpse of life in Burbank near the Warner Bros. back lot. Apparently, one got used to the noise.

> *The Warner Brothers studio was situated in the neighborhood about 500 to 1,000 feet distant from the apartment house. The deceased had been employed in the coffee shop of the studio, from which he usually returned home about 6 o'clock. The defendant was occasionally employed at the studio. That Saturday night the studio was engaged in taking a gun shooting scene in a certain film and the shooting of guns was noticeable about 1,000 feet away. Work had continued on that picture that night until about midnight. It was also in evidence that animals and fowl were kept on the studio premises; that peacocks sometimes gave shrill cries or screams; that such sounds were often heard from the studio and that frequently the neighborhood did not settle into quiet until past midnight, but that the witnesses were not disturbed by the sounds coming from the studio.*

It is worth mentioning that the cause of all the noise was the filming of a movie, fittingly entitled *Midnight Alibi*, a crime-comedy starring Richard Barthelmess.

Murderpedia.org describes the aftermath of the crime:

> *Nellie's unconventional life, tendency to take risks, and impulsive behavior converged explosively in the bedroom of her Burbank apartment moments before midnight on 24 March 1934. The Madisons' neighbors awoke to the sounds of gunfire. Eric Madison's bullet-riddled body was discovered on the apartment floor, but Nellie Madison had disappeared. The Burbank*

> *police, acting on a tip, arrested her the afternoon of 26 March, hiding in the closet of a mountain cabin eighty miles north of Los Angeles. Dozens of reporters attended her interrogation at the Burbank police station. Nellie denied killing her husband, but was forced to reveal her checkered marital history. Charged with first-degree murder and jailed while awaiting trial, Nellie Madison became the focus of massive coverage for all five daily newspapers in Los Angeles. Tall and striking, with dark hair and large brown eyes, she was likened by journalists to the deadly femme fatales featured in pulp magazines and noir novels of the period. Artists obligingly touched up photos to make her look sinister. "Her lips curl in a slow, enigmatic smile," wrote a Los Angeles Herald Examiner reporter who sat in on Madison's questioning. "She is mistress of herself and the questioners, beaten back time after time, turn away in disappointment."*

On June 23, 1934, a jury found Nellie Madison guilty of murder and sentenced her to hang. But on September 16, 1935, sixteen days before the scheduled hanging, California governor Frank Merriam commuted her sentence to life in prison on account of a sympathetic public outcry as a result of a revised newspaper portrayal of Madison as a battered victim.

Murderpedia.org concludes Madison's tale:

> *Madison spent seven-and-a-half more years in prison, lobbying continuously for a pardon, sentence commutation, or parole. On 27 March 1943, almost nine years to the day of Eric Madison's murder, she walked out of the California Institution for Women. Her years in prison had cost her youth, health, and almost "everyone I hold dear," as she wrote in one letter to the governor. In the fall of 1943, she settled in San Bernardino and married one last time, to John Wagner, a house painter. She remained in this marriage until her death in July 1953 from a stroke. Madison's life, trial, and death sentence provide a crucial window into gender ideologies and judicial practices of the 1930s and 1940s and a glimpse of the future. Her case presaged a media-driven culture based on sex and sensation and represented a very early—unusual for the time—example of a defendant's ability successfully to cite spousal battery as a defense for murder.*

The 1951 Virginia Thomason Murder: The Coincidence Killer

This next crime involves some suspended credulity: on October 27, 1951, Virginia Pauline Thomason, a pretty, twenty-four-year-old defense plant worker, was fatally wounded in Burbank as she drove to her home in Van Nuys at about 4:00 a.m. Her car rolled for two or three blocks before it came to rest against a railroad embankment near Vanowen Street and Fairview Boulevard. The police said that two shots were fired from a 30-06-caliber deer rifle by William Frank Cairns, twenty-eight, an unemployed mechanic and World War II navy veteran. Cairns gave himself up to the Van Nuys police, describing that he had shot a motorist who had angered him by pulling in front of him. The fact that the motorist was Thomason, who was a former girlfriend and had broken off relations with him, was purely coincidental, he said.

The victim's mother told reporters that her daughter had known Cairns for about two years but discontinued the relationship and filed a complaint against him in the Burbank city attorney's office, charging him with carrying a concealed weapon and threatening her life. Cairns's story was also questioned when it emerged that he was seen in a bar that his former girlfriend had been in earlier that evening. (Cairns attempted to buy her a drink but was refused.) Thomason had danced a few times with other men in the bar. Cairns, according to an eyewitness, "acted jealous."

An interesting additional feature of this case, which newspapers called "The Spurned Lover," was the levity and unconcern that Cairns displayed while at the police station. While being fingerprinted, he grinned and held his hands up for the photographer. What could he have been thinking?

Derangedlacrimes.com, on its page for "The Coincidence Killer," sums up the case:

> *At Cairns' trial there were a few bits of evidence that were difficult to explain away as coincidence. In particular nobody believed that Cairns hadn't recognized Virginia's car—he had helped her paint it a very distinctive golden color. Sadly, because there were no witnesses to the slaying, jurors were stuck with Cairns' version of the shooting. He testified that he'd fired from his moving car into Virginia's car, which he claimed was also moving. His explanation didn't tally with the physical evidence. The autopsy revealed that Virginia was within four feet of the gun when it*

was fired because powder burns were found on her left shoulder, left hand and fingers. William Frank Cairns was far luckier than he deserved to be considering the enormity of his crime. He was found guilty of manslaughter and sentenced to from one to ten years in Chino State Prison.

THE 1953 MABEL MONOHAN MURDER—*I WANT TO LIVE!*

When Wes Clark's family moved to Burbank in February 1965, one of the things about his new hometown that made an impact on Wes's nine-year-old consciousness was a drive back from a restaurant one night. His father, in sinister tones, related the story of a famous murder that had taken place in town some years back involving an elderly lady. It made the national news, and a film was made about the murderer starring one of Mrs. Clark's favorite actresses. Decades later Wes put the pieces together and realized that his father was talking about the Mabel Monohan murder, which had occurred twelve years earlier.

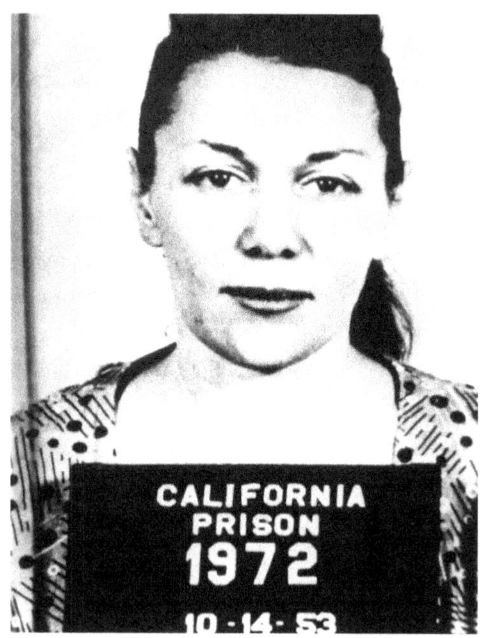

Barbara Graham, executed at San Quentin in 1955 for the murder of Mabel Monohan. *State of California.*

On March 9, 1953, sixty-four-year-old widow Mabel Monohan answered the door of her home at 1718 West Parkside Avenue. The visitor was Barbara Graham, a former prostitute, who explained that her car had broken down and asked if she could she use the telephone to call for help. Monohan opened her door and let Graham in—along with Graham's three accomplices (whom she had met via her husband, a hardened criminal and drug addict): John True, Jack Santo and Emmett Perkins. They had come to rob Monohan of $100,000 that she reputedly kept in a safe in her home. Only there wasn't a safe in the home, as the gang learned after they ransacked the premises.

Monohan was pistol-whipped, reportedly by Graham (blood was spattered on the walls and floors), and lay bleeding on the floor. She succumbed to her wounds, and her body wasn't discovered until two days later, when her gardener attempted to collect his paycheck.

The gang was caught by the Burbank police after Baxter Shorter ratted out his associates. A safe-cracker, he was terrified to learn that he was involved in a grisly murder. Shorter was kidnapped by the other gang members and, probably, killed.[42] On June 3, 1953, Perkins, Santo, True and Graham were indicted by the county grand jury on charges of conspiracy to commit burglary, robbery and murder in the death of Mabel Monohan. On June 2, 1955, Barbara Graham was taken to the San Quentin prison facility for execution. Joan Renner, in her article on derangedlacrimes.com, includes an interesting exchange:

> *Joe Feretti, one of the men in charge of her execution, strapped Barbara into the gas chamber and gave her some advice. He told her to take a deep breath, and it would go easier and quicker for her. Barbara responded, "How the hell would you know?"*

Good question.

With Barbara Graham dead, Jack Santo and Emmett Perkins also went to their deaths in the very same gas chamber some hours later.

In 1958 the charismatic and charming Susan Hayward portrayed Barbara Graham in her final days[43] in the Robert Wise production *I Want to Live!* This was the movie Wes Clark's father was referring to. (Wes's mother was an enthusiastic Susan Hayward fan.) The movie postulates that Graham was a tragic victim of circumstance. But Hayward later admitted that after doing extensive research on the real Barbara Graham, she was most likely guilty of the murder of Mabel Monohan.

1968 Cheryl Perveler Murder: *Till Death Us Do Part*

The salient facts in this complicated case for readers of Burbank lore are these: Cheryl D. Perveler, an attractive, twenty-two-year-old housewife, was shot in the head twice at about 11:30 p.m. on April 21, 1968, as she

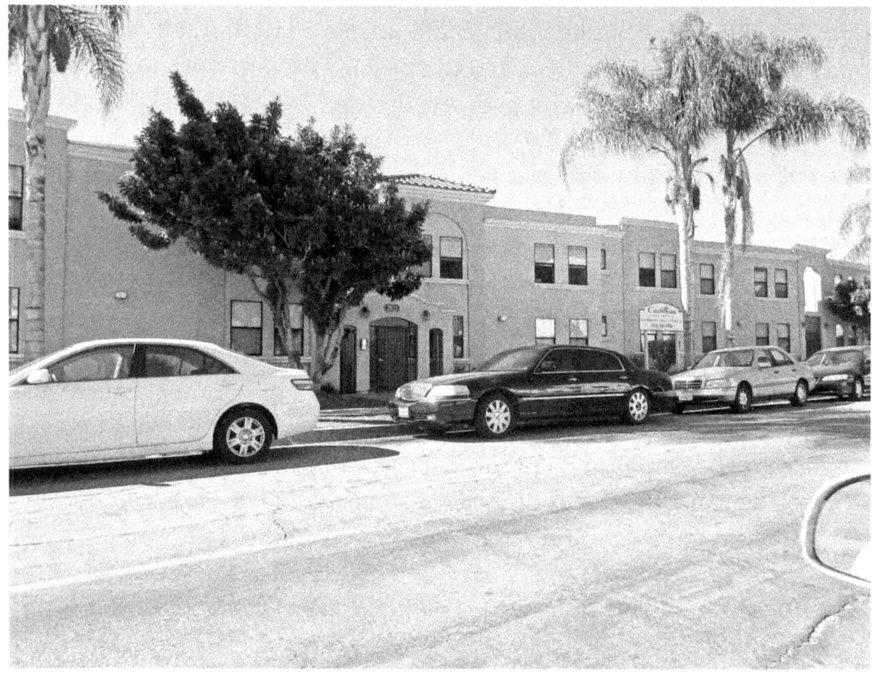

The apartment building on 2021 Grismer Street in Burbank. It is still known as the Castillian, as it was at the time of the Cheryl Perveler murder in 1968. *Michael B. McDaniel.*

parked her car in the carport of her apartment, the Castillian, on 2021 Grismer Avenue. She was rushed to Burbank Hospital, then to a county hospital, where she died without recovering consciousness. Her husband, Paul S. Perveler, a former Los Angeles police officer and the owner of a Burbank cocktail bar, was investigated by the police and arrested. Evidence suggested that Perveler's goal was to collect $100,000 in insurance money on his wife and his lover's husband, who was also killed. Perveler was eventually tried. The prosecutor in the case was Deputy District Attorney Vincent T. Bugliosi, who later achieved greater fame as the prosecutor in the Charles Manson Tate-LaBianca murders of August 1969. The Perveler conviction made his reputation.

On February 25, 1969, a Superior Court jury recommended that Paul Perveler be sentenced to death for the murders of his wife and his lover's husband. "I don't want to spend the rest of my life in prison," said Perveler at the time—but that's exactly what happened. He was originally sentenced to be executed, but when California's capital punishment law was struck down in 1972, his sentence was changed to life imprisonment. Paul S. Perveler, age seventy-eight, is still an inmate in the Mule Creek California prison as of this writing (March 2016).

This famous Burbank murder was immortalized by Bugliosi in his 1978 book *Till Death Us Do Part: A True Murder Mystery*, which was made into a television movie of the same name in 1992. The book is excellent and gives the facts in this very complicated story of murder by Paul Perveler.

A point of fact: Paul Perveler and the famous filmmaker Stanley Kubrick were first cousins.[44]

THE 1969 LOCKHEED "BOOM SHEET" SHOOTING

A lost feature of life in Burbank, at the Lockheed aircraft plant, was the "boom sheet," a formal performance notice about a worker initiated by his management. When Wes Clark worked at the Lincoln Café, the family business, he heard many complaints about boom sheets from unhappy and disgruntled Lockheed employees. On July 30, 1969, the issuance of a boom sheet had fatal consequences for three men.

Isaac Jernigan Jr., a twenty-nine-year-old Lockheed employee and president of the Black Workers Alliance, was issued a boom sheet for failing to wear safety glasses while working in a hazardous area. (Jernagin had a history of insubordination.) His response was to hand the sheet to his supervisor, Jan Domonoske; he then pulled out a snub-nosed .38 caliber revolver and fired twice at Domonoske, killing him. Having learned that the union had approved of the boom sheet, Jernigan then escaped a quickly assembled police cordon and ran almost a mile to the International Association of Machinists and Aerospace Workers headquarters at 2600 Victory Boulevard, where he requested to see Thomas E. McNett, the president of District Lodge 727. Jernagin accosted McNett and shot him three times, fatally wounding him. A Lockheed tool planner named Leonard E. Nolan tried to prevent Jernagin's escape and was also fatally shot.

Jernigan was apprehended two blocks away from the Union Hall, where he offered no resistance, and was eventually tried and convicted. On May 20, 1970, Jernigan was formally sentenced to death for the murder of the three men. However, Judge Norman R. Dowds later reduced the penalty to life imprisonment, stating that the jury had not given proper weight to the finding of five psychiatrists, who testified that Jernigan, though legally sane, was mentally ill at the time of the slayings. Isaac Jernigan does not presently show up on the online California Inmate Register.

A 1945 Bank Robbery Foiled by a Lockheed Badge

It wasn't all murder at Lockheed. Sometimes, it was bank robbery. On July 30, 1945,[45] two men, John Joseph Uckele, age twenty-six, and Stanley Matysek, twenty-three, both of Niagara Falls, New York, held up Hollywood State Bank messengers taking money to a check-cashing agency near Lockheed in Burbank. The take was $111,300. From the beginning, however, the unfortunate pair left incriminating evidence behind that led to their conviction.

First of all, the robbers' perfect fingerprints were left on the getaway car, abandoned in a eucalyptus grove off Sunset Boulevard. While the duo had remembered to remove the license plate from the car, it was found in a bush only ten feet away where it had been tossed. But the most incriminating evidence of all was part of a Lockheed worker's identification badge, left behind in a West Los Angeles garage with some of the silver loot (considered too bulky and heavy to carry). While the criminals had cut away the employee number from the badge in an effort to make it unreadable, FBI technicians determined via powerful microscopes that the ink from the badge had made an impression on the cellophane cover. The employee number was traced to John Uckele; he and his closest friend, Stanley Matysek, had disappeared from Los Angeles the day after the holdup.

The Burbank police, led by Chief Elmer Adams (whom we shall learn about later), had established stakeouts, and when the felonious pair returned to Los Angeles, they were arrested in a Beverly Hills bar; Uckele was drinking inside, Matysek was sitting in their car outside. Also in the car were eight purloined fur coats.

John Uckele and Stanley Matysek were tried and convicted, and on January 10, 1946, Matysek was sentenced to forty-two years in prison and Uckele, thirty-five years. Before sentencing, Uckele stood up and said, "Your honor, they are under the impression that I've got $100,000 some place. They're under the impression that I want to spend my time in prison and then come out and spend the money. I know I can't do that. I haven't got it and I don't know where it is." Matysek was silent.

John Uckele's sentence was cut from thirty-five to twenty years, in recognition of the fact that he cooperated with federal authorities to recover some of the money. The media trail ends here, but the question remains: Is there $100,000 buried somewhere? Perhaps in Burbank?

1950S CRIME AND CORRUPTION

Burbank began to acquire big-city problems in the 1950s, the sort of things you'd see in old films noir about police and government corruption. A May 1956 article in *Coronet* magazine, "Small Cities Can Lick Crime, Too!" described this:

> *Burbank, California, a pleasant city of 90,000 persons in the famed San Fernando Valley near Los Angeles, is a typical American community. It has well-kept homes, good schools, a symphony orchestra, an art association and 43 churches. Among its 300 industrial firms are Lockheed Aircraft Corporation, Walt Disney Productions and Warner Brothers Pictures, Inc. It's about the last place you'd look for lawlessness and civic corruption. But, on April 21, 1952, the California Crime Commission jolted the city out of its complacency by arguing that "the people of Burbank are virtually without protection against the inroads of organized crime...." Burbank was quickly turning into a "bedroom for hoodlums" because it housed some of America's most notorious underworld characters.*
>
> *Joe and Frank Sica, said to be members of the infamous Mafia, ran the Champ Cafe as a hangout for mobsters. Ted*

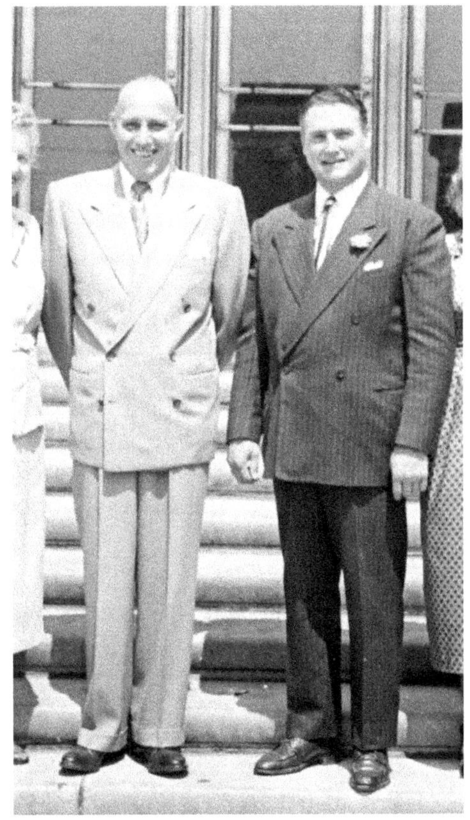

Police Chief Elmer Adams (left) and City Councilman Floyd Jolley (right) pose in the 1950s in front of city hall. *Burbank Historical Society.*

> *Lewis, reported to be associated with Detroit's Purple Gang, swaggered around town with an honorary police badge and gun permit. Mickey Cohen, recently released from prison for evading income taxes, and Ralph Maddox, a big-time bookmaker with a criminal record, both operated wide-open gambling joints. When two honest rookie policemen raided Cohen's casino at the Dincara Stock Farm[46] they were transferred to another beat and the case was dismissed on the ridiculous story that a "Rabbi Rosenberg" had been holding a meeting in order to raise some funds for Free Palestine. Maddox's horse-racing and football betting syndicate, also operated with the connivance of the police, reportedly grossed better than $2,500,000 annually.*
>
> *Chief of Police Elmer Adams,[47] on a salary of $8,500 a year, owned an expensive home and two luxury yachts, bought $250 suits at a clothing store owned by Mickey Cohen, and frequently flashed a huge roll of greenbacks. Chief Adams, as well as Floyd Jolley and Walter Mansfield of the Burbank City Council, were often guests at the home of Ralph Maddox. Mansfield made trips with him to Las Vegas; Jolley shared an expensive beach house with him at Balboa.*
>
> *If the average Burbank home owner didn't know what was going on, a small group of business and professional people did. And on August 31, 1951, key officials of Lockheed, Disney and Warner Brothers met to discuss the cancerous growth since World War II of gambling, bookmaking, prostitution, and irregularities in Burbank's city government.*

The Burbank Citizens' Crime Prevention Committee (BCCPC) was organized in October 1951; it hired investigators who ferreted out disconcerting facts about city officials, forced resignations of the guilty and corrupted and ushered in new men who had established reputations of trust. The *Coronet* article ends:

> *Exactly what did this noisy, three year campaign of fact finding, counter charges, name-calling, investigations, public hearings, red-hot elections and recalls do for Burbank? The answer: plenty!*
>
> *Burbank's new Chief of Police, Rex Andrews, is considered to be one of the most capable and incorruptible in the U.S. Formerly chief in Winnetka, Illinois, and a major in Army Intelligence in World War II, he was chosen in a nation-wide examination. He has overhauled the department, added new patrolmen, set up an in-service training program, written a duty manual, reduced gun permits from 300 to 25, recalled all "honorary"*

police badges and cards, upped patrolmen's salaries from $386 to $429 per month. Result: serious crimes have dropped 30 per cent and auto deaths 45 per cent in the last two years, while solution of crimes has increased 100 per cent.

The new Burbank City Council, under the leadership of Mayor Earl Blais, has passed a score of new ordinances based upon suggestions by the BCCPC and the Police Commission. With municipal politics laundered, a new community pride developed.... "Burbank now has the reputation of being one of the cleanest cities in the country," says John Canaday,

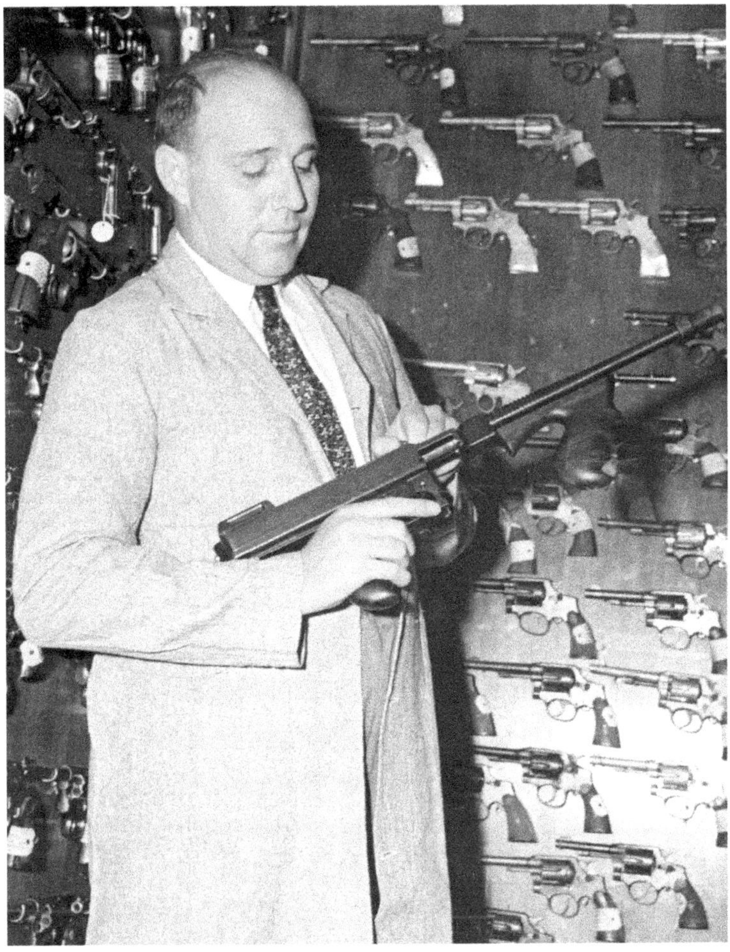

Former Burbank police chief Elmer Adams inspects a Thompson submachine gun (aka Tommy Gun). Whomever it belonged to wasn't fooling around. *Burbank Historical Society.*

Lockheed executive and one of the original founders of the BCCPC, who is now chairman. "Credit is due not only to BCCPC, but to hundreds of aroused citizens—businessmen, housewives, school teachers, factory workers and students—who learned for the first time in their lives that local government is their responsibility. It took major surgery to restore Burbank's reputation for being a good city in which to live. Now the job of the crime committee is to remind the patient occasionally that he might need a medical check-up."

9
FUN BURBANK LORE

This fun chapter provides little, inconsequential bits of this and that, Burbank anecdotes, lore and stories.

The Space Capsule of Love

Verdugo Park in Burbank once had, as a unique playground attraction, a replica of a Gemini space capsule. It was donated to the city by Weber Aircraft Company, a Burbank business. The capsule, made out of steel, was used to test the ejection seats. When the Gemini program was superseded by the Apollo space program, the capsule was donated to Burbank. In its original use, the capsule was attached to a rocket sled and fired down a track at hundreds of miles per hour; the ejection seats (with seated dummies) would be blasted clear.

A photograph (found by Mike McDaniel) dates from 1969, after the capsule had been placed in Verdugo Park, its new home.

Sadly, the capsule is no longer in place, having been removed in the early 1990s. As America and Burbank moved from the socio-industrial Cold War mode to peacetime, citizens found other uses for the attraction. A lady who works in Burbank's Parks and Recreation department stated that it was taken away "because (they had) no idea of how many kids were conceived in it!"

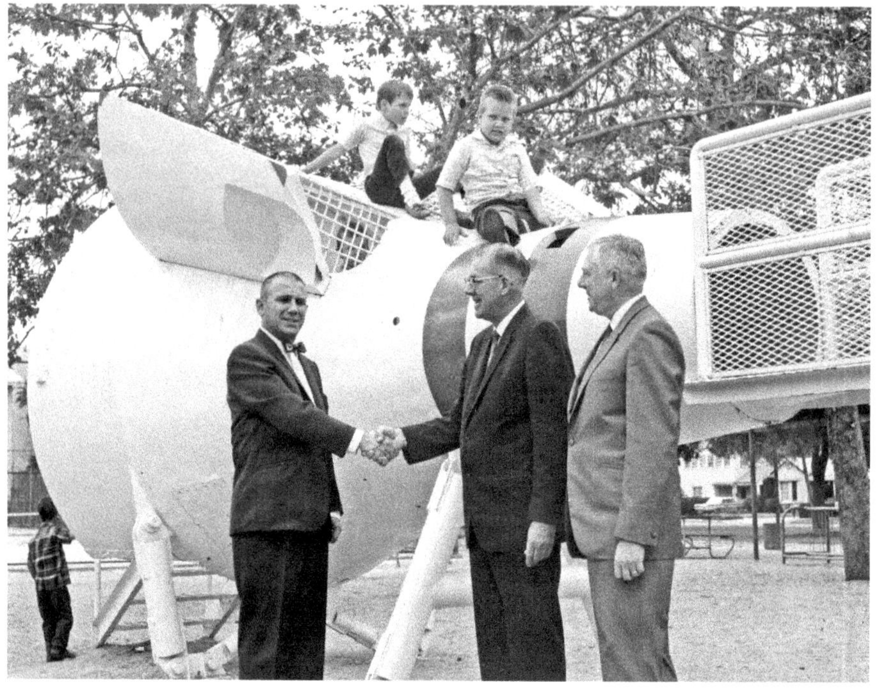

Burbank's Space Capsule of Love, in Verdugo Park, 1969. *Left to right*: C.E. Heimstadt, the vice-president of Weber Aircraft; John Whitney, the mayor of Burbank; and George Izay, the Burbank Parks and Recreation director. *Collection of Michael B. McDaniel.*

THE BREATHING BUSH

A favorite spot for Burbank lads to take easily frightened lasses was the celebrated Breathing Bush, near the intersection of Hollywood Way and the Whitnall Highway. The oleander bush breathed because of the presence of a valve for a sewer line, which stood about four feet up from the ground. When there was movement within the line, a ball at the top of the pipe would blow or suck air. The pipe went unheard during the day due to traffic noises; one had to go into the bushes at night and get near the pipe. (The appeal of the scheme to young Burbank males should be obvious.) Burbanker Bill Anderson claimed, "If you didn't know what it was it would scare the hell out of you!"[48]

Burbankia reader Rob Weaver knows who killed the Breathing Bush:

> *Steve Brown. He was my little brother's best friend. They were in about fifth grade when we took them to the Breathing Bush site late one night*

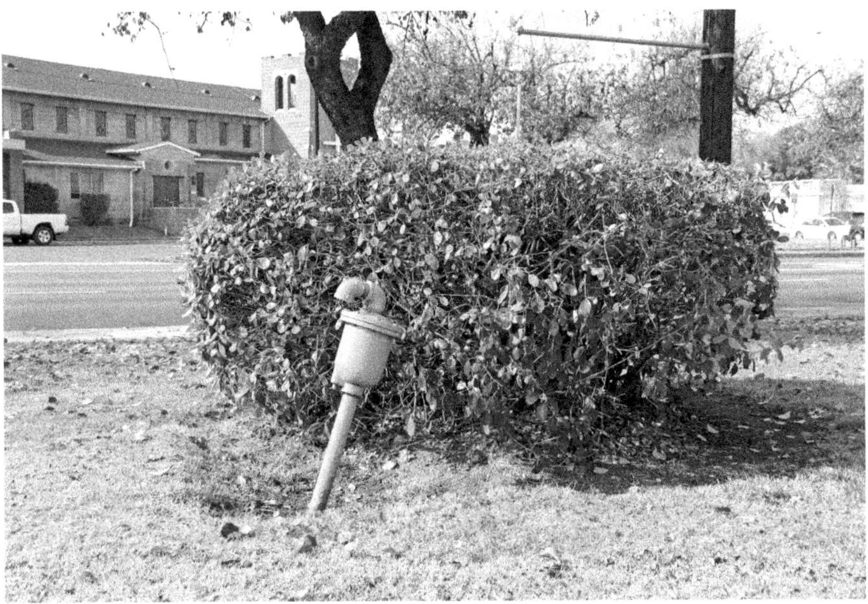

The pipe at the original breathing bush. The authors attest that it breathes no more. *Wes Clark.*

> *around 1969–1970. They just about jumped out of their skin when the bush breathed. But then on a dare, Steve, who was built like a fireplug, suddenly let out this terrific yell and ran as hard as he could into the bush. We heard a loud crack and thump and Steve, howling in pain, staggered back out of the bush. In the dirt under the bush was what looked like half a metal football with a broken pipe sticking out of the end. Silence fell upon us. The bush breathed no more. Pandemonium broke loose as we realized that Steve had killed the Breathing Bush. But then a sadness ensued as the consequences sunk in. We would no longer be bringing the unbelievers to the bush to savor their terror when the bush took a breath.*
>
> *It was a long drive back to Van Nuys.*

LOVE FROM ABOVE

Burbankia contributor Monte Thrasher has an entertaining story about viewing the valley floor from the Verdugo Hills:

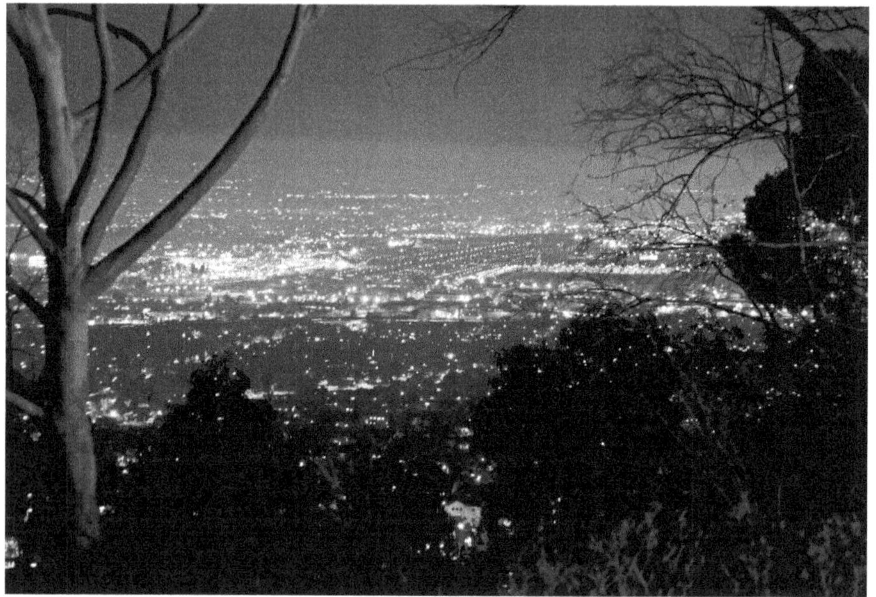

Burbank from the Verdugo Hills at night. Do you see any LOVE here? Neither do we. Things have changed; trees have grown. *Wes Clark.*

When I was a kid at Burbank High (I graduated in 1978) I heard a teenage rumor that if you climbed to the top of the local mountains and looked down upon Burbank by night, the word LOVE was spelled out in streetlights. And this is true! Of course street lighting changes with time, so it may no longer be so....As for LOVE, I'm sure the V was formed where Burbank Boulevard slices sharply into Victory Boulevard. I'm a bit vague on the other letters, though. I think Alameda Avenue meeting Victory Boulevard formed the L, and Buena Vista Street and Hollywood Way formed two horizontal strokes of the E. The O was the largest letter, and rather irregular. Somewhere there's a satellite or aerial image of Burbank at night that would resolve the issue. Actually, it's a lovely idea, of LOVE writ large right across the city; with a few strategic lights added here and there and a night-flying photographer to capture it, it would be quite a memorable image.

Burbank's UFO Landing Pad

Monte Thrasher contributes another charming bit of Burbank lore. (Warning: controlled substances were involved.)

> *I went to John Muir Middle School ("junior high," it was called then), a beautifully designed work of architecture, laid out in terraces on the Burbank hillside with a spectacular view. For many years you could simply walk into it at night. Actually, as a teenager I saw this as a brilliant idea on the part of the school authorities: since it was no challenge to get into, there was no graffiti or vandalism to declare a daring teenage breach of territory. Of course in time they built ugly iron gates and fences, so I can't go there to gaze out at the city at night and dream. Schmucks.*
>
> *Anyway, I knew a girl who lived right nearby, and Muir was her place to sit and dream or party at night. There's this gigantic concrete platform outside the cafeteria that juts like a wing from the hillside, right out into space, so it seems to hover or float. It's a sheer drop on the north and west sides, with a magnificent view I've spent many years contemplating by night. We'd get high and watch the planes land at the airport. They form a long lovely chain of lights, lining up for miles and miles across the valley to come in. I called it the diamond strand, a long wavering string of lights trailing off to the farthest distance, six or eight at any one time, always being refreshed with new lights at the end. When they come in close they turn on their brilliant landing lights. Now, the landing strip aims straight at the cafeteria platform, so the lights blast right into your eyes. They look very much like UFOs with lights around their saucer rim, dazzlingly bright, easily the brightest lights in that whole ocean of nocturnal lights.*
>
> *The runway points right at you, so when the planes came down to land, their long sloping gliding path gets foreshortened to what looked like a slow vertical drop, as if they were landing straight down. So: brilliant clusters of lights, landing straight down with slow patient grace that looked like they didn't care about gravity one bit. There's no noise at all (or so it seems) like the famously silent UFOs. It took no effort at all to pretend we were watching The Landing, aliens coming at long last to save us from our boring teenage lives.*
>
> *When they do land the brilliant lights go out, and a brief howling roar is heard; this is the plane's engines firing a braking thrust. You see the lights long before the sound reaches you, so it seems unrelated to the UFO. I hear that planes simply cut the engines and glide in, nowadays, to cut down on noise, so the roar may be gone. But the UFOs still land in Burbank, all night long.*

THE BURBANK CROSS

Here's one more bit of lost lore from Burbankia's resident fabulist, Monte Thrasher:

I moved away from Burbank recently and took a few final photos. For years I've gone on a sunset walk up towards the sagebrush and often lingered at this spot, where Country Club Drive has its fancy gate on Sunset Canyon Drive, looking straight down Olive Avenue. It's quite lovely and I've come to watch the slow changes of light and color of thirty years or so. The streetlights have gone from a sweet starlight blue in my childhood to the ugly brown crime lights of the 1980s, now being usurped by the new pure white lights. You can see the brilliant LED green traffic lights for miles across the Valley; that really struck me when I moved back a decade ago. So this lovely cross has evolved over time.

For years I've practiced a little trick of the light: blur your eyes a bit and it's easy to pretend this flat glowing spread is standing upright, like a Christmas tree, half a mile tall. I'm not sure I'd call it a cross, it seems more like a standing figure with outstretched arms. I see it sometimes as a white lady, or a vast glittering robot. It's quite distinct. I have an ancient drawing of it my late brother Mark did when we first moved to Burbank in 1974; you can see the old Van de Kamps windmill, now long gone.

AMERIO CORRADI AND HIS FAMOUS TEA CAKE

Amerio Corradi is not a nationally known name, but his culinary invention is much beloved in Burbank. From a *Los Angeles Times* obituary printed in February 2010:

Amerio Corradi—November 10, 1922–February 17, 2010—Hail to the King of Tea Cakes.

Amerio Corradi, known in Burbank, for fifty years, as the King of Tea Cakes, has passed away at the age of 87. Blessed with an irrepressible lust for life he brought to generations of Angelenos the taste of pleasure and comfort which grew into the cult of the Tea Cake.

Born in 1922 to Italian immigrant parents Rudolpho and Francesca Corradi, Amerio lived and worked his entire life in Burbank. He attended

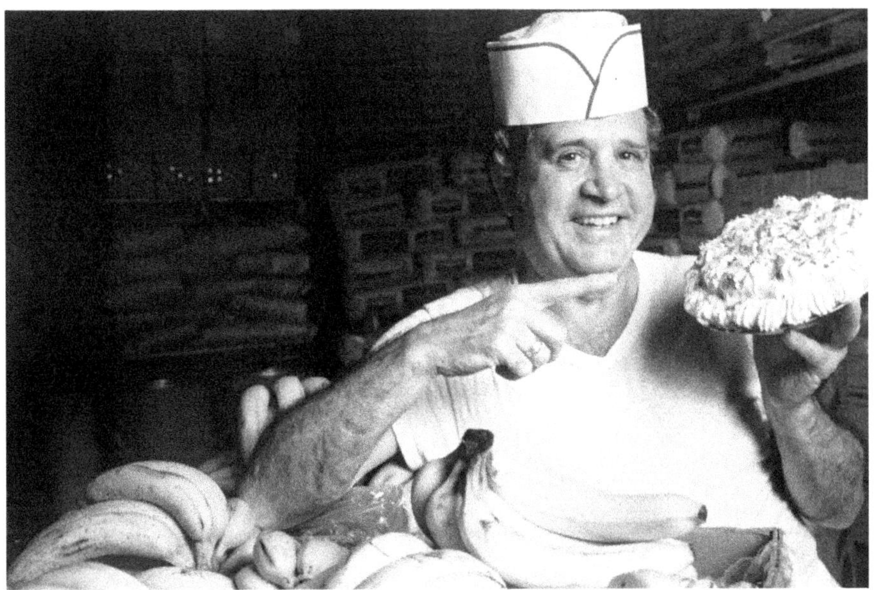

Amerio Corradi (1922–2010), King of Tea Cakes. May his memory be honored forever! *Martino's Bakery.*

Burbank High School where he met his wife Mary. In 1943 they married before he began his World War II service in the Army Corps of Engineers. Amerio distinguished himself in service during his participation in the landing on Omaha Beach on D-Day June 6, 1944. He subsequently acted as an outstanding member of his company which liberated the Buchenwald concentration camp.

Returning to Burbank in 1945 Amerio went into business with his lifelong best friend and partner Victor Martino, Jr. at Martino's Bakery which would become the largest diversified commercial bakery in Southern California with fresh daily deliveries via more than sixty trucks to the greater Southern California and Nevada areas. Martino's Bakery became a competitive force to be reckoned with using the slogan "a tasty pie, a tender crust." But the enduring legacy of Amerio Corradi and Martino's Bakery is the Tea Cake. The Tea Cake was developed by Amerio and his partner Victor at the behest of a client looking for a special light and airy cake, buttery and delicious. The result has been enjoyed by legions of people for more than fifty years.

Martino's Bakery was sold to Campbell's Soup/Pepperidge Farms in 1979. Amerio stayed on with Pepperidge Farms as a consultant for ten years. He kept his creative needs satisfied by financing and directing a retail bakery in Burbank called The Original Martino's Bakery where Tea Cakes continue to satisfy the public each and every day. Amerio had continued to be the driving force—working daily from early in the morning until very recently when he began to contemplate retirement. He is survived by countless friends and family, his loving and supportive wife Mary, son Dennis, his wife Erika; son Gerald, his wife Christie and his grandchildren Jesse, Alexys and Aron.

If you have never tried one of Burbank's legendary tea cakes, you are really missing something. In town they are exchanged almost like currency. Get thee hence to Martino's Bakery forthwith.

GLOW IN THE NIGHT

The authors are in possession of a curious black-and-white photograph dated February 22, 1955. It shows the city lights of Burbank at night with a weird, bright glow atop the foothills. A caption reads, "Burbank, Cal.—Light from the second blast in the new atomic series test at Las Vegas, Nev., blazes behind the Burbank foothills, 275 air miles away....The blast was set off at Yucca Flats with 200 military observers in trenches 4,000 yards away. Forty planes engaged in the aerial phase of the atomic test." When the authors

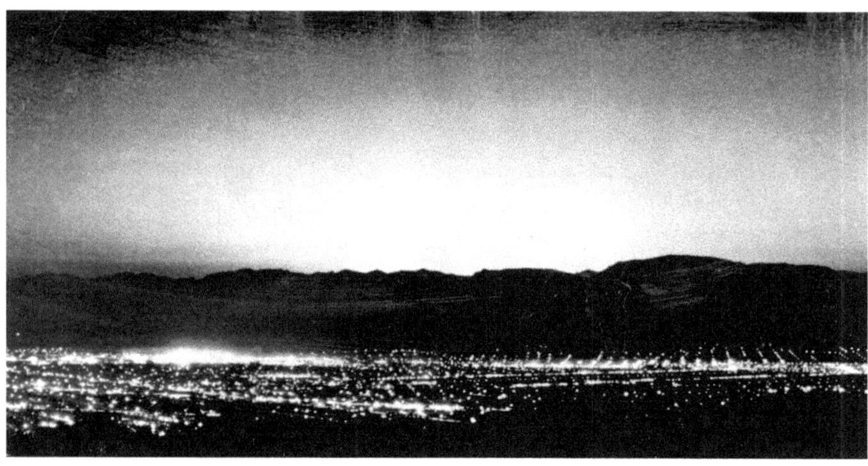

Burbank at night, with the glow of a nuclear test on the horizon, February 22, 1955. *Collection of Michael B. McDaniel.*

do their Burbankia slideshows and this photograph comes up, they imagine people doing calculations of the birthdates of family and friends for possible irradiation. Yes, that might explain them.

Blazing Saddles

Mel Brooks's 1974 comedy *Blazing Saddles* was unlike other comedies of the time, in that it featured gags involving cowboy flatulence and racial epithets and stereotypes. The world premiere in February 1974 was unique, too: at the (now demolished) Pickwick Drive-In Theater in Burbank, guests rode horses into the drive-in to view the film. There was a "Horsepitality Bar" for the film's stars, who also arrived on horseback.

Mister Ed

Every Burbanker knows that there is an exclusive section of town that is zoned for horses. What most do not know is that, reputedly, television's famous talking horse, Mister Ed, died there. The story is told in a 1994 book by the show's human star, Alan Young, *Mister Ed and Me*. The real-life Mister Ed, a horse named Bamboo Harvester, was lodged in a stable on South Sparks Street; Young visited him frequently. The horse was inadvertently given a tranquilizer by a temporary caregiver, and for reasons unknown, the horse died.

It is worth mentioning that the address given for Mister Ed's owner on the television show was "17230 Valley Spring in the San Fernando Valley." While there is a Valley Spring street in Thousand Oaks, that town is not in the San Fernando Valley. The authors suspect that this was an invented street name for a Burbank address in the horsey district of town. We haven't given Mister Ed the title of "Honorary Burbanker"—we need further documentation.[49]

Wild Parrots

Burbank may be in a heavily urbanized region of Southern California, but this doesn't mean that Burbankers don't experience an unexpected thing or two from the animal kingdom, sometimes in the skies overhead. In a March 2, 2012 article entitled "Small Wonder: The Invasions of the Parrots," *Los Angeles Times* reporter Patrick Caneday wrote the following:

> *It's a call that belongs in the jungles of Central or South America. Or in Madagascar. When I close my eyes and try to put an image to the noise, it reminds me of marbles colliding, thousands and thousands continuously crashing together in high-pitched warbles. It's the sound of exotic birds taking over the sky. Parrots have invaded Burbank....From nowhere, everywhere and elsewhere, over rooftops, trees and telephone wires, your anticipation is rewarded as aquamarine fliers overrun the sky. They speed across the blue, street by street, neighborhood by neighborhood, heading I know not where. Watching them, it seems even they don't know where they are going, flying this way and that, from every angle and in every direction. They are a loosely synchronized chaos of clamor, feathers and neon green.*

Where do they come from? Nobody is sure. One story is that when Busch Gardens in nearby Van Nuys closed in 1979, the parrots were released. Another account describes escapees from a nursery and a bird farm in Pasadena, or a simple migration north from Mexico. Whatever their origins, the birds are loud—and they occasionally favor the trees around the McDaniel home.

Murdered in Their Sleep, or Poisoning Pigeons in the Park

Who says the city fathers in Burbank don't have a heart? In October 1959, the city manager reported at a League of California Cities Conference session in San Francisco how annoying, messy pigeons are eliminated: "A day is chosen when there are no pedestrians where the birds have been gathering. Drugged grain is tossed around and in about 10 to 12 minutes the birds begin to wobble drunkenly and then quietly drop off to sleep. The pigeons are gathered up and destroyed while asleep. It's truly humane."

And only tuppence a bag.

THE BIG GAME

Without question the most important sporting event to Burbankers is the Big Game: the annual November homecoming football match between crosstown rivals Burbank High School (Bulldogs) and John Burroughs High School (Indians). Being BHS Bulldogs, it grieves your authors to report that, since 1949, when the first game was held, Burroughs has won forty-two games to Burbank High's twenty-five. The 2009 match was interesting, in that it marked the first time in the sixty-one-year history of competition that both teams finished as co-champions, with an identical 6-1 record in the Pacific League.

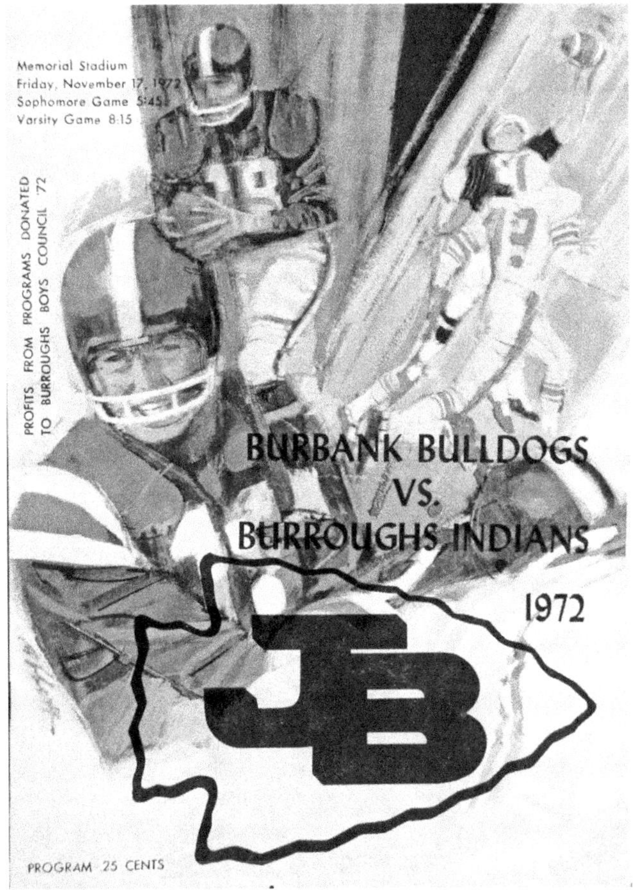

The Big Game! Nothing stimulates the competitive instincts of Burbankers like a battle between crosstown rivals Burbank and Burroughs. *Burbank Historical Society.*

SNOW!

Growing up in Burbank, where it is almost always sunny and warm, the authors were surprised to learn of the local lore that it had once snowed there. The only snow they had ever observed was atop the Verdugo Hills in early 1979, during a minor hailstorm. Yet, it did snow in Burbank, apparently twice: in January 1949 and a lesser amount in January 1950. A January 13, 1950 *Los Angeles Times* article that described the snow noted that it was of short duration and that "Burbank residents noted a steady fall of melting snow around noon at Olive Ave. and Glenoaks Blvd., Naomi St. and Glenoaks, and in Stough Park."

Wes Clark's father-in-law, Don Bilyeu, was a Burbank resident at the time and writes:

> *I remember the snow. I was married in December, 1948 and we lived in a converted garage. In this garage "conversion" the plumbing was on the outside of the building. The pipes froze and we had to go up to my folks' house to wash and brush our teeth to get ready for work. As to the amount of snow— as I recall there was about 2 to 3 inches down in the valley. A college mate of mine and I drove up Olive above the last street up above the Mormon Church and saw that there was about four to six inches up there. However, it did not last very long; I think it was melted by the next day.*

According to Jackson Mayer's *Burbank History* (1975), the 1949/1950 snowfall wasn't unique: "So heavily did it snow on December 30, 1915, that children could not go to school. But they could throw snowballs." Also, from

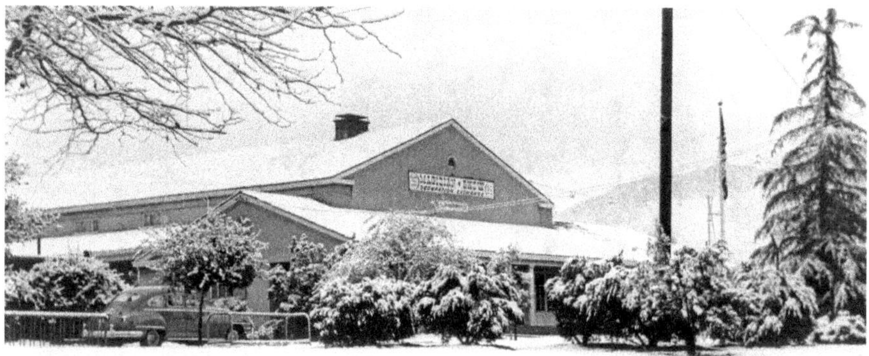

Snow at the Olive Recreational Center, 1949. We know—compared to other states, it's nothing. But it was a big deal for Burbank! *Collection of Michael B. McDaniel.*

the same source: "A freak hail storm struck the Valley on March 26, 1920, and youngsters made ice cream with the hail stones." Finally, Mayers reports, "On December 14, 1931, the Valley was white-blanketed by a driving snow storm. Heavy snow also fell on January 15, 1932."

So, sometimes snow does indeed fall in town.

THE ALLEYS OF BURBANK

Alleys are another interesting thing that distinguishes Burbank from other cities. They're everywhere, far more so than in other cities of Burbank's size. We have no idea why. When the city planners laid out the streets, for some reason they ensured that most of the lots were bordered at the rear with alleys. Also, some alleys in Burbank are granted street status with names (e.g., Colgin Court, Farley Court), even though these streets are lined with the back end of buildings.

In general, alleys in Burbank were where one got beaten up or abused in some way as a kid—at least, that was the lore in the mid-1960s. On the last day of school in fourth grade, the story in Wes Clark's classroom was that the sixth graders—who were departing Monterey Avenue Elementary School for junior high and were consequently reckless and unconcerned about school rules—lay in wait for underclassmen, whom they would drag into alleys and "scrub," that is, smear with lipstick. Wes got on his bicycle when the final bell rang and fearfully pedaled for home as if on fire. On Facebook, a fellow Burbanker confirmed the scrubbing lore and said, "Yes! Scrubbing was the *Terrors*!"

Mike McDaniel spent a lot of his childhood in alleys. He lived on an alley, thus, a lot of the action in his neighborhood took place there: bicycle dog fights, for instance. As he grew older he started noticing that people threw out a lot of things that were still good and usable. Mike found operational transistor radios that only needed a new battery. It boggled his mind why someone would chuck out a radio simply because its battery was out of juice. Mike would take things he found and trade them at a place on Glenoaks Boulevard called Jim's Used Things. Jim would either give Mike a few bucks for the stuff he found in the alley trash or trade them for World War II–era items Mike liked. For Mike, Burbank alleys proved to be a source of income. And, occasionally, a getaway route.

Once, Mike ran a stop sign on his bike and was pursued by a Burbank Police Department officer. Fearing what his strict father would say, he took

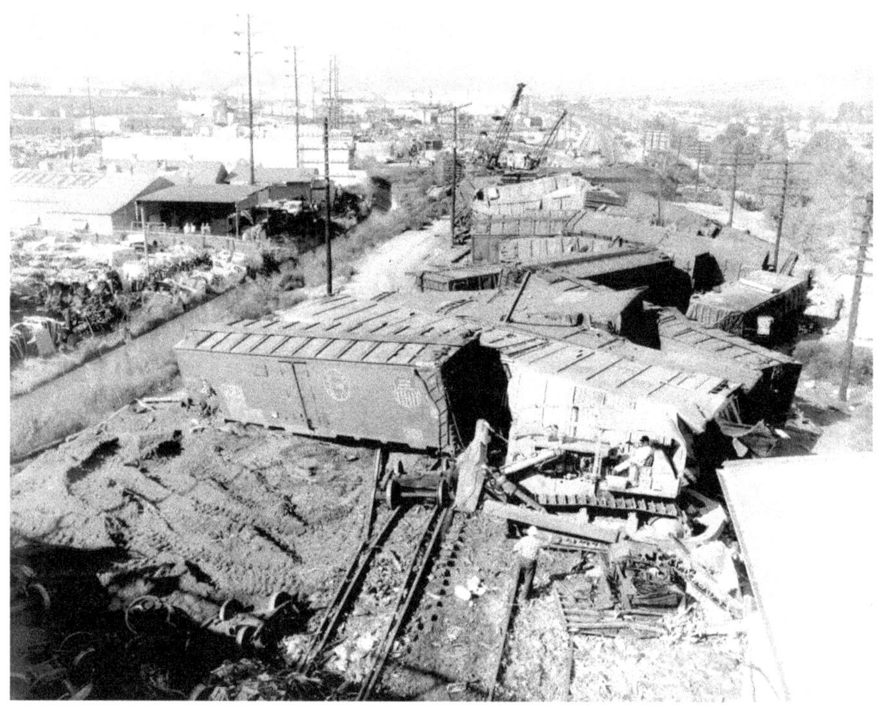

Train wrecks occur in town from time to time. This one, on December 15, 1966, is seen from the Burbank Boulevard bridge. *Collection of Michael B. McDaniel.*

a quick right and went between two apartment buildings into an alley. After a number of further evasive alley connections, this resourceful Burbanker lost the officer rather easily. Mike will always be grateful for the Burbank alleys!

Gypsy Camp

Burbanker Dianne Postal-Simmons tells an interesting story about the Burbank Gypsy camp:

> *The Gypsy camp was behind the lumber yard at the end of Chandler Boulevard where the trains came in to pick up stock; people lived in the trains. When I was in about the fourth grade there was a girl who lived there and she invited me to go to her home. She took me there after school one day. I walked into her home and she lived in one of the trains with her brother and parents. She was so sweet....I gave her some of my clothes and*

thought how cool that she lived in a train. I remember asking her if I could call my mom to tell her I came home with her and she said "We don't have a phone." She was only at our school—Edison—for a few weeks, then one day she didn't show up at school. I went to check on her and everyone was gone. This was in 1965. I wonder what happened to her.

ALBINO MIDGETS

A fanciful bit of lore entitled "The Albino Midgets of Wildwood Canyon" once appeared on a Facebook Burbank group. Jodean Ardizzone Myers says, "I remember hearing that there were a lot of albino midgets living up Wildwood Canyon and that they would chase you down the hill throwing rocks at you as they ran. Truth or fiction, I don't know, but I remember running away, not seeing anything!" Jeri Morin Valencia wrote, "Yup, that's what I heard, too! At that age I didn't even know what an albino was…all I knew was that I wanted to just stay out of their way!" Burbanker Louie Zamora confessed to being an accomplice to this particular urban legend: "I grew up in those hills, and know every square inch from bottom to the abandoned Boy Scout camp on the top! There are no albinos there and there never were. It's a fake story to scare people, and I helped to spread it. The albino feature was a part of the urban legend, but I made them into midgets to make them scarier."

At last we know.

FIGHTS AT THE UNION HALL

Burbanker Joe Modglin asks:

Who remembers the Machinist Hall party on Victory Boulevard next to Ralph's when Quiet Riot[50] was playing? It was during a full moon in 1976. The party turned into a barroom brawl with maybe 50–60 people fighting. The band got involved in the brawl and either came down to take part or were pulled down into the melee. It was like something you would see in a Hollywood movie! As the Burbank Police were arriving I was detained along with several others; gunshots went off close by and Burbank's Finest headed into that direction as we headed for home.

Wes Clark lived on Lincoln Street, not far from the distinctive International Association of Machinists (IAM) hall on Victory Boulevard that Joe speaks of; his father was a senior steward at Lockheed and so had occasion to go there many times. It was a fascinating building, of a modern industrial metal design with water courses running through the interior. The facility was often rented out for weddings; it seems that there was always some police action going on after subsequent drunkenness. There were sometimes newspaper pieces about stabbings, and Wes used to hear and see the BPD helicopters flying to and circling around the place. It got to be a standing joke in the house when they were buzzed: "Must be another Union Hall wedding reception going on."

HIGH TIMES AT ST. JOSEPH'S HOSPITAL

An unnamed Burbanker remembers:

> *About the cops and parties in Burbank: Our Friday night spot was the park behind the hospital on Buena Vista Street and Riverside Drive, St. Joseph's. We would show up just before dark.... I cannot believe that the hospital never once called the cops. We would have up to 100 drunks and stoners, with our blaring rock 'n roll (Zep, Foghat, etc.) and solid noise for hours, right behind the hospital. Once in a while, we would climb the outside back fence of the hospital to where they kept the large tanks of oxygen bottles and also nitrous oxide (laughing gas). They were not locked in those days, so most of the party would partake of the free gas. The cops would always show up at the park, one patrol car. They would turn on their flood light and shine it. It was real obvious: 50 cars, beer*

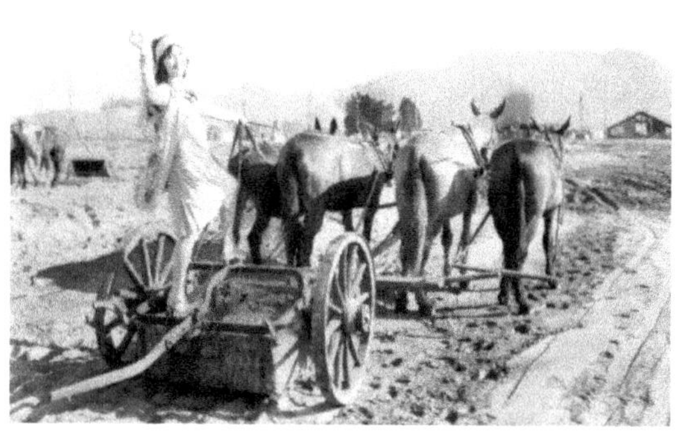

Starlet Betty Baker adopts the pose of a classical goddess with some animals used in the work of creating the Magnolia Park District, 1928. *Collection of Michael B. McDaniel.*

bottles, etc. on all ten picnic tables, but no people. We always thought that we were outsmarting the police by hiding behind the trees. It was summer and I am certain that they could hear us very well. Someone would yell (over the music) "It's the cops!" and everyone behind the trees could not stop laughing from the gas and other "vitamins." Those were certainly enjoyable times.

SCHOOL COW

Here are some especially old-time notes from Burbanker Marti Baldwin's mother, as told to her:

The Gregg Building was located on the southeast side of Olive Avenue, just above the Radio Shack (formerly the drug store). This probably took place in the mid- to late 1920s or early 1930s, but I am not sure. Apparently the man who owned the building didn't like it when anyone parked their car on his property. He would be upset if even part of their car was over the property line, and he would go out and carefully pile rocks on the part of the car that was over the line.

Another story had to do with the old John Muir School building, which was located across from Burbank High. Apparently, also in the 1920s, on Halloween, some boys swiped someone's cow and somehow got it into the school and led the cow all the way upstairs to the cupola area at the top of the building. They left the poor thing tied up. The owner didn't find it until the next morning, when its frantic mooing caused someone to go look for the source of the sound.

AIMEE SEMPLE MCPHERSON

The original Valhalla Cemetery entrance was off Hollywood Way, where the Portal of the Folded Wings structure is today. The famous Los Angeles evangelist Aimee Semple McPherson had an interest in an adjoining cemetery; she also built the Burbank Foursquare Church (via a ministerial assistant) near the corner of Providencia Avenue and Third Street. Burbank old-timer Fermer Kellogg heard McPherson preach there on Sundays.

WELL RESCUE AT CHILI JOHN'S

Burbanker Darryl Eisele relates a well rescue story from the 1940s:

In early 1941, my parents moved from a little house on Grismer Avenue to a brand new house "way out in the valley" on still-unpaved Keystone Street just off Burbank Boulevard. There were few buildings on Burbank Boulevard and the lot between Keystone and Lamer streets was deep with weeds when they moved in April 1941.

It was only a couple of weeks later when my sister Marilyn (she had just turned six) fell down an abandoned well in that lot to a depth of about 20

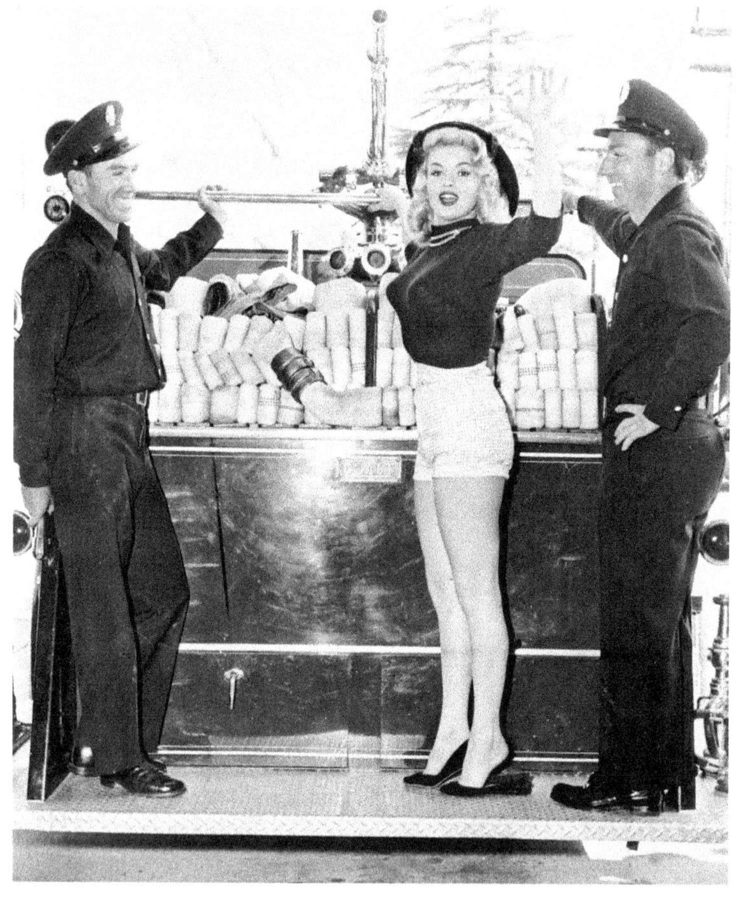

A pair of Burbank firemen (who oddly appear almost to be twins) look highly pleased to pose with Jayne Mansfield, 1955. Put out that fire, boys. *Collection of Michael B. McDaniel.*

feet, near the corner under what now is Chili John's. The fire trucks had to come from Third Street and Olive Avenue, and when they got there they discovered that their ladders were too wide to fit down the well. My dad saved the day by tying a loop in a long rope and bringing her up.

HELICOPTER CRASH

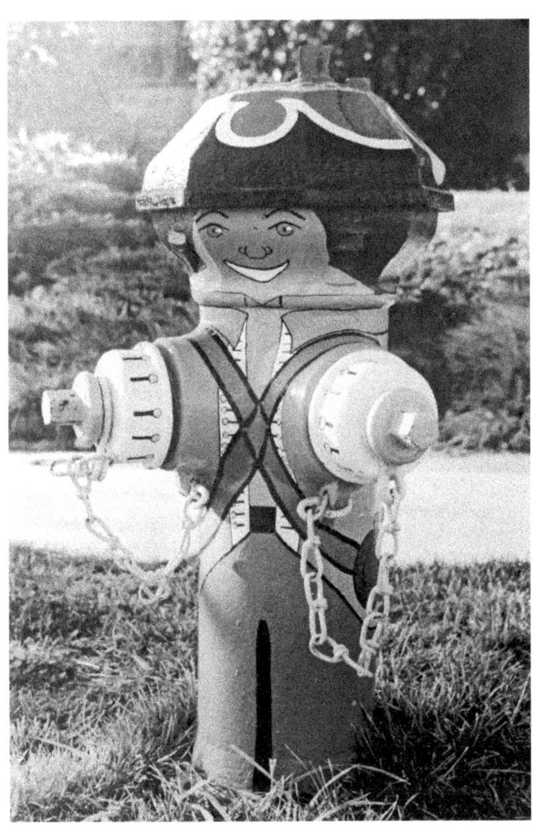

During the 1976 U.S. bicentennial, Burbankers turned ordinary fireplugs into patriotic Minutemen. *Burbank Historical Society.*

It was the talk of Monterey Avenue Elementary School. The date was January 31, 1966: "Captain" Max Schumacher, the popular helicopter pilot and KMPC Airwatch announcer, had crashed on the railroad tracks 350 feet north of the playground. He could have killed or injured children by crashing in the schoolyard, but he was somehow able to bring his badly crippled helicopter down at the railroad tracks. (A freight train had to wait while the helicopter was moved.) Schumacher was trying to land on the vacant lot near the tracks but couldn't. A sixty-seven-year-old Burbanker who lived in the area, Clyde Rose, was nearly struck by a flying piece of the tail rotor but was unhurt. Amazingly, so was Captain Max, and the helicopter was not seriously damaged. Wes Clark was one of the schoolchildren in Monterey Avenue School that day. He remembers the feeling of awe and gratitude felt by his fellow students.

Weirdly, this was not the first time Captain Max had managed to avoid a schoolyard disaster: on July 7, 1958, he managed to bring his helicopter down into a tree, avoiding the playground of the Benjamin Franklin School in Glendale.

Sadly, the clock was ticking for Captain Max. On August 30, 1966, his helicopter crashed into a Los Angeles police helicopter five hundred feet over Dodger Stadium in Los Angeles, killing both pilots and three passengers.

Burbank Titanium

Wes Clark's father, a maintenance painter at Lockheed, had a Skunk Works clearance. Wes's only tangible trophy of this is a black coffee mug with the skunk logo on it, as well as a story.

Wes Clark Sr. liked to float in the backyard pool to get a tan. But he never tanned, just burned; there were twenty or so different brands of suntan-lotion bottles on top of the dryer to support the effort. One day a cheap metal part on his float broke, the part that held the seat to the floats. So he took in the old part and had a machinist make him a new, more robust part. For reasons unknown, the machinist chose to make the part out of the high-tech titanium alloy used on the SR-71 Blackbird. It was given to Wes to install. He was amazed: it was lighter than a potato chip, and when he had to bend it ever so slightly to get it to fit, he had to pound the heck out of it with a hammer. It barely bent.

Another titanium tale, related by Ben Rich in his Skunk Works book, goes as follows: For a time, the Lockheed engineers were mystified as to why the spot welds on their SR-71 titanium parts kept failing after six or seven weeks. Sleuthing revealed that the parts were welded during the months of July and August, when the City of Burbank chlorinated the water supply to prevent the growth of algae. As it turned out, the chlorinated water used for washing after acid treatments was causing the titanium to fail. Enlightened, the engineers started using distilled water, and the problem went away.

Wes has no recollection of the chlorine used in the Clark family pool damaging his father's high-tech float part.

THE LOCKHEED SABRE JET

There used to be a bar on Empire Avenue, across the street from the Lockheed plant, called The Saber Room. It was something of a dive: the sign was made with that dark-green, fiberglass, wavy material that people used for privacy fencing around pools. The words "The Saber Room" were cut out of plywood and placed in front of the green plastic—very homemade. According to Lockheed sources, the owner came up with the name to honor that fine Lockheed Aircraft Corporation jet fighter, the F-86 Sabre (note the difference in spelling from the bar). Why not honor and attract some Lockheed customers proud of their accomplishments? The only problem, as was probably pointed out to the owner numerous times, is that the F-86 Sabre was a product of the North American Aviation Company, not Lockheed. Oops.

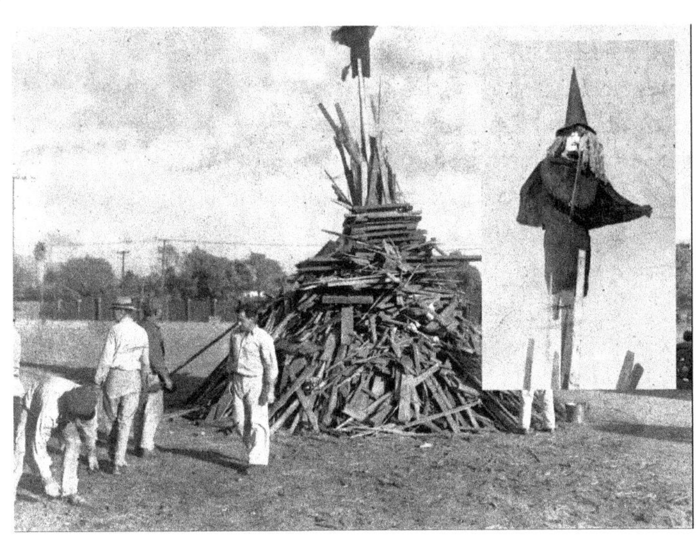

One of the Halloween events the city sponsored in the 1950s was a bonfire, with a witch placed atop the wood. The event is not allowed today, for multiple reasons. *Collection of Michael B. McDaniel.*

BURBANK'S RIDE O' FEAR

This tale comes from the 1944 *Burbank Community Book* by George Lynn Monroe, under the heading "That Famous Street Railway System":

> *That famous $10,000 street car line from the Southern Pacific depot up Olive Avenue to Eighth Street which functioned laboriously on the opening day of the Burbank Townsite Company on May 1, 1887, seems not to have been a roaring success as a transportation proposition. "Billy" Ludlow, who*

with his partner, Albert Erickson, were shouldered with the responsibility of getting the car and the passengers up the hill to the end of the line and safely back again, put in a hard day's work at it. The grade was so steep and the car so heavy that it took a team of eight horses to get the car to its destination and return. Billy says that the job back down the hill was almost as big a job as it was to get it up. Coming down, the eight horses had to be hitched on behind to keep the car from coming down too fast. Furthermore, it was intimated that only about six passengers braved the risk of making the round trip. About the only thing left of the transportation system seems to be some railroad ties which Orville Myers says he has at his home at 819 East Olive Avenue.

Ghosts in City Hall

Over the years, janitorial staff have reportedly seen ghostly apparitions in city hall at night. One of these, a woman who haunts the jail cells where the records center is now, is supposedly executed murderer Barbara Graham, who was first held in these cells after being apprehended. Another ghost is described as a man in a green military uniform with some sort of braid over one shoulder. There is no account of who he might possibly be.

Well Dressed at the Big Sunset Canyon Fire

On Saturday, December 2, 1927, a resident living near La Crescenta (on the opposite side of the Verdugo Hills) burned some trimmings from a grape vineyard on his property. The fire got out of hand, crossed over to the Burbank side of the hills and resulted in the destruction of over 110 homes in Burbank. The estimated loss in Burbank alone exceeded $550,000. We again resort to the 1944 *Burbank Community Book* by George Lynn Monroe, who describes the somewhat draconian steps the local authorities took to put out the fire:

To meet the situation civilians were pressed into service in large numbers. The police department took charge of rounding them up. Police officers went up and down the boulevard, in and out of the pool halls and other public places where crowds were in the habit of assembling, ordering all

> *to report at the fire-fighting headquarters. Voluntarily if they would and with the force of the law behind the request, if necessary. One man was arrested and put in jail because he refused to join the fire-fighters. The male part of a high-toned social event at the Elks Hall was raided by the officers for fire-fighters. They were not even given time to change their society garb for their fire-fighting clothes. As a result there were quite a number of tuxedo-attired gents noticed on the fire-fighting front. Even the women folks appeared on the fighting front with wash-boilers full of coffee and wagon boxes full of sandwiches which were distributed among the fighters, some of whom put in stretches of 24 hours without a let up.... When at its peak the situation was as nearly like what is expected at the Judgment Day as could be imagined. With sirens shrieking, men and women screaming, the wind blowing a gale and volumes of the blackest kind of smoke blackening out even the brightness of the flames.*

First fire, then water. With the Verdugo Hills made naked of vegetation due to the fire, the rainy season hit with a special force. A severe downpour resulted in mud and debris three to five feet thick making its way down the hillside, nearly covering the nine-hole golf course. The year 1927 was an eventful one.

KNOW YOUR BURBANK CANYONS

Who knew Burbank had so many canyons? The following canyons are listed, along with their current locations.

1. Sunset—Follow Country Club Drive up; this is it.
2. Wildwood—Wildwood Canyon Park.
3. Brace—Brace Canyon Road leads to this canyon.
4. Cabrini—Located more or less at Trudi Lane.
5. Craig—The end of Groton Drive.
6. Dark—Located where Barham Boulevard leads to Hollywood.
7. Deer—To the right of Country Club Drive (as you go up) across from the water tanks.
8. Fisher—Next to Cabrini, behind Villa Cabrini Academy.
9. Jeffries—At the end of Hollywood Way.
10. McClure—To the right of Brace Canyon.

11. Sennet—Not really in Burbank, but included informationally; it's across from Warner Bros.
12. Story—Starts more or less at the end of East Tujunga Avenue.
13. Elmwood—As you might expect, it starts at the end of East Elmwood Avenue.
14. Stough—Located at Stough Park.

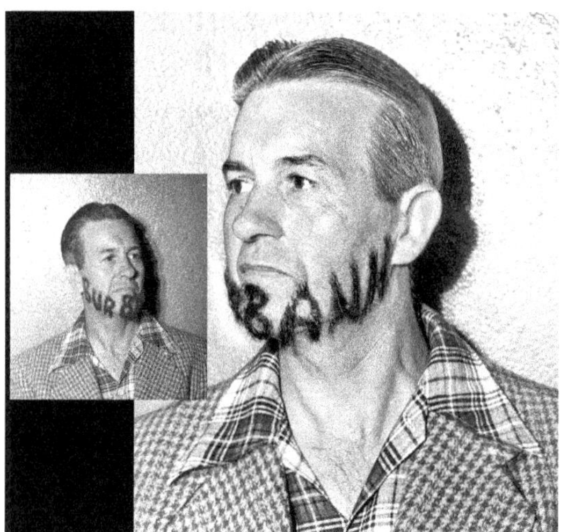

Left: It's hard to imagine a more Burbank Burbanker than Vern Sion, who, on May 21, 1951, shaved his beard to spell out Burbank for a competition. He won. *Burbank Historical Society.*

Below: Mel Keys (left), Vern Sion (center) and Volmer Jensen pose on December 29, 1964, with the first *Star Trek* USS *Enterprise* model for use by Paramount. The model, now at the Smithsonian Museum, was built at Volmer Jensen's Production Model Company on East Providencia Avenue. *Courtesy of Steven Keys.*

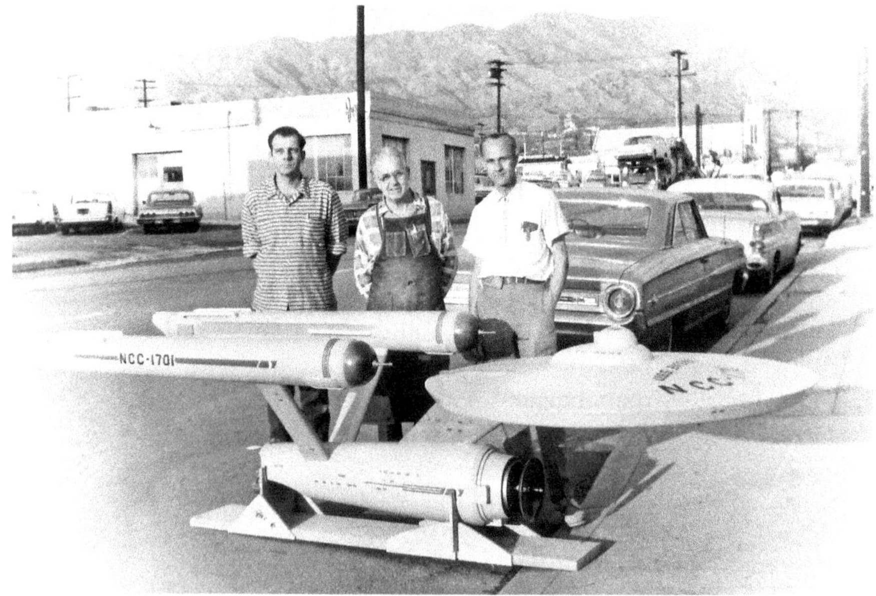

10

THE ULTIMATE SACRIFICE: BURBANK'S WARRIORS

As is the case in uncounted American communities, Burbank citizens have answered their country's call to serve in times of conflict. Burbank was a small, six-year-old incorporated city when Americans joined the effort in World War I in April 1917, yet 177 patriotic Burbankers answered the call to serve. In World War II Burbank sent thousands of men and women into the service. During the Korean War and in Vietnam, Burbank again answered with thousands of service personnel. Today, Burbank is represented by service members in the Global War on Terror (GWOT).

In all these conflicts Burbank has lost too many of its sons and daughters, who made the ultimate sacrifice for freedom. All are remembered each

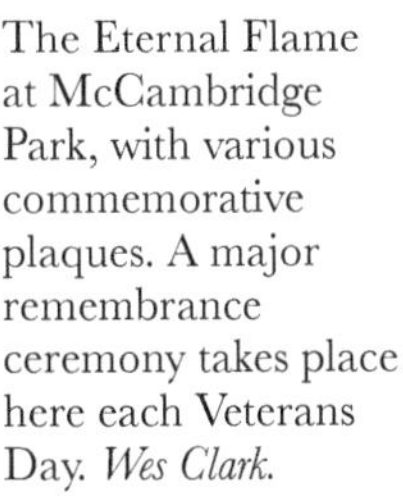

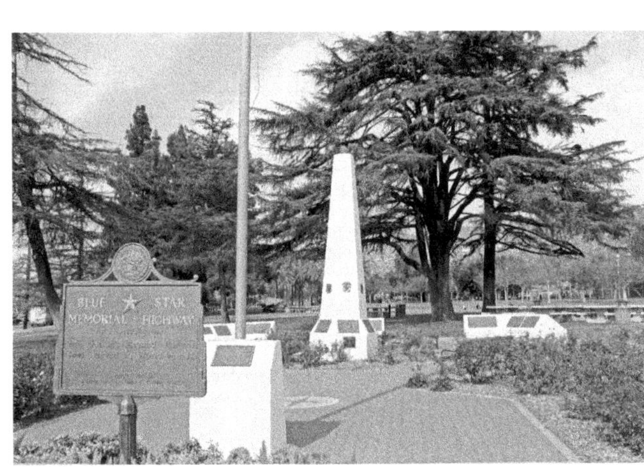

The Eternal Flame at McCambridge Park, with various commemorative plaques. A major remembrance ceremony takes place here each Veterans Day. *Wes Clark.*

Memorial Day with their names read aloud and a rose placed on the war memorial at McCambridge Park in their honor, so that they will not become part of Burbank's lost memories. Each life lost has a story. Here we highlight a few of the many.

(NOTE: Mike McDaniel has complied a substantial book of the stories, where available, of our lost Burbank veterans who served in all wars. It is a much more complete account than we can present in this chapter, and we encourage you to obtain a copy. See the bibliography.)

World War I

In World War I, Burbank lost four sons that we can account for. They are as follows: Manuel Chafino, Harry L. Colton, Ray F. Enos and James McCloud, who was awarded the Distinguished Service Cross for his actions with the Twenty-sixth Infantry Regiment, First Division, on July 19, 1918.

Burbank medical doctor Frank W. Coulter was awarded the British Distinguished Conduct Medal in 1917 by King George V at Buckingham Palace for saving the lives of wounded British soldiers during combat in France.

World War II

In World War II, Burbank lost 210 of its sons and 1 daughter in the conflict.[51] This was a rather large number for a part-rural, part-urban community of Burbank's size. What's more, Burbankers took part in the war before the United States did: Thomas Stark Hunter volunteered and flew for the 357th Squadron of the Royal Air Force. Albert O. Wedin was a sergeant in the Royal Canadian Air Force, serving as an aerial gunner.

The city's first loss was at the Japanese bombing of Pearl Harbor on December 7, 1941: Walter Leon Collier was a young Marine aboard the USS *Oklahoma*.[52] He was killed that day. A young woman, Wallace Crowder, was a WAC (Women's Army Corps) who died in a POW camp after her capture in the Pacific.

One World War II service member's death took place in Burbank: on December 22, 1943, Army Air Force lieutenant colonel William Edwin "Ed" Dyess, a survivor of the infamous Bataan Death March and a subsequent

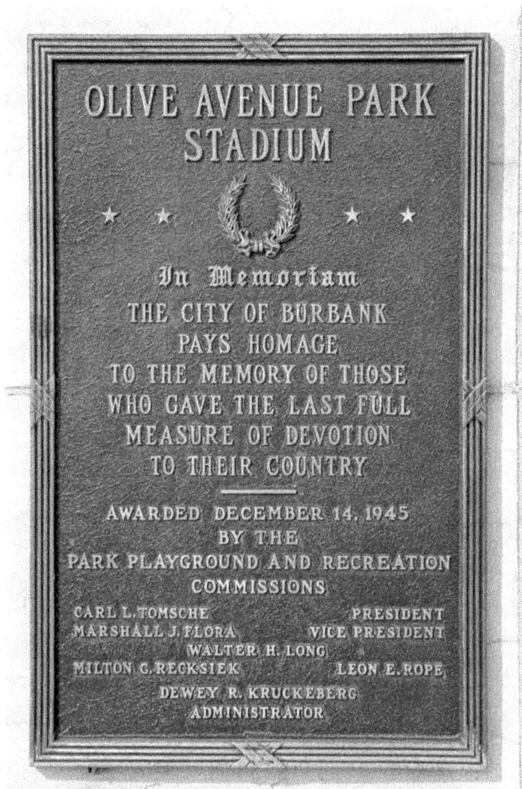

Right: The memorial plaque at the Olive Avenue Stadium. *Wes Clark.*

Below: Memorial Field at John Burroughs High School. *Wes Clark.*

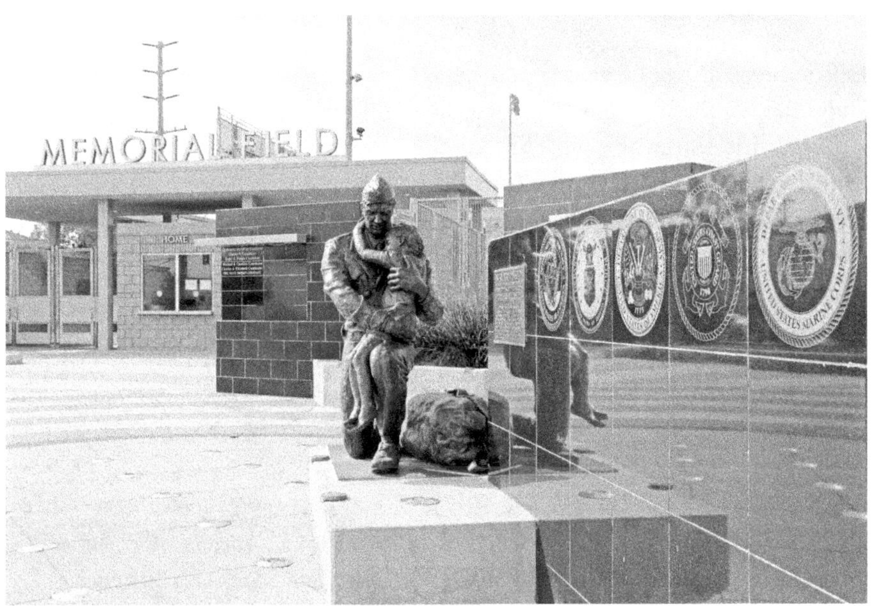

Japanese POW camp, crashed his P-38 Lightning in a vacant lot of the corner of Myers Street and Olive Avenue near St. Finbar Catholic Church. (One eyewitness reported that the P-38's left wing and left wheel struck the St. Finbar steeple.) Dyess was killed instantly. Shortly after his death, the *Chicago Tribune* received permission from the U.S. Army censorship office to print Dyess's account of his experiences on the Bataan Death March. Starting in January 1944, the story ran in serial form for weeks and was distributed nationally by over one hundred American newspapers. When the story was published in book form in 1944 as *The Dyess Story* (later titled *The Bataan Death March*), it became a bestseller. Dyess was buried in Texas.

KOREAN WAR

In the Korean War, Burbank lost twenty of its sons. Three of these young men served together in the same unit: Bobby Box, David Ellis and Edwin Giron all fought in the First Cavalry, Fifth Regiment, when they were killed. Ellis, a combat medic, died attempting to save his fellow soldiers.

VIETNAM

In Vietnam, Burbank was again called on to send its citizens off to war, and fifty-six Burbankers lost their lives in service to their country. One man became Burbank's only Medal of Honor recipient: Corporal Larry L. Maxam of the U.S. Marine Corps. Maxam served with the First Battalion, Fourth Marines, Third Marine Division. His Medal of Honor citation is illustrative of his courage and heroism:

> *Place and Date: Cam Lo District, Quang Tri province, Republic of Vietnam, 2 February 1968.*
> *For conspicuous gallantry and intrepidity at the risk of his life above and beyond the call of duty while serving as a fire team leader with Company D. The Cam Lo District Headquarters came under extremely heavy rocket, artillery, mortar, and recoilless rifle fire from a numerically superior enemy force, destroying a portion of the defensive perimeter. Cpl. Maxam, observing the enemy massing for an assault into the compound across the remaining*

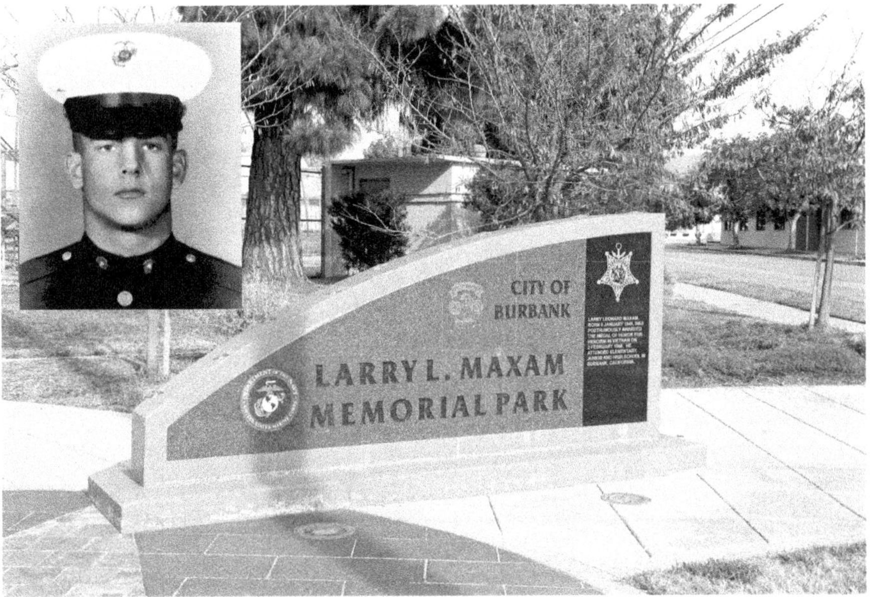

Larry L. Maxam Memorial Park on West Pacific Avenue, in honor of Burbank's only Medal of Honor recipient. *Wes Clark/U.S. Dept. of Defense.*

defensive wire, instructed his assistant fire team leader to take charge of the fire team, and unhesitatingly proceeded to the weakened section of the perimeter. Completely exposed to the concentrated enemy fire, he sustained multiple fragmentation wounds from exploding grenades as he ran to an abandoned machine gun position. Reaching the emplacement, he grasped the machine gun and commenced to deliver effective fire on the advancing enemy. As the enemy directed maximum firepower against the determined Marine, Cpl. Maxam's position received a direct hit from a rocket-propelled grenade, knocking him backwards and inflicting severe fragmentation wounds to his face and right eye. Although momentarily stunned and in intense pain, Cpl. Maxam courageously resumed his firing position and subsequently was struck again by small-arms fire. With resolute determination, he gallantly continued to deliver intense machine gun fire, causing the enemy to retreat through the defensive wire to positions of cover. In a desperate attempt to silence his weapon, the North Vietnamese threw hand grenades and directed recoilless rifle fire against him, inflicting two additional wounds. Too weak to reload his machinegun, Cpl. Maxam fell to a prone position and valiantly continued to deliver effective fire with his rifle. After one and a half hours, during which he was hit repeatedly by fragments from exploding grenades

and concentrated small-arms fire, he succumbed to his wounds, having successfully defended nearly half of the perimeter single-handedly. Cpl. Maxam's aggressive fighting spirit, inspiring valor and selfless devotion to duty reflected great credit upon himself and the Marine Corps and upheld the highest traditions of the U.S. Naval Service. He gallantly gave his life for his country.
Signed, Richard M. Nixon

In 2010 the City of Burbank renamed Pacific Park Larry L. Maxam Park, in recognition of Burbank's only Medal of Honor recipient.

GLOBAL WAR ON TERROR

As of this writing, Burbank has lost one of its sons in the Global War on Terror, David J. Hart, who died on January 8, 2008, during Operation Iraqi Freedom. From an article by the *Associated Press*:

Daniel Hart said he grew up emulating his brother, David—picking up the bass guitar because that's what his brother played. He went on nighttime hikes with his brother and both slept under the stars in the freezing cold. "He was the toughest guy I knew, and he was always OK," Daniel Hart said. "And knowing that, it made me OK." Hart, 22, of Lake View Terrace, Calif., died Jan. 8 after he was wounded in a battle around Samarra. He was assigned to Fort Campbell. Hart grew up in Burbank and was home schooled, said his mother, Cherie Hart. Later, the family moved to the Lakeview Terrace campus of Youth with a Mission, a Christian ministry organization with an international reach. Hart went on missions to Romania, Tahiti, New Zealand and other countries. "David lived up to his name, which in Hebrew means: 'well beloved,' 'dear,'" said his father, Jack Hart, during a memorial service. Spc. Richard Gilbert said his buddy would sacrifice to help others succeed. "If we were going on a run and someone fell back, he would fall back to help that soldier make the run." He also is survived by his wife, Nicole.

Burbankers who lost their lives were awarded the following for their valor in service to their country: Medal of Honor (1), Navy Crosses (3), Distinguished Service Crosses (4), Distinguished Flying Crosses (8), Air

Medals (meritorious achievement while in aerial flight) (35), Bronze Stars (acts of heroism in combat) (2), Silver Stars (gallantry in action against the enemy) (4), Prisoner of War Medals (7) and Purple Hearts (wounds received in combat) (229).

Burbank soldiers and airmen are also remembered on monuments in towns across Europe for their service. One town decorates their memorial near Mont-Dol in France, where the name of Burbanker Quentin L. Sandahl, a navigator, appears. Also, a Netherlands memorial is made from the propeller of a bomber that crashed near a town; Burbanker Warren F. Neilson was a gunner on this plane. Finally, Burbanker Myron Kendal Strickland is remembered on a memorial in Arlington National Cemetery.

The authors wish to memorialize the names of the Burbankers who never returned home, to remember their sacrifice.

To those who died
HONOR and ETERNAL REST;
To those still in bondage
REMEMBRANCE and HOPE;
To those who returned
GRATITUDE and PEACE.

(This inscription appears on the plaque dedicated on November 11, 1988, at McCambridge Park, 1515 North Glenoaks Boulevard in Burbank.)

Appendix

HONOR ROLL OF THE DEAD

World War I

Manuel Chafino
Harry Leslie Colton
Ray Fredrick Enos
James McCloud

World War II

Edwin V. Anderson
Herbert E. Anderson Jr.
Winston H. Arnold
Lee Bargaehr
Warren A. Barker
Clinton D. Barton
Neville A. Barton Jr.
Kenneth Bell
Harold Bettle Jr.
James A. Beyea
Warren R. Blakeman
Donald Blakesly
Arthur R. Boade
Rex Bobbie
Herman L. Bower
Louis Brammer
Donald N. Broman
Floyd L. Broman
Richard H. Bunbau
Albert B. Bylund
H.H. Campbell
David Carillo
Delbert Ben Carr
Robert W. Chambers

Glen E. Chapman
John Morris Chase
Fernando Chavez
John Chovanec
Charles Christofer
Jack Clark
Alfred W. Cole
Walter Collier (Pearl Harbor)
Roy Conyero
Paul G. Cosandier
Norvin F. Craig
Claire C. Cross
Wallace Crowder
James G. Davis
Tello DeSantis
C.W. Dickens
Robert A. Dibb
Ronald Dinsmoor
John A. Dorgan
Perry L. Dryer
Warren C. Dunaway
Richard H. Dunbar
Richard E. Dunkleberger
Edwin L. Ebinger
A.O. Elierman
Glen O. Elliot
Harley A. Ellis
Keith Edwin Ellis
Webb D. Ellmaker
N.J. Ellrott
Eugene Loyd Farthing
Robert A. Frank
Leo Fratella
Raymond O. Fulford
James H. Gamblin
Reuben Garcia
George Gene
Edward G. Genz
Charles A. Gettys
Douglas Lawrence Goff
Raymond Gonzales
Edwin S. Green
John R. Gugerty
Joesph H. Hackwell
Edward J. Hadraba
C.F. Hagerstrom
Gaylord Grant Hanley
Jack Henry Harder
Patrick Harman
Alvin Hart
Warren G. Haviland
Archie F. Havilland Jr.
Richard Hayward
Lawrence Headly
Ole E. Henrickson
Harol P. Hepburn
George Herren
Robert A. Herzog
Herman H. Hetzel
Howard Hickenlooper
Donald Hinshaw
Norman A. Hollis
Felton E. Horton
Robert W. Howard
Thomas Hunter
Aubrey Hurren
Kurt Francis Jennings
Glen E. Jewett
Arvin E. Johnson
Robert Johnson
Forest J. Johnston Jr.
Wayne A. Jones
Ernest L. Kearne
Richard Kimble
William F. Kinzy
William N. Kirkland
Max Kruger
Thomas Lake

Donald A. Landis
James Landsberger
Albert Lemmon
Melvin Leiberman
Sam Leiberman
Gordon R. Lofgren
John S. Lombart
Charles S. Lonergan
Harry Long
Lawrence R. Long
Earl Louden
Eugene Madole
Wilbur C. Mattern
William F. McChesney
Vernon McElmurray
Jack McHenry
Robert McNish
Wm. A. Messina
George Milburn
William Montandon
Joe Morris
William J. Morrison
Troy B. Mullinix
Alvan Mussen
Douglas L. Mutschler
James Williams Myers
Norman L. Myers
Wesley N. Myers
Warren F. Neilson
Carl V. Nelson Jr.
Harold Nelson
Frank C. O'Donnell
Fred W. Oettel
Peter Ogborn
Billy B. Parker
Robert Spencer Patterson
William A. Pelkey
Floyd Penry
Jack R. Peres
John Pilkington
John Frederick Ploof
J.A. Pritchard Jr.
James G. Purdy
Barthelmess Quinte
Glenn Raine
Douglas Richards
Joseph D. Risdon
Gerald Roberts
Virgil Robertson
B.C. Robinson
Fred C. Rowland
William A. Rutledge
John Samorian
Quentin Sandahl
Daniel Saunder
Creighton Schaefer
George R. Schaffer
Roy Clifford Scheer
Robert E. Schmidt
C.E. Schmiedeke
Robert L. Schug
Paul Schwartz
W.E. Seagren
Arthur B. Sherman
J.J. Signorelli
Nathan Silver
Jess Edward Simpson
Edwin Slocomb
Roger A. Smith
Elmer Snodgrass
Wm Alexander Snyder
Dudley M. Steele Jr.
Sam Stimolo Jr.
Clark D. Stone
Myron K. Strickland
William Stripe
August W. Sulflow
Joseph M. Sundeen

Richard Sussman
Ray Swenson
Philip B. Taylor Jr.
Walter Merle Taylor
William E. Taylor
Charles R. Teele
Robert Tegart
Milton A. Tolman
Charles Franklin Townsend
Nelson Troop
Richard Tull
Don Van Atta
Walter Vernon
Lloyd Waid
Bernard P. Walmsley
Wm Taylor Wattenberger
Ray Weber
Albert O. Wedin
Robert P. Westbrook
Arthur White
Robert V. Wickers
Donald L. Wickersham
Jack Wiles
Johnson B. Wiles Jr.
Richard D. Williams
Robert K. Wilson
Ronald H. Winget
Albert A. Wyatt
William H. York
John T. Zimmerman

KOREAN WAR

William J. Barnes
Donald S. Bills Jr.
Bobby S. Box
Edward L. Conyers
Foster L. Delmar
Max L. DeRossett
James Homer Elliott
David M. Ellis
Edwin Giron
Curtis A. Hatfield
William C. Karin
Charles F. Kirk
George R. Klein
Alfred J. Ledger Jr.
Burton H. Levenson
Michael La Magna
Arnold Nalley
Larry R. Shiner
Jon D. Varney
Robert V. Wilson

(Note: This enumeration differs from the names on the plaques for the Korean War at McCambridge Park, which accidentally listed names of veterans who were not killed. This list is the correct one.)

VIETNAM WAR

Jerry Joe Allen
Robin Annis
James M. Ball
Steven P. Barnett
Christopher P. Battaglia
Arthur "Skip" E. Bedal
James A. Beene
William H. Bric III
Brian E. Bullock
Felix A. Calderon
Robert J. Campbell
Donald E. Close
Michael L. Corrigan
Thomas B. Daily
John A DeRoo
Frank A. Difiglia
Douglas Dispensiero
Reese C. Elia Jr.
Allan L. Elmore
Daniel P. Elsass
Terry M. Enriquez
James H. Flickinger
Steven D. Francis
John A. Gero
Wayne E. Halstead
Stephen P. Hanson
Norbert P. Holzapel
Robert K. Houle
Scott W. Iggulden
Douglas R. Johnson
George F. Keiper
Steve M. Kenoffel
James W. Kerr
Ronald R. King
Howard L. Klenske
Edward L. Krausman
Edward R. LeTourneau
Von M. Liebernecht
Larry L. Maxam (Medal of Honor)
Gary T. McClain
Michael McKeever
David Moreland
Donald L. Morrison
Andrew J. Payne Jr.
Stephen D. Pleasant
William C. Proctor Jr.
Paul V. Quaglieri
Robert W. Robinson
David Salisbury
Charles P. Searles
Sal Silva
Larry Stephan
Guenter R. Thonues
Kenneth J. Webb
Ray Leonard Willman
Jack P. Wilson Jr.

GLOBAL WAR ON TERROR

David J. Hart (Afghanistan)

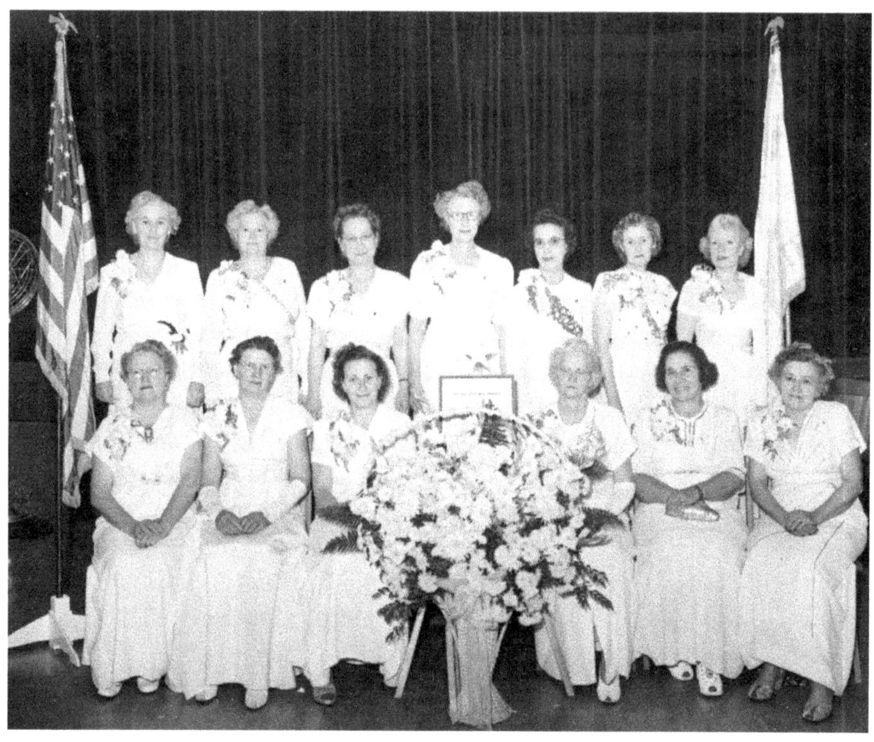

A portrait in fortitude: Burbank's Gold Star Mothers, late 1940s/early 1950s. Each of these women lost a son in war. Their smiles indicate a courage only a relative few in society can understand. *Collection of Michael B. McDaniel.*

NOTES

Chapter 1

1. What do we call residents of Burbank? "Burbankers" or "Burbankians?" The matter is in some dispute on the various Burbank-related Facebook groups. It is not a matter of world-shaking importance, but the authors are fond of "Burbanker" because it has historical weight. In the *Burbank Times* of November 30, 1889, we find the following note from the editor: "Gano Henry, Jr., has opened a boarding stable at 110 Upper Main Street, Los Angeles. Mr. H. is an old Burbanker and his friends in this section ought not to forget his place of business when they drive into town."
2. The Los Angeles River: The *Beverly Hillbillies'* Jed Clampett once looked down upon it and its cement channel and described it as "Pitiful, pitiful." Elly May added, "Properly, there ain't sufficient water down there to moist down a good-sized crawdad, is there Pa?"
3. There are old-timers who insist that San Fernando, as it runs through the downtown district, is properly a "road" and not a "boulevard," as maps today have it. We have been reprimanded about this on our Burbankia website. So "road" it is.
4. Your authors are Burbank High School Bulldogs (class of '74) and, as such, note with pride that our high school actually predates the incorporated city. Take that, crosstown rival Burroughs High.
5. This classic Burbank photograph served as an inner-sleeve illustration for Warner Bros. records during the 1970s; the LP label proudly featured a palm tree–lined street and the words, "Burbank, Home of Warner Bros. Records."

6. The ubiquitous Disney "Buena Vista" designation for various related companies refers to the street on which the studios are located. All Burbankers are happy to point this out. The street and its name predate the 1939 construction of the studio, by the way.

Chapter 2

7. The first battle was fought more or less in the same place in 1831.
8. Nearly all of the reference publications cited here are available to view on the Burbankia website.
9. Mike McDaniel has heard the question more than once, "Why are there airplanes on the tops of the signs?"
10. It still exists as Rocky's.
11. Indeed. Do a Google image search and see for yourself.
12. Wrestling and roller derby fans may recall his "Whoooaaaaa Nelly!" from local telecasts.
13. R. Lee Ermey was a memorable recent speaker.

Chapter 3

14. The authors' search for a copy of this apparently lost film continues.
15. Wes Clark's dad's favorite was one of Alice Cooper, wearing smeary eyeliner, in 1971: "What in the hell is *that*?"
16. Frankie Burke, who absolutely channels James Cagney in this film.
17. That's right: Shangri-La is in Burbank. Reflect on that next time you're at the corner of Verdugo Avenue and Hollywood Way. Do you feel any younger?
18. If this sounds familiar, it's because the premise was reworked in 1980 as *Xanadu*, a film starring Olivia Newton-John and Gene Kelly.
19. "Captain Hook," which aired on December 17, 1974.
20. In the 1960s there were plenty of vacant lots in town to be commemorated. The authors used to play in them. Back then, Burbank was known for vacant lots and a curious superabundance of alleys.
21. Some ripe quotes: "I'm not too thrilled about the [San Fernando] Valley as an aesthetic concept. . . . To me, [it] represents a number of very evil things." "I've always hated the Valley. It's a most depressing place."

22. Forest Lawn is in Glendale or Los Angeles, Johnny.
23. There are newspaper stories suggesting that this is changing.

CHAPTER 4

24. The moniker has generally fallen out of use, to be found only in history books like this.
25. John Burroughs High School was used for exterior shots.
26. Wes Clark's father and mother are also buried near the structure.

CHAPTER 5

27. How's that for musical diversity?
28. He was the senior music director at RKO Radio Pictures and earned Academy Award nominations for his work on *The Fallen Sparrow*, *Higher and Higher* and *None but the Lonely Heart*.
29. An earlier Burbank Municipal Band was organized in late 1923, led by a fellow named Hubert Snow White.
30. You can see them perform in the Warner Bros. film *Wings for the Eagle* (1942), scenes of which were filmed in the plant.
31. Your authors were handed their Burbank High School diplomas at the site during a pleasant June 1974 evening.

CHAPTER 6

32. Amusingly, a 1910 description of Fawkes's vehicle incorporates a gas bag for lift and suspension.
33. Fawkes seems to have had a problem with Burbank existing as a city outside Los Angeles; in January 1912, the year after the city incorporated, he filed a petition before the Burbank Board of Trustees calling for an election to vote on dis-incorporating the city. Nothing came of it.
34. You can see it on Britishpathe.com.
35. Being large men, your authors feel a special affection for him.
36. He carried brickmaking supplies to sites.
37. Probably reflecting the common anti-Semitism of the times, a short caption mentions that "he is not a member of the House of David."

Chapter 7

38. However, he lost a 1910 comeback bout, "The Fight of the Century," with Jack Johnson.
39. A street in Burbank was named for him.
40. One of the wrestling stars was Gorgeous George.

Chapter 8

41. It's a mile south of the home on the 1600 block of North Lincoln Street where Wes Clark was raised.
42. Shorter's body was never found, and he was declared legally dead in 1960.
43. Hayward won the Best Actress in a Leading Role Academy Award for it.
44. Kubrick's mother was Paul Perveler's maternal aunt.
45. Twenty-four years to the day before the boom sheet murder, it may be noted.
46. The interior of this casino is depicted in the 2013 film *Gangster Squad*. The site is memorialized by Dincara Road in Burbank.
47. He's called "Elmer Jackson" in the movie *Gangster Squad* (2013), where he is shown dining with Mickey Cohen at a swank Los Angeles nightclub.

Chapter 9

48. The authors confess to never having heard this phenomenon.
49. We can no longer go right to the source and ask the horse.
50. You will recall from the musical chapter that guitarist Randy Rhoads and drummer Drew Forsyth were Burbankers.

Chapter 10

51. Prior to Mike McDaniel's research, only 163 veterans were officially listed.
52. The *Oklahoma* was badly damaged and decommissioned in 1944.

BIBLIOGRAPHY

Books

Bugliosi, Vincent. *Till Death Us Do Part: A True Murder Mystery*. New York: W.W. Norton & Company Inc., 1978.

Burbank Centennial History, 1911–2011: Celebrating Our Past and Embracing Our Future. St. Louis, MO: Reedy Press, 2011.

Burbank High School. *The Blue and White Wave High*. Burbank, CA: self-published, 2008.

Burbank Unified School District. *A History of Burbank*. Burbank, CA: City of Burbank, 1967.

Keffer, Frank M. *History of San Fernando Valley in Two Parts Narrative and Biographical*. Plainfield, WI: Stillman Printing Company, 1934.

Marshall, Garry. *Wake Me When It's Funny: How to Break into Show Business and Stay There*. Avon, MA: Adams Media Corporation, 1995.

Mayers, Jackson. *Burbank History*. Burbank, CA: James W. Anderson, 1975.

McAleer, John. *Packed and Loaded: Conversations with James M. Cain.* Ann Arbor, MI: Nimble Books, 2010.

McCoy, Tim, and Ronald McCoy. *Tim McCoy Remembers the West.* Lincoln: University of Nebraska, Bison Books, 1977.

McDaniel, Michael B. *Burbank Veterans Memorial Book.* Burbank, CA: self-published, 2015.

Merritt, Christopher, and Dominic Priore. *Pacific Ocean Park: The Rise and Fall of Los Angeles' Space Age Nautical Pleasure Pier.* Port Townsend, WA: Process Media, 2014.

Monroe, George Lynn. *Burbank Community Book.* Burbank, CA: A.H. Cawston, 1944.

Odd, Gilbert. *Encyclopedia of Boxing.* Wingdale, NY: Crescent Books, 1988.

Perry, E. Caswell. *Burbank: An Illustrated History.* Northridge, CA: Windsor Publications, Inc., 1987.

Reynolds, Debbie, and David Patrick Columbia. *Debbie: My Life.* New York: William Morrow & Company, 1988.

Rich, Ben R., and Leo Janos. *Skunk Works.* New York: Little, Brown and Company, 1994.

Schonauer, Erin K., and Jamie C. Schonauer. *Images of America: Early Burbank.* Mount Pleasant, SC: Arcadia Publishing, 2014.

Strickland, Mary Jane, and Theodore X. Garcia. *A History of Burbank: A Special Place in History.* Burbank, CA: Burbank Historical Society, 2000.

Young, Alan. *Mister Ed and Me and More!* New York: Geordie Press, 1994.

Pamphlets and Booklets

Burbank Chamber of Commerce. *A Brief History of Burbank, California.* Burbank, CA: City of Burbank, 1961.

———. *Burbank—Its Place in the Sun.* Burbank, CA: self-published, 1930.

Burbank Merchants' Association. *Your Burbank Home.* Burbank, CA: Valley Printing Company, 1928.

Burbank Security Trust and Savings Bank. *Ranchos de Los Santos—The Story of Burbank.* Burbank, CA: self-published, 1927.

Burbank Senior High School. *BHS 70th Memories.* Burbank, CA: self-published, 1978.

City of Burbank, California. *Annual Report for the Fiscal Year Ended June 30, 1950.* Burbank, CA: City of Burbank, 1950.

City of Burbank Public Information Office. *Burbank—City of Pride and Progress.* Burbank, CA: City of Burbank, 1981.

Gold Star Mothers Memorial Scrapbook. In possession of Mike McDaniel.

Henry, Leroy Freedom Hill. *Freedom from Fond Friends*. Burbank, CA: Freedom Hill Press, 1919.

———. *Freedom Hill, the Place of Evergreen Happiness*. Burbank, CA: Freedom Hill Press, 1919.

———. *Henry's Glass Eye Story*. Burbank, CA: Freedom Hill Press, 1920.

A History of the Desert Wolf (the 121 AAA Gun Battalion) 1940–1945. N.p., 1946.

Lockheed Aircraft Corporation. *Of Men and Stars—A History of Lockheed Aircraft Corporation.* Burbank, CA: Lockheed Aircraft Corporation, 1958.

Magnolia Park Chamber of Commerce. *The Story of Burbank from Her Eventful Pioneer Days.* Burbank, CA: self-published, 1954.

Walt Disney Studio. *Burbank, California—Gateway to the San Fernando Valley.* Burbank, CA: self-published, 1947.

Newspapers and Magazines

Albert, Katherine. "Harper B. Henry—Inventor and Originator of the Azonic Language and Alphabet." *Los Angeles Times*, August 31, 1924.

Braxton, Greg. "Fear Lives Where Street Stops but Cars Don't." *Los Angeles Times*, November 19, 1995.

Chen, Vivien Lou. "Burbank Permit for X-Rated Film Stirs Image Issue." *Los Angeles Times*, October 27, 1994.

Einstoss, Ron. "Jury Overruled on Death for Slayer." *Los Angeles Times*, May 21, 1970.

Hamilton, Andrew. "Small Cities Can Lick Crime, Too!" *Coronet*, May 1956.

Jeunesse Magazine (Paris). "*Embarquons-nous en Fusee Interplanetaire*!" May 7, 1939.

Los Angeles Times. "Armed Suspects Jailed in Holdup of Messengers Netting $111,300." September 27, 1945.

———. "Bumpless Vehicles." July 3, 1934.

———. "Car Find Spurs Bandit Hunt." August 2, 1945.

———. "Chapel to Honor First U.S. Saint." December 30, 1973.

———. "Charges to Be Filed in Burbank Slayings." August 1, 1969.

———. "Clock to Aid Aerial Navigation." July 7, 1941.

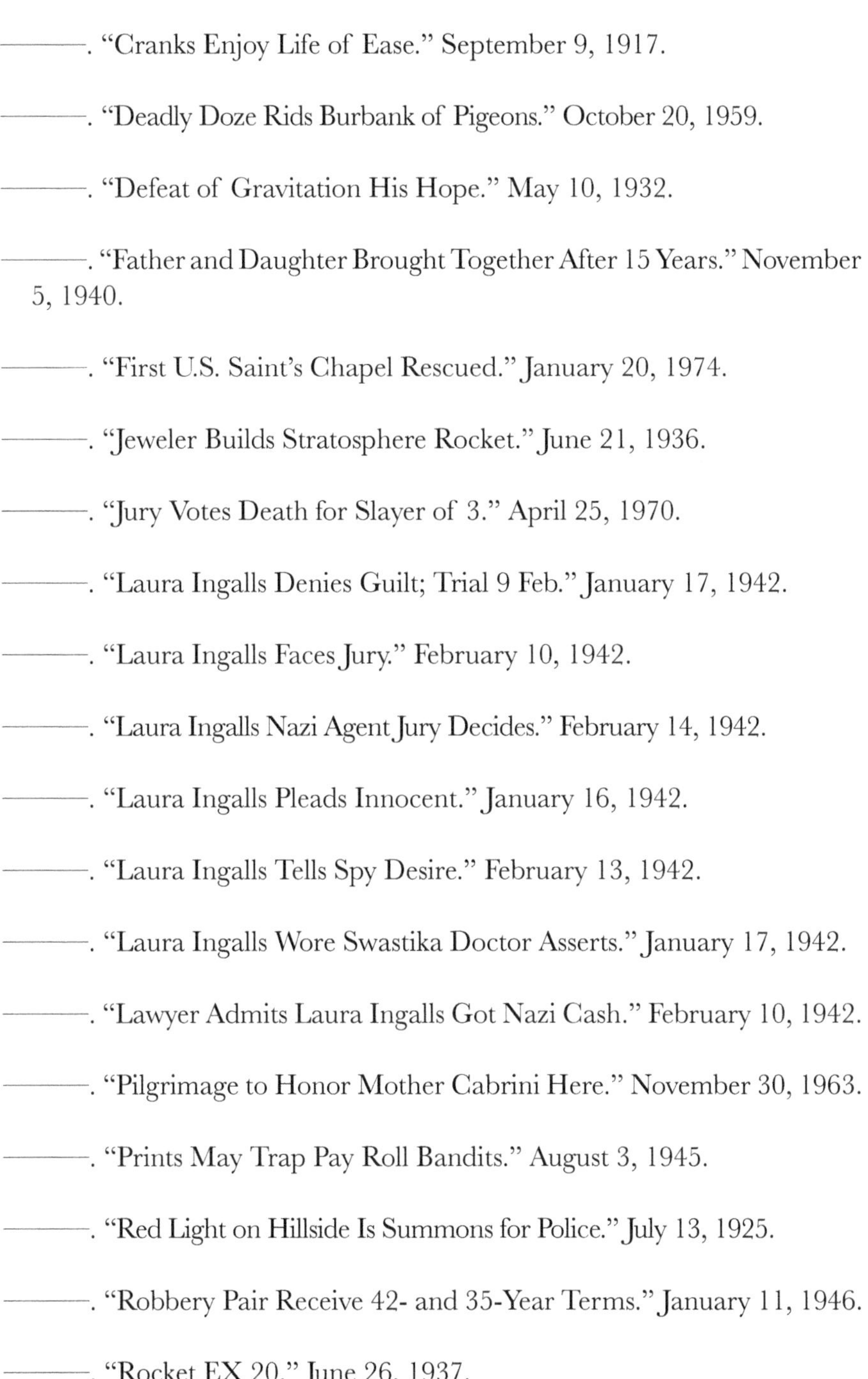

———. "Cranks Enjoy Life of Ease." September 9, 1917.

———. "Deadly Doze Rids Burbank of Pigeons." October 20, 1959.

———. "Defeat of Gravitation His Hope." May 10, 1932.

———. "Father and Daughter Brought Together After 15 Years." November 5, 1940.

———. "First U.S. Saint's Chapel Rescued." January 20, 1974.

———. "Jeweler Builds Stratosphere Rocket." June 21, 1936.

———. "Jury Votes Death for Slayer of 3." April 25, 1970.

———. "Laura Ingalls Denies Guilt; Trial 9 Feb." January 17, 1942.

———. "Laura Ingalls Faces Jury." February 10, 1942.

———. "Laura Ingalls Nazi Agent Jury Decides." February 14, 1942.

———. "Laura Ingalls Pleads Innocent." January 16, 1942.

———. "Laura Ingalls Tells Spy Desire." February 13, 1942.

———. "Laura Ingalls Wore Swastika Doctor Asserts." January 17, 1942.

———. "Lawyer Admits Laura Ingalls Got Nazi Cash." February 10, 1942.

———. "Pilgrimage to Honor Mother Cabrini Here." November 30, 1963.

———. "Prints May Trap Pay Roll Bandits." August 3, 1945.

———. "Red Light on Hillside Is Summons for Police." July 13, 1925.

———. "Robbery Pair Receive 42- and 35-Year Terms." January 11, 1946.

———. "Rocket EX 20." June 26, 1937.

———. "Rocket Plane Displayed at Theater." October 15, 1930.

———. "Tiny Chapel at Villa Cabrini Escaped Fires." May 15, 1960.

———. "Twelve Second Watch." May 30, 1937.

———. "2000 Pilgrims Honor First American Saint." December 2, 1957.

———. "Weather Thwarts Poirier's Launch." February 8, 1931.

———. "Weeds Would Fuel Ship." January 24, 1931.

Maltun, Alan. "Family Unhurt So Far: Owners Ask Burbank City Council to Buy Accident-Prone House, Hit 12 Times." *Los Angeles Times*, December 30, 1979.

———. "Owners Ask Burbank City Council to Buy Accident-Prone House, Hit 12 Times." *Los Angeles Times*, December 23, 1979.

Quinn, James. "Couple Hope New Traffic Barrier Will Keep Cars from Crashing into Garage." *Los Angeles Times*, October 10, 1976.

———. "Couple Tired of Cars Smashing Into Home." *Los Angeles Times*, October 19, 1975.

Schenectady Gazette. "Group to Begin Life Anew on Tiny Island." November 14, 1947.

Shippey, Lee. "Lee Side o' L.A." *Los Angeles Times*, March 16, 1929.

Time. "Planet Plans." February 9, 1931.

Reports

Burbank Historical Society. "Famous People Who Lived in Burbank," undated.

Report of the Burbank Citizens' Crime Prevention Committee (BCCPC) to the City Council of the City of Burbank, June 16, 1953.

Websites

Ancestry.com (various veteran-related databases). http://ancestry.com.

Burbank, California (blog). "Stanley Kubrick's Burbank Connection: The Notorious Killer Paul Perveler Was His First Cousin." https://semichorus.wordpress.com.

Burbank Chorale. "About Us." http://www.burbankchorale.org/about_us.

Burbank Community Band. "Band History." http://www.burbankband.org/b_history.html.

Burbankers Remember. "High Times at St. Joseph's Hospital." http://wesclark.com/burbank/burbankers_remember.html.

Burbank Historical Society. "A Bit of History." http://www.burbankhistoricalsoc.org/a-bit-of-history.

BurbankNBeyond. "The Big Game." http://www.burbanknbeyond.com.

Burbank Philharmonic Orchestra. "About Us." http://burbankphilharmonic.org.

Cassingham, Curt. Burbank Police Boys' Band. http://www.curtcass.com/bpbb/curt.html.

Bibliography

Clark, Wes, and Mike McDaniel. Burbankia. http://wesclark.com/burbank.

Cox's Corner Profiles. "Jim Jeffries, the Boilermaker . . . You Never Seen an Athlete Like Him." http://coxscorner.tripod.com/jeffries.html.

Del Casher personal website. http://delcasher.com.

Deranged L.A. Crimes. "Dead Woman Walking: Barbara Graham." http://derangedlacrimes.com/?p=1570.

———. "The Coincidence Killer." http://derangedlacrimes.com/?p=4035.

Dixon, Richard. "Catalina Street," "The Ranch (1946)," "Warner's Jungle (1945)." Burbankers Remember. http://wesclark.com/burbank/burbankers_remember.html.

Facebook. "You Know You're from Burbank If…" www.facebook.com.

Fold3.com (various veteran-related databases). http://fold3.com.

Internet Movie Database. http://imdb.com.

Library of Congress image database. http://loc.gov.

Lockheed Martin. "Our History." http://lockheedmartin.com/us/100years/stories.html.

Murderpedia.org. "Nellie May Madison." http://murderpedia.org/female.M/m/madison-nellie-may.htm.

PardonPower.com. "Laura H. Ingalls—Just One Flight Too Many!" http://www.pardonpower.com/2010/11/laura-h-ingalls-just-one-flight-too.html.

Portal of the Folded Wings, Shrine to Navigation. http://www.portalofthefoldedwings.net.

Postal-Simmons, Dianne. "Burbank Gypsy Camp." Burbankers Remember. http://wesclark.com/burbank/burbankers_remember.html.

The Smoke House. "Tales from the Smoke House." http://www.smokehouse1946.com/smokehouse_legacy.html.

Songfacts. "It's a Small World." http://www.songfacts.com/detail.php?id=4691.

Starlight Bowl. http://www.starlightbowl.com.

Thrasher, Monte. "Love from Above," "Burbank's UFO Landing Pad," "The Burbank Cross." Burbankers Remember. http://wesclark.com/burbank/burbankers_remember.html.

Underwood, John. "Volmer Jensen Remembered." Soaring Society of America. http://www.ssa.org/FinalGlide?id=662.

U.S. Patent and Trademark Office database for live and expired patents (Maurice Poirier, J.W. Fawkes). http://uspto.gov.

U.S. Patent and Trademark Office database for live and expired trademarks (Alshire, A/S, 101 Strings). http://uspto.gov.

Wikipedia. "'Athena' (song)." https://en.wikipedia.org/wiki/Athena_(song).

———. "Burbank, California, 'Notable People.'" https://en.wikipedia.org/wiki/Burbank,_California.

———. "Hollywood Black Friday." https://en.wikipedia.org/wiki/Hollywood_Black_Friday.

———. "Jeffries, James J." https://en.wikipedia.org/wiki/James_J._Jeffries.

———. "Patsy Awards." https://en.wikipedia.org/wiki/PATSY_Award.

———. "Randy Rhoads." https://en.wikipedia.org/wiki/Randy_Rhoads.

———. *"A Toot and a Snore in '74."* https://en.wikipedia.org/wiki/A_Toot_and_a_Snore_in_%2774.

———. "Volmer VJ-23 Swingwing." https://en.wikipedia.org/wiki/Volmer_VJ-23_Swingwing.

WisconsinHistory.org. "Wreck of the Lady Elgin and rescue work of E.W. Spencer." http://www.wisconsinhistory.org/Content.aspx?dsNav=N:4294963828-4294963788&dsRecordDetails=R:BA9961.

Yannicos, Trina. "John, Paul, George and Bob: Did The Beatles Really Eat at Bob's Big Boy?" http://www.examiner.com/article/john-paul-george-and-bob-did-the-beatles-really-eat-at-bob-s-big-boy.

E-MAIL AND OTHER

Barefoot Ted, e-mail messages to Wes Clark, April 4, 2016.

Brian Schneider, e-mail message to Wes Clark, June 8, 2012.

Justin Rousellot, e-mail message to Wes Clark, September 17, 2015.

Rob Clampett, phone conversation with Wes Clark, March 16, 2016.

Steven Keys, e-mail messages to Wes Clark, February 24, 2016.

Tim Conway, e-mail messages to Wes Clark, April 4, 2016.

INDEX

Index

C

G

H

I

J

K

L

M

Q

R

S

T

ABOUT THE AUTHORS

Wes Clark was born in Los Angeles, but his family moved to Burbank when he was eight; he was educated in Burbank schools. He met Mike McDaniel in 1972, and they graduated from Burbank Senior High School in 1974. They have always been intensely interested in history. Clark lives in Springfield, Virginia, with his wife of thirty-five years—they have three kids and five grandchildren. An electrical engineer, he works for the United States Patent and Trademark Office.

Mike Mc Daniel was born in the now-disappeared Burbank Community Hospital and has lived in Burbank in the same house for nearly sixty years. He attended all-Burbank schools. Mike still lives in Burbank and has been married for thirty-six years; he and his wife have five children. Mike has worked for the City of Burbank for thirty years and is the supervisor of the City Print Shop (printing being a vocation he learned in high school).

We thank our biology teacher for having the foresight to seat us together in class so we could be friends for the past forty-one years! An interest in history is one of the many things we have in common—hence this book.

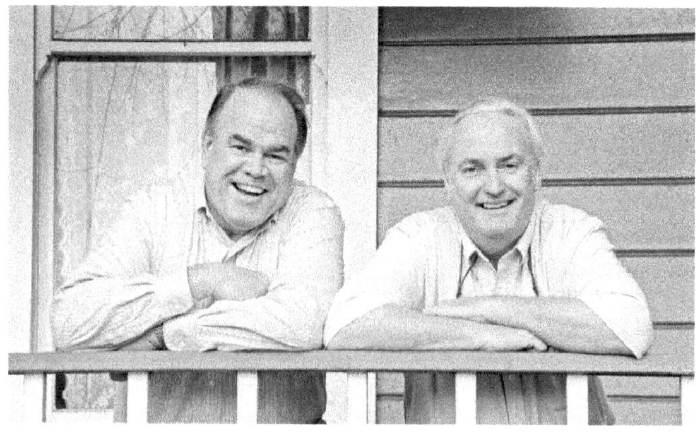

www.ingramcontent.com/pod-product-compliance
Lightning Source LLC
LaVergne TN
LVHW010936100826
845153LV00001B/60

9781540200778